Competition and Regulation in Utility Markets

Competition and Regulation in Utility Markets

Edited by

Colin Robinson

Professor of Economics, University of Surrey, UK

In association with the Institute of Economic Affairs and the
London Business School

Edward Elgar

Cheltenham, UK • Northampton, MA, USA

Published by
Edward Elgar Publishing Limited
Glensanda House
Montpellier Parade
Cheltenham
Glos GL50 1UA
UK

Edward Elgar Publishing, Inc.
136 West Street
Suite 202
Northampton
Massachusetts 01060
USA

A catalogue record for this book
is available from the British Library

Library of Congress Cataloging in Publication Data
Competition and regulation in utility markets / edited by Colin Robinson.
    p. cm.
"In association with the Institute of Economic Affairs and the London Business School."
Includes bibliographical references and index.
    1. Electric utilities—Deregulation—Great Britain. 2. Gas industry—Deregulation—Great Britain. 3. Telecommunications—Deregulation—Great Britain. 4. Competition—Great Britain. I. Robinson, Colin, 1932–

   HD9685.G72 C66 2003
   363.6'0941—dc21

2002037942

ISBN 1 84376 230 7
Printed and bound in Great Britain by MPG Books Ltd, Bodmin, Cornwall

Contents

List of figures, tables and boxes   vii
Abbreviations and acronyms   ix
Notes on the authors   xi
Introduction by Colin Robinson   xxi

1   UK transport policy, 1997–2001   1
    Stephen Glaister
    Chairman's comments   56
    Tom Winsor
2   Electricity: regulatory developments around the world   61
    Stephen Littlechild
    Chairman's comments   88
    Eileen Marshall
3   Prospects for gas supply and demand and their implications
    with special reference to the UK   91
    Alexander G. Kemp and Linda Stephen
    Chairman's comments   119
    Callum McCarthy
4   The ingredients of effective competition policy   121
    Irwin M. Stelzer
    Chairman's comments   134
    Derek Morris
5   Regulatory incentives and deregulation in telecommunications   138
    Leonard Waverman
    Chairman's comments   160
    David Edmonds
6   An end to economic regulation?   162
    Robert W. Crandall
    Chairman's comments   186
    Penelope Rowlatt
7   Mutualization and debt-only vehicles: which way for RPI–X
    regulation?   187
    David Currie
    Chairman's comments   199
    Philip Fletcher

Contents

8 International mergers: the view from a national authority   203
   John Vickers
9 Liberalizing postal services   219
   John Dodgson
   Chairman's comments   236
   Graham Corbett

Index   239

List of figures, tables and boxes

FIGURES

1.1	Growth of traffic in vehicle-kilometres, 1950–2000	5
1.2	Price indices relative to gross household income, 1964–2000	6
1.3	Motoring fuel price indices relative to the Retail Price Index, 1987–2001	8
1.4	Growth of traffic on various road types, 1982–2000	9
1.5	Urban days with low pollution, 1993–2000	13
1.6	Rural days with low pollution, 1993 -2000	14
1.7	Road fatalities per bn motor-vehicle-kilometres, 1969–99	15
1.8	Rail fatalities per bn passenger-kilometres, 1969–99	16
1.9	Household expenditure on different modes of transport	19
1.10	Bus-passenger-kilometres, 1969–99	21
1.11	Bus vehicle-kilometres, 1969–99	21
1.12	British Railways passenger-kilometres, 1908–98	24
1.13	Train-kilometres, 1969–99	25
1.14	Goods moved by road and by rail, 1953–99	28
1.15	Freight tonne-kilometres: market shares	28
1.16	Total subsidies to London commuter railways, 1997–2004	32
1.17	Historic under-investment in the Underground, 1970–2000	34
1.18	London Underground: track and signalling failures, 1994–2001	36
1.19	London Underground: percentage of scheduled kilometres not operated, 1997–2002	37
1.20	Public sector net investment as a percentage of GDP, 1990–99	38
1.21	Strategic roads: public expenditure, 1991–2011	39
1.22	Local transport: public expenditure and private investment, 1991–2011	41
1.23	Rail: public expenditure and private investment, 1991–2011	47
1.24	London: public expenditure and private investment, 1991–2011	49
3.1	Potential gas production by field category, medium case, 2001–10	96
3.2	Potential gas production by producing area, medium case, 2001–10	98
3.3	UK production and capacity at St Fergus, medium case, 2001–10	100

3.4 UK production and capacity at Teesside, medium case, 2001–10 101
3.5 UK production and capacity at Barrow, medium case, 2001–10 102
3.6 UK production and capacity at Theddlethorpe, medium case, 2001–10 102
3.7 UK production and capacity at Easington and Dimlington, medium case, 2001–10 104
3.8 UK production and capacity at Bacton, medium case, 2001–10 104
3.9 Potential UK gas production and UK demand, medium case, 2001–10 105
3.10 Potential UK gas production and UK demand including exports, medium case, 2001–10 107
5.1 Supply of and demand for regulation 153
9.1 The burden of the USO 221
9.2 Delivery cost index for the UK 222
9.3 Inland mail volumes, 1991/92 to 2000/2001 223
9.4 Labour productivity, 1991/92 to 2000/2001 225

TABLES

1.1 Responses of traffic to fuel prices and income 7
1.2 Expenditure 1999–2000 and needs for next ten years 41
3.1 Significant exploration success rates, 2001–15, medium case 93
3.2 Number of exploration wells, 2000–2015 94
3.3 UKCS mean discovery size, 2000–2015 94
5.1 Oftel activities summary, 2000–2001 149
6.1 The scope of economic regulation in the USA, 1975 and 2001 163
6.2 The effects of deregulation in the USA 167
9.1 Consignia letter mail postal costs by activity 224
9.2 Distribution of Consignia inland letter traffics by weight band, 1999–2000 233
9.3 Distribution of Consignia inland letter traffics by price band, 1999–2000 233

BOX

9.1 The Deutsche Post predatory pricing ruling 229

Abbreviations and acronyms

ADSL	asynchronous digital subscriber line
BKA	Bundeskartellamt (German Federal Cartel Office)
Capex	capital expenditure
CEGB	Central Electricity Generating Board
CHP	combined heat and power
CRTC	Canadian Radio-Television and Telecommunications Commission
DETR	Department of Environment, Transport and the Regions
DOES	Director General of Electricity Supply
DLEC	data local exchange competitors
DPAG	Deutsche PostAG
DTAG	Deutsche Telekom AG
DSL	digital subscriber line
DTI	Department of Trade and Industry
DWR	Department of Water Resources (California)
ECMR	European Community Merger Regulation
ECNZ	Electricity Corporation of New Zealand
FAC	fully allocated cost
FCC	Federal Communications Commission (USA)
FSU	Former Soviet Union
GE	General Electric
GLA	Greater London Authority
HSE	Health and Safety Executive
ISDN	integrated services digital network
IEA	International Energy Agency
ISP	Internet Service Provider
kps	kilobytes per second
LNG	liquefied natural gas
LPG	liquefied petroleum gas
LRIC	long run incremental cost
MALC	Market Abuse Licence Condition
MMC	Monopolies and Mergers Commission
NAC	net avoided cost
NAO	National Audit Office
NARUC	National Association of Regulatory Utility Commissioners

NECA	National Electricity Code Administrator (Australia)
NERA	National Economic Research Associates
NETA	new electricity trading arrangements
NGC	National Grid Company
NTS	National Transmission System
Ofcom	Office of Communications
Offer	Office of Electricity Regulation
Ofgas	Office of Gas Supply
Ofgem	Office of Gas and Electricity Markets
OFT	Office of Fair Trading
Oftel	Office of Telecommunications
Opex	operating expenditure
OPRAF	Office of Passenger Rail Franchising
PFI	Private Finance Initiative
PPP	public-private partnership
PUC	Public Utility Commission
PX	Power Exchange
RegTP	Regulierungsbehörcle für Telekommunication und Post
ROR	rate of return
SMP	system marginal price
SRA	Strategic Rail Authority
SSL	subsurface lines
sSRA	shadow Strategic Rail Authority
TELRIC	Total Element Long Run Incremental Cost
TfL	Transport for London
UKCS	UK Continental Shelf
UPS	Universal Postal Service
USF	universal service fund
USO	Universal Service Obligation
WAR	weighted average measure of regulation

The authors

Graham Corbett was appointed Chairman of the Postal Services Commission in March 2000. He was previously a deputy chairman of the Competition Commission. He is also chairman of Ricability, a charity concerned with research and information for consumers with disabilities.

Corbett was born in 1934. He qualified as a chartered accountant and was for 12 years the Senior Partner of Peat Marwick's continental European firm based in Paris. He then moved to the commercial world to become the chief financial officer and a main board director of Eurotunnel. He was awarded a CBE in 1994 for services to transport.

Robert W. Crandall is a Senior Fellow in the Economic Studies Program of the Brookings Institution. His research has focused on telecommunications regulation, cable television regulation, the effects of trade policy in the steel and automobile industries, environmental policy, and the changing regional structure of the US economy. His current research focuses on competition in the telecommunications sector and the development of broadband services. His book on universal service, *Who Pays for 'Universal Service'?* (written with Leonard Waverman of the London Business School), was published by Brookings in 2000. He was also a contributor, with Professor Jerry Hausman of MIT, to the recently published Brookings book, *Deregulation of Network Industries: What's Next?* (edited by Sam Peltzman and Clifford Winston).

Crandall was a Johnson Research Fellow at the Brookings Institution and has taught economics at Northwestern University, MIT, the University of Maryland, the George Washington University, and the Stanford in Washington program. Before assuming his current position at Brookings, he served as assistant, acting, and deputy director for the Council on Wage and Price Stability.

Crandall is the author of *Talk is Cheap: The Promise of Regulatory Reform in North American Telecommunications* (with Leonard Waverman) (Brookings Institution, 1996); *Cable TV: Regulation or Competition?* (with Harold Furchtgott-Roth) (Brookings Institution, 1996); *The Extra Mile: Rethinking Energy Policy for Automotive Transportation* (with Pietro Nivola) (Brookings Institution, 1995); *After the Breakup: The U.S. Telecommunications Sector in a More Competitive Era*; *Manufacturing on the Move*; *Changing the Rules:*

Technological Change, International Competition, and Regulation in Com-munications (with Kenneth Flamm) (Brookings Institution, 1991), and numerous journal articles.

He holds an MS and a Ph.D. in economics from Northwestern University.

David Currie is Chairman of Ofcom, the new UK Communications regulator, and Dean of City University's Cass Business School. Previously he was Professor of Economics and Deputy Dean at London Business School, where he directed the School's Regulation Initiative and before that the Centre for Economic Forecasting. In his earlier career, he worked in the City and in con-sultancy and held a Chair at Queen Mary, University of London. He has held visiting appointments at the International Monetary Fund, the Bank of England, the European University Institute and the University of Manchester, and has acted as consultant to the OECD and the European Commission. In October 1996, he joined the House of Lords as Lord Currie of Marylebone, where he sits on the crossbenches.

John Dodgson is a director in NERA's London Office. He is a senior member of NERA's Transport team, and heads NERA's work on European postal matters. John's work in transportation covers all the modes: air, road, rail and ports. He has directed projects for a number of major clients, including the European Commission, the UK Civil Aviation Authority, the Department of the Environment, Transport and the Regions (DETR), the Office of the Rail Regulator and the Strategic Rail Authority.

Before joining NERA at the end of 1996, John was an academic at the University of Liverpool. He has also taught at Universidad Carlos III in Madrid, and at the University of British Columbia. He has published extensively on applied economics, in particular transportation economics. Work has included: identification of predatory behaviour in the airline and bus industries; deter-mination of optimal levels of public transport subsidies; appraisal and evaluation in the transport sector; reorganization of the rail industry; and modelling of greenhouse gases and other environmental effects of the transport sector. His work in the postal sector has included estimation of the impacts of liberalizing cross-border mail, and the calculation of Universal Service Obligation burdens.

David Edmonds is Director General of Telecommunications, the independent telecommunications regulator. He is also a Board member of the Office of Com-munications, the new UK communications regulatory body. He held various posts in the Department of the Environment from 1966 to 1984 and was then appointed Chief Executive of the Housing Corporation, which became the major instrument for delivering the government's social housing programme from

1991 to 1997. He was Managing Director, Group Central Services at NatWest Group and a member coordinating work on the Group's preparation for European economic and monetary union. He also chaired the Group's charitable foundations and was responsible for creating the Lothbury Gallery in the City.

Philip Fletcher was appointed as the Director General of Water Services on 1 August 2000. He has served in major management roles, primarily with public finance and procurement emphasis. He has gained wide experience in partnerships between government, business and voluntary sectors.

Fletcher's previous post was Receiver for the Metropolitan Police District. The Receiver had statutory responsibility for the administration of the Metropolitan Police Fund and for ensuring that distributions from the fund were made only with proper authority. He was a full member of the Commissioner's management team but was separately accountable to the Home Secretary. He was in charge of finance, procurement, internal audit and property services (as the legal owner of all Metropolitan Police property).

After joining the Metropolitan Police in 1996, Fletcher carried out projects to develop greater value in procurement, improve financial management, and he reviewed central support services.

Educated at Marlborough College and Trinity College, Oxford, where he read history, Fletcher joined the Ministry of Public Buildings and Works in 1968. It later merged into the Department of Environment in 1970 (now DETR). At the Department, Fletcher's experience spanned environmental pollution control, the construction industry, housing, finance, and planning and land use.

He was promoted to Under-Secretary in 1986 as Director of Central Finance, Department of Environment, where he took part in discussions leading up to the privatization of the water industry in England and Wales in 1989. He became Director of Planning and Development Control in 1990, where he initiated and oversaw the government's review of land use.

Fletcher was appointed head of the Property Services Agency (PSA) in 1993 on promotion to Deputy Secretary. He completed the privatization of the PSA and transferred to head the Cities and Countryside Group in 1994.

Stephen Glaister is Professor of Transport and Infrastructure at Imperial College, London.

He was a member of the UK government's first Advisory Committee on Trunk Road Assessment, and has been Specialist Advisor to the Parliamentary Select Committee on Transport.

He was a non-executive director of London Regional Transport from 1984 until 1993 and in July 2000 he became a member of the Board of Transport for London.

Between 1993 and spring 2001 he was an economic adviser to the Rail Regulator. He is an adviser to the Commission for Integrated Transport. He has published widely on transport and also on regulation in the telecommunications, water and gas industries. In 1998 he was awarded the CBE for services to public transport.

Alexander G. Kemp worked for Shell and the University of Strathclyde before returning to take up an appointment at Aberdeen where he is now Schlumberger Professor of Petroleum Economics. He has also held a visiting appointment at the University of Nairobi. He has specialized in petroleum economics since the early days of North Sea exploration, and has over 180 publications in this field, including *Petroleum Tax Analysis: North Sea*, with David Rose (*Financial Times*, 1983), *Petroleum Rent Collection Around the World* (Institute for Research on Public Policy, 1988), *An Economic Analysis of Petroleum Exploitation Systems in Ireland, the UK, Norway, Denmark and the Netherlands* (with Alan Gray) (Price Waterhouse, 1988), and *The UK North Sea Southern Basin Fiscal System* (with Graham Kellas) (British Institute for Energy Economics, 1988). He has contributed papers to *Economica, Energy Economics, Energy Journal, Energy Policy, Geopolitics of Energy, Journal of Oil and Gas Finance and Accounting, Natural Resources Forum, Oxford Energy Forum, Scottish Economic Bulletin, Scottish Journal of Political Economy, Oxford Review of Economic Policy* and *World Oil*. He has acted as consultant on petroleum contracts and legislation to commercial companies and national governments as well as to the United Nations, World Bank and Commonwealth Secretariat. He was a specialist adviser to the House of Commons Select Committee on Energy until its abolition in 1992. Since 1993 he has been a member of the Panel of Independent Advisers to the Minister for Energy. He has been appointed by the Cabinet Office to write the official history of North Sea oil and gas. He is a member of the Economic Advisory Panel to PILOT, the joint government–industry body on North Sea oil and gas.

Stephen Littlechild was UK Director General of Electricity Supply (DGES) for nearly ten years. He was in charge of the Office of Electricity Regulation (Offer), from its foundation in September 1989, to December 1998. Previously he advised ministers on the regulatory regime for British Telecom and the water industry. In 1983, he proposed the RPI–X approach to price controls, which has since been widely adopted for regulating utilities in the UK and overseas. He was a member of the Monopolies and Mergers Commission for six years. Before 1989, he acted as a consultant to public and private sector organizations, including HM Treasury, several UK government departments, NZ Treasury, the World Bank, AT & T, Bell Telephone Laboratories and General Motors.

Professor Littlechild graduated as Bachelor of Commerce from the University of Birmingham in 1964. He did postgraduate work at Stanford University (Operations Research program) 1965–67, Northwestern University (Engineering faculty) 1967–68, and the University of Texas at Austin (Graduate School of Business) 1968–69, obtaining his Ph.D. there in 1969. He did postdoctoral research at UCLA and Northwestern. From 1972 to 1975 he was Professor of Applied Economics and Head of the Economics, Econometrics, Statistics and Marketing Subject Group at Aston Management Centre. He was Professor of Commerce and Head of the Department of Industrial Economics and Business Studies at the University of Birmingham from 1975 to 1989. During 1979–80 he was a visiting professor or research fellow at Stanford University, New York University, University of Chicago and Virginia Polytechnic and Institute. Since 1994, he has been an honorary professor in the University of Birmingham Business School.

Professor Littlechild's publications include *Operational Research for Managers* (Philip Allan, 1976), *The Fallacy of the Mixed Economy* (IEA, 1978), *Elements of Telecommunications Economics* (Institute of Electrical Engineers, 1979), *Energy Strategies for the UK* (with K.G. Vaidya) (Allen and Unwin, 1982), *Regulation of British Telecommunications' Profitability* (Department of Industry, 1983), *Economic Regulation of Privatized Water Authorities* (HMSO, 1986), and over 60 articles.

Since stepping down as DGES at the end of 1998, Professor Littlechild has engaged in lecturing and consulting for government departments, regulatory bodies, universities, research institutes, regulated companies and international organizations including the World Bank. He has been involved since January 1999 in policy discussions in the USA, Mexico, India, Brazil, Australia, New Zealand, Poland, Thailand, the Philippines, Spain, Germany, Argentina and Italy, as well as in the UK. In May 1999, Stanford University conferred on him the Zale Award for Scholarship and Public Service. He was awarded an Honorary D.Sc. by the University of Birmingham in 2001.

Eileen Marshall worked as a stockbroker in the City of London before becoming a university lecturer, then senior lecturer, in industrial economics. Her research specialism was in energy economics and she acted as consultant to many companies and bodies.

Dr Marshall took up the position of Director of Regulation and Business Affairs with the Office of Electricity Regulation (Offer) in October 1989. In April 1994, she was appointed Chief Economic Adviser and Director of Regulation and Business Affairs at the Office of Gas Supply (Ofgas). Her responsibilities covered the full range of Ofgas policy issues, including the setting of price controls and the introduction of domestic competition. In

January 1997, while retaining her previous responsibilities at Ofgas, Dr Marshall became a part-time economic adviser to Offer, and from autumn 1997 led the Review of Electricity Trading Arrangements. In January 1998, she was awarded the CBE for services to regulatory policy. In June 1999, the former regulatory offices, Ofgas and Offer, were merged and renamed the Office of Gas and Electricity Markets (Ofgem). Dr Marshall took up the new position of Deputy Director General, with particular responsibility for competition and trading arrangements.

Callum McCarthy is the first energy regulator for the UK. He was appointed Director General of Gas Supply on 1 November 1998, and Director General of Electricity Supply on 1 January 1999. Both appointments are effective until 31 October 2003.

A Graduate of Oxford University, McCarthy also has a Ph.D. in economics from Stirling University and an MS from the Graduate School of Business at Stanford University (USA), where he was a Sloan Fellow. On graduating in 1965, he joined ICI as an economist and operations researcher. He moved to the Department of Trade and Industry in 1972, where he held a number of posts, including Principal Private Secretary to Roy Hattersley when he was Secretary of State for Prices and Consumer Protection, and to Norman Tebbit when he was Secretary of State for Trade and Industry.

McCarthy left the DTI in 1985, having reached the grade of under-secretary, and joined Kleinwort Benson as Director of Corporate Finance. In 1989, he joined BZW as Managing Director and Deputy Head of Corporate Finance. In 1993, he was appointed Chief Executive Officer of Barclays Bank's operations in Japan, where he served until 1996, when he became responsible for their businesses in North America.

Callum McCarthy is married with three children. His wife has a Ph.D. from Sussex University.

Derek Morris is Chairman of the Competition Commission (formerly the Monopolies and Mergers Commission). He first joined the MMC in 1991 as a member, becoming a deputy chairman in 1995 and chairman in 1998. Having studied politics, philosophy and economics at Oxford from 1964 to 1967, and then for a D.Phil. in economics at Nuffield College, he took up a research fellowship at the Centre for Business and Industrial Studies at Warwick University. Then, from 1970 until 1998, he was fellow and tutor in economics at Oriel College, Oxford.

During this time he wrote numerous books and articles, primarily in the field of industrial economics. Books included *The Economics System in the UK* (third edition, Oxford University Press, 1985); *Unquoted Companies* (Macmillan,

1984); *Industrial Economics and Organisation* (Oxford University Press, 1979, second edition, 1991); and *Chinese State Owned Enterprises and Economic Reform* (Clarendon Press, 1983) (the last three written with D. Hay). Other academic activities included chairmanship of the economics sub-faculty and then Social Studies faculty at Oxford and editorial board responsibilities for the *Journal of Industrial Economics*, the *Oxford Review of Economic Policy*, *Oxford Economic Papers*, among others.

Other activities have included three years on secondment as economic director of the National Economic Development Council, chairman of Oxford Economic Forecasting Ltd. He has also been involved for over 20 years in various types of advisory and consultancy work, initially in the field of competition policy but more recently for the Asian Development Bank, in helping to design and implement economic reform measures in China and Central Asia.

He was knighted in the 2002 New Year Honors list.

Colin Robinson was educated at the University of Manchester, and then worked for 11 years as a business economist before being appointed to the Chair of Economics at the University of Surrey in 1968.

Professor Robinson has written more than 20 books and monographs and over 150 papers, mainly on energy economics and policy. For the IEA, he has written *A Policy for Fuel?* (IEA Occasional Paper no. 31, 1969); *Competition for Fuel* (Supplement to Occasional Paper no. 31, 1971); *The Energy 'Crisis' and British Coal* (IEA Hobart Paper no. 59, 1974); (with Eileen Marshall) *What Future for British Coal?* (IEA Hobart Paper no. 89, 1981) and *Can Coal Be Saved?* (IEA Hobart Paper no. 105, 1985); *Competition in Electricity? The Government's Proposals for Privatising Electricity Supply* (IEA Inquiry no. 2, March 1988); *Making a Market in Energy* (IEA Current Controversies no. 3, December 1992) and *Energy Policy: Errors, Illusions and Market Realities* (IEA Occasional Paper no. 90, October 1993). He has contributed chapters to *Privatisation & Competition* (IEA Hobart Paperback no. 28, 1989) and to four volumes in the *Regulating Utilities* series. His most recent publication for the IEA, written with John Blundell, the Institute's General Director, is *Regulation Without the State* (IEA Occasional Paper no. 109, 1999).

Professor Robinson became a member of the IEA's Advisory Council in 1982 and was its editorial director from 1992 to August 2002. He was appointed a trustee of the Wincott Foundation in 1993. He received the British Institute of Energy Economists' award as 'Economist of the Year 1992' and the 'Outstanding Contribution to the Profession' award in 1998 from the International Association for Energy Economists.

Penelope Rowlatt trained at Oxford University as a theoretical physicist, and became an economist after raising a family. She worked for some years in HM Treasury and the (then) Department of Energy before becoming a director, first of National Economic Research Associates, and subsequently of Europe Economics. She is now a freelance consultant trading under the name Alexander Economics. She has been on the RPI Advisory Committee and the Royal Commission for Environmental Pollution, and was a lay member of the Restrictive Practices Court. Currently, she is Treasurer of the Royal Economic Society and a member of the Better Regulation Task Force.

Irwin M. Stelzer is a senior fellow and director of Hudson Institute's regulatory studies program. Before joining Hudson Institute in 1998, Stelzer was resident scholar and director of regulatory policy studies at the American Enterprise Institute. He also is the US economic and political columnist for *The Sunday Times* (London) and *The Courier Mail* (Australia), a contributing editor of *The Weekly Standard*, a member of the Publication Committee of *The Public Interest*, and a member of the board of the Regulatory Policy Institute (Oxford).

Stelzer founded National Economic Research Associates, Inc. (NERA) in 1961 and served as its president until a few years after its sale in 1983 to Marsh & McLennan. He also has served as managing director of the investment banking firm of Rothschild Inc. and as director of the Energy and Environmental Policy Center at Harvard University.

As a consultant to several US and UK industries with a variety of commercial and policy problems, Stelzer advises on market strategy, pricing and antitrust issues, and regulatory matters.

His academic career includes teaching appointments at Cornell University, the University of Connecticut, and New York University, and an associate membership of Nuffield College, Oxford. He is a former member of the Litigation and Administrative Practice Faculty of the Practicing Law Institute. He served on the Massachusetts Institute of Technology Visiting Committee for the Department of Economics, and has been a teaching member of Columbia University's Continuing Legal Education Programs.

Stelzer received his bachelor's and master's degrees from New York University and his doctorate in economics from Cornell University. He has written and lectured on economic and policy developments in the USA and UK. He has written extensively on policy issues such as America's competitive position in the world economy, optimum regulatory policies, the consequences of European integration, and factors affecting and impeding economic growth. He has served as economics editor of the *Antitrust Bulletin* and is the author of *Selected Antitrust Cases: Landmark Decisions* (Richard D.

Irwin, seventh edition, 1986) and *The Antitrust Laws: A Primer* (American Enterprise Institute, Washington, DC, fourth edition, 2001).

Linda Stephen is Research Fellow in Petroleum Economics at the University of Aberdeen. She is a graduate in Economics from the University of Aberdeen. For several years she has undertaken research on the economics of North Sea oil and gas and has co-authored many papers with Professor Kemp on this subject. These have appeared in books and journals including *Energy Policy*, *Continental Shelf Research*, and *Oxford Review of Economic Policy*.

John Vickers has been Director General of Fair Trading since 1 October 2000. Before that he spent two and a half years as Chief Economist at the Bank of England, and was a member of the Monetary Policy Committee. Most of his career has been spent teaching economics at Oxford University, where he was made the Drummond Professor of Political Economy in 1991. He has published widely on privatization, regulation and competition. He is a fellow of the British Academy, the Econometric Society and All Souls College, Oxford.

Leonard Waverman is Professor of Economics and Director of the Regulation Initiative and Global Communications Consortium at the London Business School. He has recently been appointed Director of the Economic and Social Research Council's E-Society Research Programme and has been awarded a research grant from the Leverhulme Trust for 'The social/economic impact of information and communication technology'. He is also a non-executive Board member of Ofgem – the UK's Gas and electric Market Authority. Professor Waverman has received the honour of *Chevalier dans l'Ordre des Palmes Academiques* of the Goverment of France.

Tom Winsor was appointed Rail Regulator and International Rail Regulator with effect from 5 July 1999.

He was born in 1957 and brought up in Broughty Ferry, Dundee. He was educated at Grove Academy, Broughty Ferry and then at the University of Edinburgh, where he graduated with an LL.B. (Scots Law) in 1979. As a solicitor, he qualified first in Scotland, where he is a Writer to the Signet, and subsequently in England and Wales. After general practice in Dundee, he took a postgraduate qualification in oil and gas law at the Centre for Energy, Petroleum and Mineral Law and Policy of the University of Dundee.

In the course of his legal career, Tom Winsor specialized first in UK and international oil and gas law, later adding electricity, regulation, railways and public law. He joined Denton Hall as a partner in 1991, where he was responsible for the design of the regulatory regime for the electricity industry in Northern Ireland. In 1993 he was seconded to the Office of the Rail Regulator as Chief Legal Adviser and later as General Counsel. He returned to his partnership at Denton Hall in 1995 as head of the railways department, part of the firm's energy and infrastructure practice.

Tom Winsor is an honorary lecturer at the Centre for Energy, Petroleum and Mineral Law and Policy of the University of Dundee, where he directed the UK Oil and Gas Law summer course from 1993 to 1997. He is married, with one daughter, and lives in Kent, travelling daily to his office in London by train.

Introduction

Colin Robinson

The eleventh annual series of Beesley Lectures on Regulation, jointly arranged by the Institute of Economic Affairs and the London Business School and named after Michael Beesley, was held in the autumn of 2001. The chapters in this volume are revised versions of the papers given in the series and they are, as usual, followed by comments made by the chairmen: the chairman in most cases is the relevant regulator. There is one exception in this volume. A lecture on merger control, due to have been given by Frederic Jenny, did not take place because of the speaker's illness. Fortunately, however, the chairman for the evening, John Vickers, was able instead to give a paper on international mergers which appears here as Chapter 8 without any subsequent chairman's comment.

Since the early days of the Lectures on Regulation in the early 1990s, a great deal of experience has accumulated of how and how not to design and operate regulatory systems. This growing experience is reflected in the increasing detail and sophistication of the papers given in the series.

In the first chapter, Professor Stephen Glaister provides a very wide-ranging review of the development of transport policy and of trends in various modes of transport in Britain. Glaister argues that, though the present government early on declared transport to be a key policy area, the 'delivery of policy' has not been a success. It was unwise to cut spending on major road schemes; transport policy in London has become less, not more, integrated; buses have been neglected; policy for the railways has been confused; and the quality of service on the London Underground has deteriorated. The government now needs to carry out an 'objective analysis of the facts' and create a realistic funding mechanism.

Tom Winsor, commenting on the chapter, says that it would have been better, in the case of the London Underground, for the government to have opted for licence regulation rather than contracts between the public sector and the infra-structure companies. He also discusses investor confidence in the railways, which he argues is best maintained by having an independent railway regulator. Investors want to avoid uncertainty; hence firm regulation is required.

Governments all round the world have privatized and deregulated their elec-tricity industries. In Chapter 2 Professor Stephen Littlechild explains to what extent there is a 'standard model' of regulation and what are the departures from that model. He surveys the approaches taken by various countries to competition in generation, competition in retail supply and wholesale trading arrangements. He concludes that there is scope for improved regulation to promote competitive markets and to avoid unnecessary intervention. Littlechild is critical of attempts at cost–benefit analyses of regulatory actions which consume regulatory time and effort: regulators are already thinking seriously about the way forward.

In her comment, Dr Eileen Marshall is generally in agreement with the Littlechild chapter. She argues for *ex ante* sector-specific regulation, with regulatory offices independent of the political process, and suggests that such offices are more likely to be established at the time of privatization rather than afterwards: because independent regulation is seen as reducing political uncertainty, it tends to increase share values and hence revenues from privatizations. Dr Marshall also points out that the establishment of NETA was a remarkable feat for all concerned, with 97 per cent of power being traded in voluntary markets.

In Chapter 3, Professor Alexander Kemp and Linda Stephen discuss the rising demand for natural gas in Western Europe, and more particularly the UK, relative to the supply. They expect UK production to peak within a few years, with rising imports thereafter. Net imports into Western Europe will also become substantial by 2010. Infrastructure will have to be expanded in the context of a liberalizing but regulated gas market. According to Kemp and Stephen, in the UK the basic industry structure has been settled, but that is not so on the Continent, where infrastructure provision and gas supply are often in the hands of the same organization. All parties would benefit from a settled structure and regulatory framework.

Callum McCarthy, in his comments, points to the uncertainty surrounding econometric estimates of future gas demand. Investment and operational decisions made by Transco are bound to be complex: Ofgem has therefore devised a system which gives incentives to Transco to respond to demand changes and which gives producers firm contractual rights to deliver gas to the National Transmission System. The new regime, which is a considerable advance on anything previously in place, will provide greater certainty both for Transco and for the producers.

Dr Irwin Stelzer, in Chapter 4, considers the ingredients of an effective competition policy. He lists the economic and social advantages of such a policy, including both microeconomic benefits and the expected boost to productivity growth. However, he argues, competition authorities are prone to make three conceptual errors: 'to equate bigness with evil'; 'to equate market share with market power'; and to fail to recognize the restraint placed on the behaviour of incumbents by the threat of entry. He would also like existing procedures to be studied to see if they can be made fairer to the parties and if the flow of information can be improved.

Commenting on Stelzer's chapter, Dr Derek Morris points to evidence which he believes shows that the British competition authorities do not make the 'conceptual errors' identified by Stelzer. He argues that markets which are quite close to being fully contestable may, in practice, be difficult to enter. Outside full contestability, the threat of entry will not necessarily constrain incumbents to behave competitively. He agrees about the need to improve information flows between the Competition Commission and the parties to inquiries.

Chapter 5 is a contribution by Professor Leonard Waverman on regulatory incentives and deregulation in telecommunications. He sees regulation as an attempt to 'mirror competitive actions', though an attempt that can never be completely successful. 'Uncontractability' (inability to write down all possible contingencies that may arise) is a particular problem. He suggests a regulatory cap regime that will limit 'regulatory creep'. Waverman expresses some concerns about Ofcom, whose scope and power appear too large. He would minimize regulation of broadband, reduce regulation of mobiles and change the design of auctions for 3G licences to try to 'place the spectrum in the best hands'.

David Edmonds defends the 3G auction and is also doubtful that 'regulatory creep' is a serious issue. He points to the growth of regulatory departments in regulated companies as a means of supporting their own existence. He sees Oftel's task as promoting competition for the benefit of consumers. Edmonds argues that moving from sectoral regulation to regulation under the Competition Act would make for more complex, not simpler inquiries. He supports Ofcom, which is, he says, designed to be both a sectoral regulator and a competition authority.

Dr Robert Crandall would like to see less 'economic' regulation (Chapter 6). His statistics show that economic regulation has already declined substantially in the USA because of the deregulation movement of the 1980s and 1990s, though there are a number of sectors (such as housing, agriculture, water and health care) where there are government controls of output or prices. The gains from deregulation, in terms of productive and allocative efficiency, have been impressive, though there are distributional implications. Further deregulation could bring more benefits as there are now few 'natural monopolies'. He sees telecommunications and electricity as candidates for more deregulation.

In her comment, Penelope Rowlatt says that Dr Crandall's chapter is the first 'really serious argument put forward for a total deregulation of the utilities'. In Britain debate has been mainly about the best way to regulate rather than about abolishing regulation. She commends Crandall's emphasis on the distributional aspects of regulation which is, she says, appropriate in the British context, given the decline in prices in some of the utilities and the changes in prices paid by different groups of consumers.

Professor David Currie considers, in Chapter 7, the case made for mutualization and for the use of debt-only vehicles, in the water industry and elsewhere, and also discusses whether the RPI–X regulatory model continues to be relevant. He is doubtful of the benefits of mutuals as compared with the equity ownership which applies to most regulated utilities in Britain: he fears mutuals and similar structures are 'prone to confused or poor decision-making processes in the event of difficulty' whereas, in such circumstances, under the equity model there is an 'established route for changing the management'. He suggests some 'modest reforms' to the RPI–X system, designed to improve the incentives for long-term investment in capacity expansion but argues that, in general, RPI–X has delivered 'enormous benefits'.

Philip Fletcher points out that experience in the water sector is that, under RPI–X, an industry can cope with a very large investment programme. He also agrees with David Currie that the equity model has so far worked well for water. He distinguishes between debt-only vehicles like Glas Cymru, and the earlier Kelda proposal for a community asset mutual which was rejected by the regulator. In his view the regulator should not try to dictate the structure of a regulated industry – for instance, forcing companies to go for higher gearing. There are risks in high gearing and 'you can only go very highly geared once'.

Chapter 8 is a contribution by John Vickers on international mergers, written before the 2002 Enterprise Act and the review of the European Community Merger Regulation, in which he explores the idea that internationalized merger control is more effective than national control. He describes the UK system of merger control, including the latest legislation which removes ministers from the process, and its relationship to the EU regime. He argues that it is those mergers which affect competition in 'inherently international' markets which may require international remedies, rather than those which affect only national markets. He sees several reasons for more international control, including the enhanced effectiveness of remedies in cases where those remedies are international. More coordination among national competition authorities is required.

John Dodgson considers the liberalization of postal services, principally in the UK, in Chapter 9. Pressures to liberalize have, he says, come from two sources – the European Commission and Postcomm. Provision of a universal postal service has in the past required that the postal operator be given a protected sector in which it has a monopoly: liberalization means the end of this monopoly. Dodgson concludes that there is considerable uncertainty about the outcome of liberalization. Postcomm should encourage liberalization as much as possible, but regulation, as well as competition, will be needed to protect consumers. However, Consignia may not react appropriately to an RPI–X regime, in which case the debate about whether Consignia should remain in the public sector may well be reopened.

In his comments, Graham Corbett asks whether a universal postal service, accompanied by a uniform tariff, might 'owe as much to commercial self-interest as to dictat': if so, the regulator could relax the measures designed to protect both of them. Encouraging entry to the postal market will be difficult, says Corbett, and the regulator may have to take some positive steps if there is to be vigorous rivalry. A cultural transformation in Consignia will be required to discourage resistance to change and to provide better and more reliable postal services to consumers.

The chapters in this volume show how the regulatory scene in Britain is changing, even though on the surface the essentials of the regime established at the time of privatization remain. The RPI–X system of price control, established in the early days when the regulatory regime was being formulated, has stood the test of time and, though occasionally questioned, is still the basis of regulatory control. The equity model was another pillar of the system. It too remains, though in some industries, notably water, new forms of organization with higher gearing have appeared, apparently as a response to price reviews which were seen as too harsh by the companies concerned.

But, while these two pillars of the regime remain more or less intact, there are signs of change. The rest of the EU is generally regarded as having lagged behind the UK in its regulatory regimes, but EU regulation is now becoming more of an issue. On the domestic scene, there appears to be some repoliticization of the utilities, which may threaten a third pillar of the regime – the independence of regulatory offices from political control. Most obviously, this is so in the railways where, in the aftermath of some serious accidents and financial problems, control has moved back to the government, which now takes responsibility for much of what happens as part of its transport policy. Even in gas and electricity, where privatization and subsequent regulation have been most successful in terms of providing tangible benefits to consumers, incipient signs of political intervention have appeared in the form of the return of energy policy. The eventual form of this policy still has to be determined, but clearly it could have a major impact on the privatized energy utilities and, in some circumstances, could result in the regulators being bypassed.

The question of whether political control of the utilities is returning, and whether or not such control is desirable, are bound to be principal themes of future Beesley Series, which will continue to examine the evolution of the British regulatory regime in comparison with what is happening in other countries.

1.   UK Transport Policy, 1997–2001

Stephen Glaister

INTRODUCTION

This chapter is an appraisal of the land transport policies of the 1997 Labour government. I compare public statements of aspirations and policy against the actual outcomes as measured in the official statistics.[1] Some suggestions for the future are offered.

The chapter is an overview and must skate over much of the detail. A number of smaller-scale initiatives may have been successful, but shortage of space precludes mentioning them here.

The overall conclusion is that the statistics indicate that very little was achieved 'on the ground'. There was a great deal of talk but little effective action. The 1997–2001 government made a number of important statements of new policies and achieved some changes in law and administration that may well prove to have been influential over the longer term.

THE DEVELOPMENT OF POLICY

In opposition the Labour Party had identified transport as being an important area of policy. Soon after the 1997 election the Labour government stated the problems it considered to be obvious and widely accepted, and some of the appropriate actions it also considered to be obvious.

The Consultation Document

The Consultation Document, *Developing an Integrated Transport Policy* (DETR, 1997a) was published in August 1997 with some supporting documents, most notably a useful set of facts and figures as they were known at the time. It was a dispassionate account of the issues. In many respects these were perceived in a similar way to those set out in discussion papers issued in the late days of the previous, Conservative, administration. Among other things it asserted: 'the forecast growth in road traffic is clearly unacceptable'. Appraisal of policy options and investment proposals in term of their costs and benefits was to 'remain at the heart of decision making and central to the review process'. Those responding to the consultation were to bear in mind 'the tight constraints on public funding'.

The overall objectives of policy were imprecise and couched in the 'correct' language of the time:

- 'a safe and efficient transport system'
- 'a better, more integrated public transport system'
- 'a more environmentally sustainable transport system'
- 'better and more strategic integration of transport and land use planning'.

The new government had already made a move towards the last objective by creating a unified Department of Environment, Transport and the Regions. This was intended to bring transport, environment and land use planning policies under the direction of the one Secretary of State (the Deputy Prime Minister), a move that recognized the fundamental interdependencies of these policies and one that had been advocated by the professionals for many years.

The GLA Act

In March 1998 the government announced its proposal for a public–private partnership (PPP) to rejuvenate the London Underground – important because it was one of the first and by far the largest of the new public–private partnerships. Soon afterwards it published *A Mayor and Assembly for London*, the White Paper presaging the Greater London Authority Act, 1999. This created the directly elected Greater London Assembly and directly elected, executive London Mayor. The GLA took its powers in July 2000. It is too early to judge what improvements it will succeed in making but, in principle, the GLA Act is of great importance in attempting to create a devolved Authority for London, including the Transport for London Board with specific powers over transport. At the time of writing (September 2001) the PPP for the Underground was still under negotiation and so control of the Underground resides with central government: the intention is that it will transfer to the GLA after completion of the PPP contracts.

Congestion Charging and Hypothecation of its Revenues

The GLA Act contains one feature new to British government that is innovative and in due course may prove to be of immense importance: the power to hypothecate the revenue from a government-imposed user charge – in this case a charge for the use of roads in London. The legislation insists that the revenues be used for transport purposes within the area. This could be regarded as hypothecation of a tax and such 'ring-fencing' of tax revenues has been stoutly resisted by the UK Treasury in all fields of public administration. Without it, introduction of this thoroughly sensible 'polluter pays' charge would be politically infeasible. This innovation must have been a consequence of a victory in an enormously hard-fought battle between the DETR and the Treasury.

The Transport Act 2000 and the Creation of the Strategic Rail Authority

The power to levy congestion charges is extended to cities outside London in the Transport Act 2000.

One of the other important provisions of the Transport Act 2000 is to create the Strategic Rail Authority (SRA). This is designed to correct a widely perceived weakness of the legislation that created the structure for the privatized railway (the Railways Act 1993): the lack of an effective body to take a lead in developing schemes to increase the capacity of the railway. In fact, the predecessor body, the Office of Passenger Rail Franchising, had been acting as the SRA in 'shadow' form more or less since the publication of the Transport White Paper in July of 1998.

The 1998 Transport White Paper

The 1998 White Paper, *A New Deal for Transport: Better for Everyone* (DETR, 1998b), is generally considered to have been a poorly focused and indecisive document. The White Paper was sometimes aptly described as 'carry on consulting'. Foster (2001) describes it as 'a collection of small initiatives which could equally well have been produced by the previous government'. The intention to create the SRA was one of the few genuinely 'white' parts in it. It was apparent that the government had come to realize that the transport problem is less tractable than they had thought in the early days of their Consultation Document.

The 2000 *Ten Year Plan*

In December 1999 the Deputy Prime Minister announced a new initiative: the start of a process of producing a ten-year plan for transport. The first such plan, *Transport 2010*, was published in July 2000 and relates to the ten years starting in April 2001 (DETR, 2000). Whilst the content of this plan is criticized below, the concept of a long-term plan that is revised from time to time is thoroughly sensible and was widely welcomed. Indeed, it is indispensable in an industry where the assets are so long lived.

ROAD TRAFFIC

The Aspiration to Cut Traffic

From the beginning, the 1997 government recognized the prime importance for the general public of the subject of 'traffic'. The government had a clear aspiration to reduce traffic and to mitigate its effect on the environment.

There was some recognition in the Consultation Document of what causes traffic growth. However, when the Deputy Prime Minister said in a notorious statement:

> I will have failed, if in five years' time there are not many more people using public transport and far fewer journeys by car. It's a tall order, but I urge you to hold me to it[2]

it was unclear how he intended to achieve this in the light of the facts identified in the Consultation Document.

The Growth of Traffic

Figure 1.1 shows traffic by vehicle type since 1950, highlighting the extraordinary growth in car traffic over this period. Clearly visible are the impact of the economic boom in the 1980s, the stagnation during the recession in the early 1990s and the renewed growth, at a lower rate, in the late 1990s.

The reasons for car traffic increases
Increases in car traffic have come about principally because real standards of living have risen and the costs of owning and running cars have not risen as fast, as illustrated in Figure 1.2. Many more people can afford to own and to run a car than used to be the case.

Note how public transport fares have broadly kept pace with real incomes – as one would expect since public transport relies heavily on labour for its major input – whilst the cost of car purchase has fallen markedly. This is a reflection of the technical progress in design and manufacture of motor vehicles over the decades. Not only are they cheaper, but they are better-quality items and they last longer. The fluctuations in the price of fuel have been considerable. Relative to prices generally, the price of fuel is now about the same as it was in 1964, though it has been substantially more expensive at times.

The official forecasts of traffic (DETR, 1997 and 2001c) have a good scientific foundation and I see no reason to dispute them. The growth they predict is mainly a consequence of assuming the continuation of the normal rate of increase of prosperity that we have enjoyed in the past, together with a general decline in motoring costs.

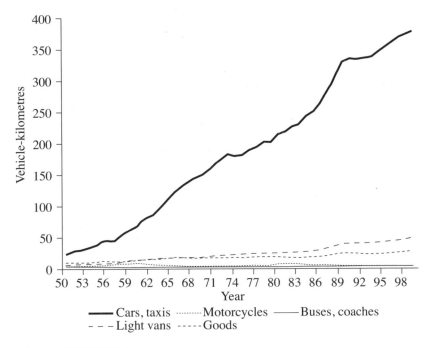

Source: DETR (2001c).

Figure 1.1 Growth of traffic in vehicle-kilometres, 1950–2000

Demographic factors

Other factors contribute to traffic growth. One is the striking growth in the number of households – especially one-person households. This is a source of concern in housing policy and it also has implications for the average number of cars owned per household.

There are other important demographic forces. A particularly important example concerns older people. We can expect an increase in the number of active older persons, especially women, living on their own. In 1996 only 7 per cent of women on their own and over the age of 75 had a driving licence (Glaister and Graham, 1996). Many of them never learned to drive. But 70 per cent of today's women aged between 40 and 49 hold a driving licence and young women are learning to drive just as much as young men. As the decades pass the older generations will wish to own and use cars in much higher numbers than their predecessors.

The benefits of mobility

Benefits of mobility represent a contradiction to the generally accepted aspiration to *reduce* traffic. Improved mobility for older persons will be an

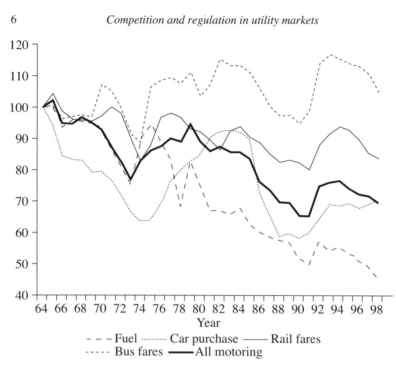

Source: DETR (2001b).

Figure 1.2   Price indices relative to gross household income, 1964–2000

enormous benefit both to us and to younger generations. We will be able to
stay self-sufficient to a greater degree and our quality of life will be enhanced.
There will be savings for health and social services if home visits can be
avoided. Anybody who asserts that the growth in the number of cars should be
stopped should be willing to say whether and how growth among the older
population is to be accommodated.

The extraordinary growth in mobility for the population as a whole represents
an important improvement in the general quality of life. The average household
that spends money on motoring now spends well over £50 per week – the same
order of magnitude as other 'necessities of life', housing and food. This is
people's free choice, and the fact the figure is so high is a reflection of how
many other goods and services they are willing to sacrifice for the privilege.

The responsiveness of traffic to prices
The variation in fuel prices over time and across space allows statistical exploration of the extent to which people do respond to changes in the price of fuel
that they face. Table 1.1 records a summary of the conclusions from a review
of the literature (Glaister and Graham, 2002).[3]

Table 1.1   Responses of traffic to fuel prices and income

	Immediate impact (%)	Long-run Impact (%)
Effect of 10% fuel price rise on traffic	−1.5	−3
Effect of 10% fuel price rise on fuel consumption	−3	−7
Effect of 10% rise in incomes		12

These figures illustrate the distinction between the immediate, or short-run, effects and the long-run effects. There is also a distinction between the effect on *traffic* and the larger effect on *fuel consumption*. The difference comes about because people are able to adjust the way they drive and the fuel efficiency of the cars they use.

The role of fuel taxation and the fuel tax escalator
There is good evidence that people do respond, especially over the kind of time horizon that transport policy should be considering. Raising taxation can be used as a means to reduce both traffic and the quantity of fuel burned.

At one time there seemed to be a general acceptance within government that the price of fuel had some effect on fuel consumption and on traffic. The outgoing Conservative government had instigated an automatic 'fuel tax escalator' of 5 per cent per year above inflation. Although there were allegations that this was really a means of raising tax revenues for a government that was in financial straits, the official justifications given included that it was to reduce traffic growth or to make a contribution towards mitigation of the damage caused by traffic-generated air pollution.

The new government embraced and reinforced this policy, increasing the escalator from 5 to 6 per cent per year. The consequence of this policy can be seen in the motoring fuel price index in Figure 1.3. Petrol had been cheap by European standards, but by 2000 the UK had the most expensive petrol in Europe. The proportion of the final price that is tax rose from 44 per cent in 1980 per cent to 82 per cent in 1999.

In the recent debates on motoring taxes the public has focused on the cost of fuel and the rate of fuel duty, neglecting the fact that the increases have been largely offset by rapid falls in the costs of purchasing cars. However, the composite index representing *all* the costs of motoring has remained remarkably constant relative to the RPI since 1964, as shown in Figure 1.3. Taxes on car purchase and on insurance are taxes on ownership (as distinct from use) that deserve consideration as part of any review of motoring taxation. The annual licence disc is another element of the cost of vehicle ownership. This was reduced for smaller vehicles in the November 2000 statement.

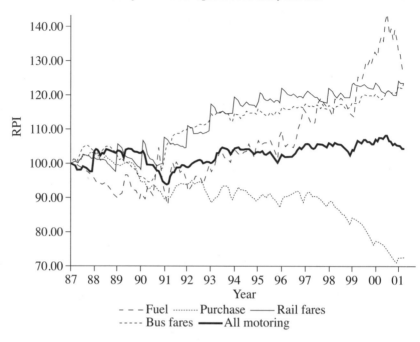

Source: DETR (2001b).

*Figure 1.3   Motoring fuel price indices relative to the Retail Price Index,
            1987–2001*

Labour's Effect on Traffic

Figure 1.4 shows what has happened to traffic on various road types since 1982,
with the graph 'stretched' to show seasonally adjusted quarterly annual running
rate for 1999 and 2000.

   The growth pattern is repeated for all road types. Note that total traffic growth
was low during 1999 and 2000, with a noticeable dip corresponding to the peak
in fuel prices and the fuel price protests in September 2000. An analysis by
P. Hathaway of the effect of the fuel 'protest' on road traffic (DETR, 2001c)
is that road traffic in the third quarter of 2000 was reduced by nearly two
percentage points as a result of the disruption caused by the fuel protest.

   Between January 1998 and July 2000 the fuel price index rose by 23 per cent
above inflation. Assuming a traffic elasticity of –0.3, this would be expected
to reduce traffic by about 7 per cent over the two and a half years, or an average
of 2.8 per cent per year. This is of the same order as the growth that would be
expected as a result of economic growth. So, the evidence on traffic is consistent

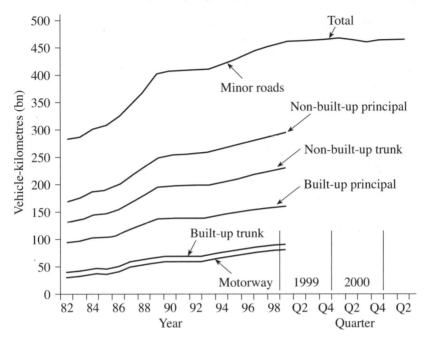

Source: DETR (2001c).

Figure 1.4   Growth of traffic on various road types, 1982–2000

with the view that the government did indeed manage almost to halt traffic growth over a period of two years or so. This was not achieved by any complicated transport policy, but by the simple policy of increasing fuel tax, supported by world crude oil prices.

Policy Reversal: the Fuel Tax Protest

In the summer and autumn of 2000 there was an increase in the world price of crude oil, which combined with the fuel price escalator to cause the acceleration in the final price of fuel visible in Figure 1.3. This ignited the fuel protests of the autumn.

The government as a whole responded quickly. The Chancellor of the Exchequer reversed the trend in fuel taxation. He was to be heard on the radio claiming that traffic did *not* respond to fuel prices, so the reduction would not contribute to traffic growth. This was contrary to the evidence and it repudiated cornerstones of transport policy on both traffic and the environment.

The concessions announced in the November 2000 Pre-Budget Report equate approximately to a 6 per cent fall in the pump price of fuel, relative to an inflation-matching increase. Hence, in the long run traffic will be about 6×0.3 $= 1.8$ per cent higher and fuel consumption $6 \times 0.7 = 4.2$ per cent higher than it would otherwise have been. This contrasts with the policy in the first years of the Labour government of increasing the duty on fuel by 6 per cent per year above inflation. Since duty represents on the order of 80 per cent of the pump price, this policy would have offset the 3 per cent or so annual growth due to rising real incomes by about $6 \times 0.8 \times 0.3 = 1.4$ per cent.

By the end of 1999, on the advice of the Commission for Integrated Transport (a body first proposed in the White Paper), John Prescott had apparently become reconciled to the view that no country in the world would cut traffic in absolute terms while its economy is growing (Foster, 2001, p. 282).

As fuel tax is reduced in response to the fuel price protests, traffic will start to respond to whatever economic growth there is. The latest traffic figures (DTLR, 2001c) confirm that traffic has started to grow again in response to the reduction in fuel prices.

THE POLITICAL ECONOMY OF ROAD FUEL PRICES

The fuel crisis was a first stirring in the UK of a new force to which policy has only begun to respond: the motoring majority. Over the last couple of decades the car has become much more easily and cheaply available to a majority of the population. Travel patterns and land uses have changed fundamentally in response to this. Two thirds of households have at least one car, and three quarters of adults live in a household that has a car.

Changes in fuel prices directly affect the daily lives of a far greater number of people than used to be the case. Industry and commerce have altered the way they function to take advantage of the cheapness and reliability of road as the generally preferred mode for moving their goods.

The revenues from fuel taxation have gradually grown to be a major source of funds for general government expenditure. In 1975 tax revenues from the road sector were £13 bn and public spending on roads was a little lower at £11.5 bn. By 1997 tax revenue had increased to £31 bn, yet spending had fallen to £6 bn. It is small wonder that taxation and public spending on road transport have become more politically sensitive than they once were (Coates, 1999).

It will no longer be possible for the Chancellor to set rates of taxation on transport at each budget in isolation from those responsible for transport policy in other departments of state, or from the overall policy strategists. This was clearly illustrated by the government's statements presaging the Chancellor's Pre-Budget Report on Wednesday 8 November 2000. They clearly stated that a reduction in revenues from road taxation would have direct implications for other public spending programmes.

Future Fuel Costs

Fuel prices are made up from the US$ price of crude oil and the rate of taxation. A fuller analysis of different scenarios on the price of crude oil and on fuel taxation policies is now required. The main scenario in the *Ten Year Plan* document assumes that the rate of fuel duty is constant, but that the cost of motoring per vehicle-mile falls by 20 per cent because the price of crude oil is assumed to fall from $28 to $16 per barrel, and technological improvements in vehicle efficiencies continue. These benefits are assumed to be passed on to motorists in full. The document does discuss one alternative scenario in which motoring costs are held constant. This demonstrates how different the outcomes could be (p. 87). Instead of congestion improving by 6 per cent, it would improve by 12 per cent.

FUEL TAXATION AND ENVIRONMENTAL POLICY

Increasing taxation was a deliberate emissions-reducing policy as well as a traffic-reducing policy in the first three years of the 1997 government. The White Paper affirms this in several places. For instance, under the section heading 'Sending the Right Signals' it states:

> The use of economic instruments, such as pricing measures and taxation, is an important way of influencing travel choice. Such measures can help to ensure that all costs, including environmental costs, are reflected in the price of transport.
>
> We have sent clear signals about the need to use transport more sustainably, consistent with the Chancellor of the Exchequer's 'statement of intent' on using environmental taxes in combination with other instruments to achieve environmental objectives ...
>
> We already use duty on different fuels as a way of influencing demand for road transport and as an incentive to consumers to buy more fuel efficient and less polluting vehicles ...
>
> Increasing fuel duty has proved an effective way of directly influencing CO_2 emissions from road transport as part of our strategy for tackling climate change ... (Paragraphs 4.118–4.121)

Carbon Dioxide Emissions

The *Ten Year Plan* illustrates how holding motoring costs constant, rather than allowing them to fall as assumed in the plan, would be expected to reduce CO_2 emissions by 6 per cent, rather than the 3 per cent claimed for the plan (p. 87).

The Labour Party's 1997 Manifesto made a commitment to reduce carbon dioxide emissions to 20 per cent below their 1990 levels by 2010. Transport accounts for about one third of carbon dioxide emissions, and on current policies it seems unlikely that transport will achieve that target. To move towards this will require the large-scale adoption of the fuel-efficiency benefit that available technology can already offer for conventional fuels. Some new fuels, such as natural gas, LPG (liquefied petroleum gas) and possibly hydrogen, offer the prospect of real advance in mitigating air pollution problems. But they will only be adopted on the required scale if motorists are given the financial incentive to do so.

Air Quality

The general public are particularly worried about transport-generated air pollution and its effect on health. The hard evidence on the danger to health of transport emissions is controversial and inconclusive. Sansom et al. (2001) give a good survey of the recent evidence on the health costs of transport emissions.

The Consultation Document said little explicitly about air pollution. By the time of the White Paper, policy had explicitly responded to the general public's concern that traffic-generated emissions were damaging to their health: 'We must do everything we can to cut this loss of life by improving air quality ...' (paragraph 2.7).

Figures 1.5 and 1.6 show measures of four air pollutants at a selection of rural and urban sites. The Internet now carries a bewildering quantity of raw information taken – almost in real time – from a large number of measuring sites.[4] There are many possible ways of summarizing the information. These two graphs show the number of days in the respective year that there was neither moderate nor high pollution, for each of the four air pollutants. Unfortunately not all sites have records extending back more than a year or so. The data shown in the figures are averages across those sites where data have been recorded for a number of years. They are not representative in any statistical sense.

Taking these graphs at face value, it is apparent that the situation was worsening in the early 1990s. But around 1997 or 1998 there was a marked improvement, especially in particulates. These are the small particles produced predominantly by diesel engines, and this is one of the pollutants for which there is convincing evidence of health damage.

There are several reasons for the improvements: the widespread introduction of low-sulphur fuels; the fitting of catalytic converters and smoke traps; and, importantly, the imposition of more demanding technical standards for the efficiency and environmental performance of modern engines. The improvements are particularly marked at some of the dense urban sites, such as those in inner London. These are the places where there is a high density of people around to be affected by the pollution.

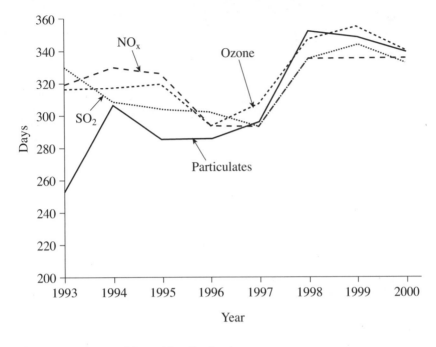

Source: www.aeat.co.uk/netcen/airqual/statbase/

Figure 1.5   Urban days with low pollution, 1993–2000

Air pollution did improve within the period of the Labour government, but it is not clear that government can claim credit for more than continuing with an existing trend.

This is a considerable success story, especially in the light of the growth in traffic. The prospects for further improvements are good. There are still a number of heavily offending vehicles (many of them old, diesel-powered) and there is scope for more effective enforcement of the laws. Technical improvements in engine and vehicle design also still have a great deal to offer in improved fuel consumption and reduced emissions.

Conclusion on Fuel Taxation

The overall conclusion is that whilst rises in fuel taxation do have a part to play in facing motorists with the 'correct' costs of their decisions, they are unlikely to achieve the government's objectives on their own at politically acceptable levels. Nor should they, because they are such a blunt instrument. Set high enough to have a useful effect in congested cities, they would cause unwarranted

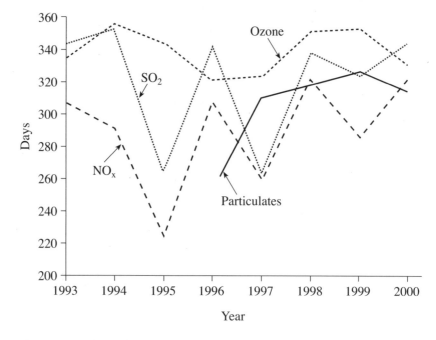

Source: www.aeat.co.uk/netcen/airqual/statbase/

Figure 1.6   Rural days with low pollution, 1993–2000

damage to the interests of those in less damaging circumstances, such as the country areas. Further, the incidence of fuel tax increases on some poorer groups may be thought to be undesirable (discussed in Glaister and Graham, 2002).

SAFETY

Understandably, governments always make strong statements about safety. The White Paper recognized the magnitude of the problem of road deaths and notes the considerable past achievements: 'By 1997 the number of deaths on the road had fallen by 36% to 3,599 and the number of serious casualties had declined by 42% to 42,967' (paragraph 3.218). The *Ten Year Plan* (paragraph 7.4) records a target of further reducing these by 40 per cent.

Figure 1.7 confirms how dramatic has been the improvement in road safety over the last three decades. But it also shows how further improvements are proving to be more and more difficult to achieve. Indeed, little progress has actually been achieved in recent years. There are effective means still available to reduce road deaths and injuries substantially. Many of them involve the spending of relatively small amounts of money on local road improvements. One of the most productive means would be to reduce average speeds, for instance by rigorous enforcement of speed limits, through implementation of speed cameras and other means. The government seems to have been ambivalent in its attitude to policies to achieve this, as have other governments before. Speed cameras have been found to be highly effective if properly enforced, but in July and August 2001 the representatives of senior police officers were displaying a reluctance to risk 'alienating' the motorist by over-zealous enforcement.

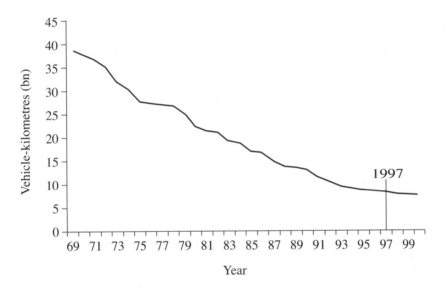

Source: *Road Casualties in Great Britain* (DETR, annual).

Figure 1.7   *Road fatalities per bn motor-vehicle-kilometres, 1969–99*

Figure 1.8 shows the safety performance on the railways.[5] As with road fatalities, there has been a remarkable continual improvement in the safety performance of the railway. Serious rail accidents are much less frequent than road accidents, so the profile of fatalities is less regular. There is some suggestion of an increase in the rate after 1997 (the railway was fully privatized in 1996). Some of this may be accounted for by an increase in suicides and drunken behaviour by the general public.

Railway safety certainly became a highly controversial subject under that government. Labour had opposed railway privatization before they formed the

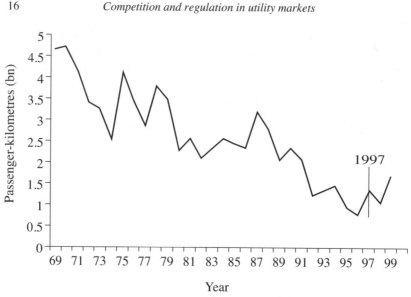

Source: Evans (2001).

Figure 1.8   Rail fatalities per bn passenger-kilometres, 1969–99

government and it had been unpopular with the public. Ministers reacted strongly to the two major accidents in west London, and Railtrack themselves responded in the name of safety to an accident due to a broken rail at Hatfield in a way that destroyed the performance of the industry and the confidence of both passengers and investors. However, Evans (2002) notes that

> Although the Hatfield accident has had an unprecedented effect on the operation of the railway, in statistical terms what happened in the year 2000 was remarkably in line with [previous] estimates. It follows that the occurrence of the Hatfield accident itself has not led to more than minor revisions to estimates of train accident risk.

It will be some years before we have sufficient perspective to know whether there was a statistically significant increase in the railway accident rate under the Labour government, and what the role of privatization in this might have been.

Railway safety policy appears to have lost perspective under the Labour governments. It is likely that when the several official inquiries into the subject have been published, government and the safety regulators will insist on greatly increased safety expenditure at a cost that will not be justified by the benefits secured, and where that same money would save very many more lives if it were diverted to the much less safe roads.

Sadly, the 1997 government was no more successful than its predecessors in improving the rigour of the public debate on the allocation of the available resources so as to create the safest possible overall transport system.

INTEGRATION

The word 'integration' appears consistently in Labour government statements on transport policy – indeed, the 1997 Consultation Document had it in its title. Although used a great deal, its meaning has not been clearly defined. The Consultation Document hints at two, distinct meanings: 'a better, more integrated public transport system ...' and 'better and more strategic integration of transport and land use planning'.

The first of these seems to refer, for example, to easier interchange between modes or services on the physical system. It is hard to know how one would measure progress on this. On the basis of casual observation, there does not seem to have been much change over the period of the Labour government.

The more significant interpretation has been the attempt to integrate *policy*. Here a positive beginning was made with the agglomeration of the transport, environment and land use planning functions within the one department of state, the DETR. This turned out to be a large and somewhat unwieldy department. Most commentators agree that land use policy is at least as important in the long term in determining transport and environmental objectives as are more direct approaches, so this seemed a logical move. I am not in a position to judge whether, in practice, it has made a difference. Foster (2001) says 'there [were no] immediate benefits realised from joining up transport, environmental and planning policies in the creation of DETR'. The 2001 government removed the environmental responsibilities.

As we have noted in other sections, policy was not successfully integrated in other respects. Fuel taxes were not successfully tied to traffic management or environmental objectives for long. The White Paper made the reasonable claim that this was beginning to be achieved. However, the policy reversals after the fuel protests have thrown this attempt at integration into disarray.

Transport policy integration in London has yet to be achieved, with the SRA responsible for the commuter railway, Transport for London (TfL) responsible for the buses and London Regional Transport (a nationalized industry) still responsible for the London Underground. Although the intention is to transfer this to TfL, the government is resolutely determined to fragment the Underground into four parts and enshrine the new structure in 30-year commercial contracts. This will prevent the devolved London government from achieving unified management control.

SOCIAL INCLUSION

Like 'integration', 'social inclusion' is another ill-defined term that was frequently mentioned in the transport context by the 1997 government. It clearly had something to do with a wish to help the poor or disadvantaged – particularly to the extent that improving access to transport facilities could mitigate the disadvantage.

It is hard to identify much active transport policy in the first Labour government that actually promoted social inclusion. There is no doubt that the Labour government was firmly pro-rail and less actively pro-bus or pro-car, as illustrated by the thrust of the *Ten Year Plan*. Some might argue that spending on rail helps the poor and the socially excluded. However, as a generalization, the poor and the socially excluded do not use railways much. This is illustrated in Figure 1.9, which shows average weekly spending on different modes of transport by households of various types. The household types are ordered in increasing total weekly expenditure along the horizontal axis: lone state pensioners had an average expenditure of £83 per week and, at the other end of the spectrum, households with three or more adults and children spent £519 per week. The relationship between income and spending on rail is clear: anything that benefits the generality of rail users is more likely to benefit the rich rather than the poor.

Spending on buses is also shown. Much more is spent on buses than on rail in most of the lower income categories. Also, the level of spend is much more uniform across income levels; the more so if one ignores the two right-hand categories (households with more than two adults) and allows for the availability of fares concessions to pensioners. The poorest, pensioner groups, spend between two and six times more on buses than on rail. It is disappointing that the *Ten Year Plan* only aspires to a modest 10 per cent growth in bus travel, when the bus is a much more commonly used mode.

The biggest surprise is in the figures for expenditure on motoring (note the different scale for the vertical axis from the other two panels). The poorest group averages nearly £2 per week on motoring, which is 15 times more than on rail. The next two groups spend 50 to 80 times more on motoring than on rail. The use of the car has become so pervasive that it may well be the case that if governments wish to help the poor then it is more effective to find a way of helping the lower-income motorist than the generality of rail users.

The *Ten Year Plan* says that, among other objectives it will 'enhance access and opportunity in rural areas' and 'reduce social exclusion' (paragraph 1.9). Yet it is far from clear by what mechanisms it will achieve these two objectives. In fact, the Plan is really directed at meeting other objectives and it is most unlikely to do much to help the poor and the socially excluded – who are more likely to be helped by direct cash grants or other aspects of social policy.

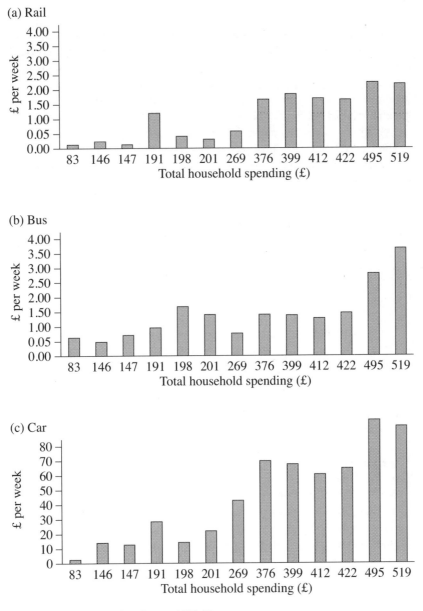

Source: Family Expenditure Survey, 1996–97.

Figure 1.9 Household expenditure on different modes of transport

BUSES

The bus is a far more important mode of public transport than the train. Yet Labour's policy towards it has been strangely muted. Labour strongly opposed the 1985 deregulation and privatization of local bus services and subsequently criticized the way it operated. When they took power they inherited a lightly regulated industry (outside London) over which neither central nor local government had much control, beyond the ability to purchase non-commercially viable services on competitive contract. Fares could not be regulated.

The Consultation Document noted that 'The bus is a vastly under-utilised and under-valued transport resource, which we need to use much more effectively' (paragraph 19). It spoke of restoring a degree of regulation and route franchising:

> Regulation will help achieve efficient, high quality bus services at the local level ... we believe that changes are needed to allow the bus to play its full part in an integrated transport policy ... it can help by reducing congestion and pollution by attracting people out of their cars ... (Paragraph 21)

It also mentioned the option of expanding the 'quality partnership' approach which had already been introduced in some areas.

The White Paper reiterated these thoughts, but given that it recognized buses as 'the workhorses of the public transport system' (paragraph 3.13), the document gives them remarkably little attention. It did announce the intention to legislate to give powers to local authorities to enter into 'Quality Contracts' for bus services. These involve operators bidding for exclusive rights to run bus services on the basis of a local authority service specification and performance targets. These powers are contained in the Transport Act 2000, but there has been little action in implementing the idea.

The Labour government introduced a few, minor grant schemes such as the Rural Bus Grant.

The *Ten Year Plan* claims progress on buses: bus quality partnerships in 120 towns and cities, bus industry investment up by over 30 per cent (funded by the private owners) and nearly 2000 new or enhanced rural bus services in England (paragraph 2.3). However, at the aggregate level, actual achievement in promoting the use of buses has been modest, as Figure 1.10 shows. This is in spite of some success in increasing the volume of bus service on offer, a continuation of a trend established under Conservative governments (Figure 1.11). The plan is also modest in its aspirations for the future of buses, since it expects a growth of only 10 per cent over the ten-year period (paragraph 6.62).

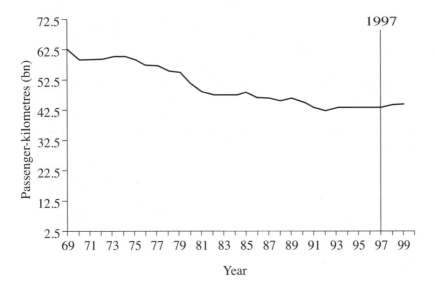

Source: DETR (2001c)

Figure 1.10   Bus-passenger-kilometres (bn), 1969–99

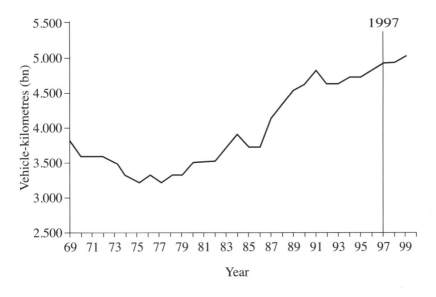

Source: DETR (2001c)

Figure 1.11   Bus vehicle-kilometres (bn), 1969–99

RAILWAYS

Problematic Railways Policy

Railways policy proved to be a major problem for the Labour government. In opposition Labour had opposed rail privatization throughout its development. On achieving power Labour decided not to implement the policy of renationalizing the railways. Instead, they chose to work within the structure they had inherited.

The Consultation Document was vague about railways policy. The White Paper also says surprisingly little about the railways, beyond endorsing the freight operator's 'aspirational target' to double traffic and noting that 'there is clearly scope for increased use of the passenger railway' (paragraph 3.27), recognizing that this would require investment in new capacity and recording that Railtrack had estimated that it would complete a solution to the railway congestion problems by 2006 (paragraph 3.31).

The delayed Strategic Authority

The major railways policy initiative in the White Paper was the promise to convert the Office of Passenger Rail Franchising into a Strategic Rail Authority (SRA). This would

> provide a clear, coherent and strategic programme for the development of our railways ... [and] will provide a focus for strategic planning of the passenger and freight railways with appropriate powers to influence the behaviour of key industry players. (Paragraphs 4.12 and 4.14)

It was generally accepted that this would rectify one of the shortcomings of the privatized rail structure. However, in the event the relevant legislation proved to have difficulty in finding parliamentary time and was then delayed until the end of 2000 by controversy over the privatization of National Air Traffic Control Services. Such was the lack of determination on the part of the government that it took all of two and a half years for legislation firmly promised in the White Paper to reach the statute book.

The delayed franchise renegotiations

As the Transport Bill became ensnared in parliamentary bureaucracy, and feeling under pressure to be taking some action on railways policy, the Secretary of State announced a programme of 'franchise renegotiations'. Many of the train-operating franchises are seven-year contracts due to expire in 2003–04. There were persistent complaints from the public about the standards of service being achieved by some of the train-operating companies. The SRA (operating in 'shadow' form as sSRA until it obtained its legal powers in early 2001) was instructed to commence renegotiation of the agreements. This policy did not seem fully to recognize that the franchises are legally binding commercial contracts that could not be repudiated by one side. Not surprisingly the progress of negotiating changes has proved slow. No contracts changed during the first Labour government. Agreement was reached that one franchise would terminate and change hands before the contract reached full term, but at the end of July 2001 even that transition still had not been completed. Outline agreement on some other, London local franchises has been reached, but it is unclear exactly when transfer might occur.

The SRA seems to be convinced of the view that because of the need to secure long-term investment, it is advantageous to agree long tenures for the contracts. Twenty years is the term that seems to have been favoured. It is ironic that the administration that was so frustrated by its inability to alter the seven-year contracts it inherited is so determined to commit to contracts as long as 20 years (and 30 years in the case of the London Underground infrastructure contracts).

The East Coast Main Line franchise has become a notorious case. The SRA invited re-bids for the franchise and received them from the incumbent, Great North Eastern Railway (GNER) and from Virgin Trains. The SRA seems to have had difficulty agreeing a decision with government. In July 2001 the Secretary of State in the second Labour government unexpectedly announced that neither long-term offer would be accepted, but the existing contract would be extended by a mere two years.

The lack of a Strategic Rail Authority strategy
A full statement of the (shadow) SRA Strategic Plan has been expected and then delayed on more than one occasion, and it is not now expected to appear before late autumn 2001.[6] Meanwhile, an outline *Strategic Agenda* was published on 13 March 2001.[7] This document is essentially a restatement of the objectives of the *Ten Year Plan*, both in respect of the amounts of money to be spent and the objectives it will pursue. The document says 'The challenge for the SRA is to achieve both consensus and momentum among the many public sector interests in transport, and to obtain value for money for the funds they will commit' (p. 24). However, it does not say any more about how the SRA might interpret the concept of value for money. When listing individual rail schemes in outline, the document simply identifies the extent to which each scheme might contribute towards the *Ten Year Plan* objectives.

Published information about value for money from specific rail investment schemes is hard to come by. Two illustrative computations are to be found in Railtrack's 2000 *Network Management Statement* (vol. 1, p. 74). Unfortunately little detail is given there about the methods used, although it is clear that the basis is not directly comparable to the longstanding method used for economic assessment of trunk roads.

Rail growth under privatization and further growth under the *Ten Year Plan*

Unlike the 1998 White Paper, the 2000 *Ten Year Plan* puts the railway in its centre. It envisages a 50 per cent increase in passenger traffic (and an 80 per cent increase in freight traffic).

Figure 1.12 shows the history of railway patronage since 1908. The figure is 'stretched' to show detailed quarterly data (at the annual running rate) for the four quarters starting spring 2000. It is remarkably stable, in spite of the two world wars, the Beeching rationalizations of the 1960s, the advent of the motor car and many other social changes.

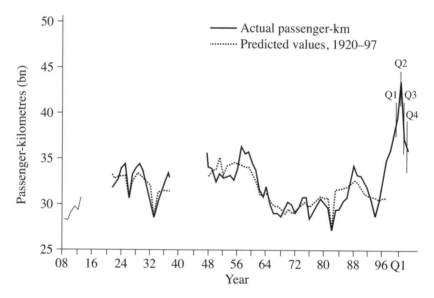

Sources: Glaister (1999) and SRA (2001).

Figure 1.12   British Railways passenger-kilometres, 1908–98

This historical perspective reveals how ambitious is the target to increase patronage by 50 per cent. As the figure shows, extraordinary growth was established after privatization and it continued throughout most of the first Labour term. Quality of service generally improved for some years after privatization. It started to decline, partly as a consequence of congestion of trains on the network. Figure 1.13 shows how the volume of service offered increased. The architects of rail privatization did not anticipate this problem of success.

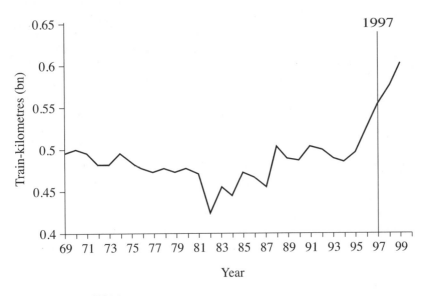

Source: DETR (2001c).

Figure 1.13   Train-kilometres (bn), 1969–99

Catastrophic decline

The growth in the period after privatization was far more than can be explained by conventional responses to increasing economic activity or reduction in fares. As Figure 1.12 shows, at its peak in the summer of 2000 patronage was at a level without historical precedent. Something must have been going right.

None of this growth could be claimed as a credit for the Labour government – though it was, of course, consistent with their overall transport policy. To have presided over the disastrous decline after the Hatfield accident must be seen as an acute embarrassment.

The failing railways policy

Before government can make a sensible change of policy towards the railway it must diagnose the problems with the present structure. Arguably, it worked reasonably well in the early years. We have seen how rapidly patronage and the volume of train service were both growing. As Figure 1.23 below shows, private investment was increasing rapidly, continuing a trend started under the Conservatives. Surprisingly, in view of the Labour Party's historical commitment to railways, *public* expenditure was also falling, again continuing the trend set under the Conservatives. This was the direct consequence of the reducing schedules of payments enshrined in the passenger franchise contracts, and it was a central aim of the Conservative rail privatization policy. The Labour government continued the policy of accepting the improved financial performance of the railway in the form of a reduced call on the Exchequer, rather than ploughing the saving back into the industry.

If privatization seemed to be progressing successfully, there were at least three things that were not satisfactory. First, the general public were unhappy with the very concept of rail privatization, many of their concerns having been articulated by Labour over many years while in opposition. Commentators and the public were unreceptive to data that seemed to show that things were improving. Two major accidents reinforced their scepticism, and government took the opportunity to add to the adverse comment. Then a third accident with the broken rail at Hatfield in autumn 2000 led to an embattled Railtrack taking precautionary action that destroyed the train service performance and the confidence of both the general public and investors.

Second, as the number of trains on the system increased, they tended to obstruct one another and the improvements in service reliability started to be reversed. The only way to accommodate extra services without compromising reliability is to invest in extra capacity. Railtrack claimed that the regime of charges did not give them sufficient incentive to do this. This difficulty was one that the creation of the SRA was intended to correct, but it has taken so long to move into action that it has yet to have any impact.

Third, Railtrack seemed to have difficulty in meeting the targets it had agreed with the regulator for reducing the number of service failures for which they were responsible.

Finally, there was doubt about whether Railtrack were investing as much as they should have been in maintaining the assets – a task that the access charges were supposed to remunerate them.

These two last problems caused particular friction with the rail regulator. The failure to maintain the assets adequately may have been a contributory factor to the Hatfield accident. This in turn has very seriously damaged the share values and long-term prospects for the company.

What went wrong?
The reasons for this set of failures must be ascertained. Some of the unanswered questions are:

- Were the commercial incentives wrongly set? These were revised in the regulator's Periodic Review of autumn 2001.

- Did the company fail to respond to incentives in a way that was in its long-term commercial interest?
- If so, why?
- Were the particular senior executives deficient, or was the company too large and too geographically spread out to manage effectively?

Excessive government intervention

One factor that may have been damaging is the fact that governments have a much greater propensity to intervene in the railway than in the other privatized utilities. This is at least partly because large public subsidies are paid. One consequence is that the management knows that if things turn out badly the government will rescue them. This blunts the normal incentive to be efficient and prudent. An example is presented by the high-speed upgrade of the West Coast Main Line. This was a highly risky commercial venture, willingly signed up to by Railtrack. But it later transpired that Railtrack had poor information about the costs of delivering the required outputs. In the event the finances of this project have had to be rescued by at least one substantial grant from the Exchequer.

FREIGHT

The Consultation Document does not say much about inland freight, except that 'The Government wants to see more passengers and freight travel by rail ...' (paragraph 15). The White Paper has a section on 'sustainable distribution', which actually makes few concrete proposals beyond some adjustments in permitted maximum lorry weights and promising to work with local authorities to direct lorries away from unsuitable areas.

A Failure to Shift Freight from Road to Rail

The more significant statement was that the main rail freight operator had an 'aspiration' target of doubling its tonne-kilometres over five years and tripling it over ten, and that the government 'endorse[d] these targets' (paragraph 3.32–3.33). Nothing is said about whether these targets were realistic or what, in practical terms, might be done to help meet them. Many commentators thought them to be hopelessly unrealistic. As Figures 1.14 and 1.15 show, this has so far been shown to be the case. Rail freight has grown a little and has achieved a slight improvement in its market share relative to road – both trends that had started under the Conservatives.

If it was a policy aim to shift freight from road to rail, the figures indicate that it has been largely unsuccessful so far.

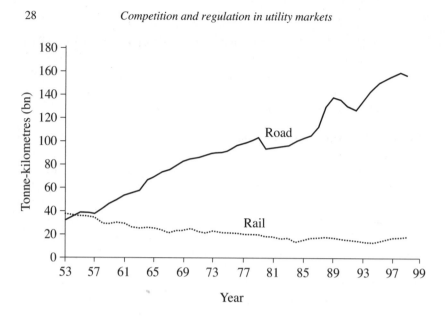

Source: DETR (2001c).

Figure 1.14   Goods moved by road and by rail (bn tonne-kilometres), 1953–99

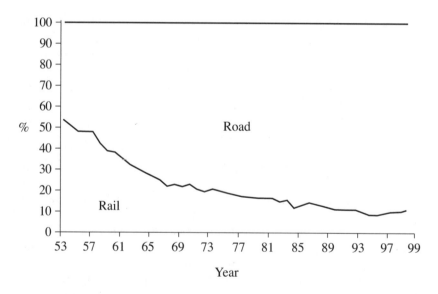

Source: DETR (2001c).

Figure 1.15   Freight tonne-kilometres: market shares

In view of the shortage of capacity for passenger trains, one wonders whether adequate consideration has been given to whether it is sensible to attempt to provide for rail freight movements on the scale the government has in mind. Differences in running speeds between different types of train greatly restrict the effective capacity that can be delivered from the infrastructure. If there were no freight trains it would be easier to reduce the speed differences between trains, thus releasing a disproportionate increase in capacity for the remaining passenger services. The ultimate test would be to compute the full incremental system cost of a freight train and see the extent to which customers (private or government) were willing to pay it.

CHARGING

Road Taxes

One of the most fundamental aspects of policy integration is charges and taxes. I have noted that the attempt to use road taxation rates as a way of reflecting capacity shortages and environmental damages started well, but was abandoned under political pressure.

Road Tolls

There has been some discussion of introducing tolls on inter-urban roads, but that appears to have been dropped – apart from continuing the development of the privately financed, tolled, Birmingham North Relief Road which Labour inherited from the Conservatives.

Congestion Charging

The introduction of the powers for local authorities to levy congestion charges or a workplace parking levy was extremely important. Sooner or later it will have to be implemented as the only way of rationing increasingly scarce road space.

Although many authorities have expressed a strong interest – and the *Ten Year Plan* speaks in terms of local charging being introduced in around eighty cities – the political realities still have to be worked out. All eyes are on the scheme being developed by Mayor Livingstone for London, for introduction in early 2003. It is crucial that this works well enough to demonstrate the considerable benefits congestion charging has to offer, as the *Ten Year Plan* assumes, in addition to being an important source of local revenues. Should the scheme fail, the policy will be discredited and become impossible to reintroduce for a long time.

Whilst some local authorities were initially keen on the idea of the workplace parking levy as a simpler alternative, many have become less enthusiastic as the political and enforcement problems grow more readily apparent. There is also now some doubt about the resolve of some authorities that were initially attracted by the idea of congestion charging.

Public Transport Fares

Fares policies on rail were broadly as inherited from the Conservatives: increases 1 per cent less than inflation on those national railway fares that are regulated (by the SRA) and 1 per cent more than inflation on the London Underground.

Bus fares outside London have remained deregulated and thus determined in the market.

LONDON

The 1997 Labour government quickly formulated a policy of creating a new, devolved local government for London. The legislation is contained in the Greater London Authority Act 1999. The executive mayor and the Greater London Assembly were duly elected in May 2000.

It is generally accepted that the single most important feature of this legislation was the attempt to create a locally accountable executive authority – Transport for London – to oversee transport in the capital and chaired by the mayor. From the point of view of an integrated transport policy the legislation has two major weaknesses: policy control of the commuter railway remains with the national SRA (essentially an agent of central government) and the London Underground has, so far, remained under the control of London Regional Transport (a nationalized industry).

London Commuter Rail Services

The relationship between the franchising director (now the chairman of the SRA) and the GLA is defined in Section 196 of the Greater London Act 1999. At first sight it may seem that the Act gives the GLA considerable sway over the SRA concerning policy in the London area. However, caveats may in practice mean that the mayor can only achieve something that the SRA would not do in any case if the Secretary of State does not prohibit it and if the mayor funds it in full. Given the limited budget likely to be available to the mayor in relation to the other demands for infrastructure investment, the funding requirement is likely to be a severe constraint.

There are potential policy conflicts between the SRA and the GLA. The GLA is elected by and accountable to residents of greater London. But London is the hub of the national rail system. Three quarters of the nation's rail traffic is accounted for by train-operating companies that serve London. Over 30 per cent of all passenger travel and over 60 per cent of passenger travel by public transport in the London area is by the railway under the patronage of the SRA. London is the destination for a large number of long-distance trips. Many of these are made by commuters serving the London economy, but many are not. The mayor and TfL are particularly concerned about frequency of service, reliability and crowding on the local parts of the network. But the train operators will no doubt regard the longer-distance traffic as more financially attractive. The approaches to London are already severely capacity-constrained. So the SRA will find it a more severe claim on its budget to promote the local service, and, in any case, it has a national perspective. The GLA may wish to improve rail services in certain areas as part of its regional development policies, but it is unclear that these considerations would play any part in the criteria being applied by the SRA.

There are also major interfaces to be considered. The commuter railway deposits large numbers of passengers at certain locations, and many of these wish to travel onwards by Underground or bus. Capacity has to be found for them in an already overcrowded system. Some of the proposals reportedly involve large-scale tunnelling under London. They will clearly have significant engineering, passenger numbers and revenue implications for the TfL system.

Renegotiation of London Rail Franchises

The chairman of the SRA says in his *Strategic Agenda* that 'The SRA attaches great importance to working with local, regional and devolved government. ... The SRA is working well with Transport for London on the rail elements of [the Mayor's] Transport Strategy ...' (pp. 25 and 26).

In accordance with government policy the SRA has already adopted an aggressive programme of passenger franchise renegotiations. By late October 2000 the sSRA had already announced the results of two of these renegotiations, both in the London commuter area – in spite of the fact it did not then have legal powers beyond those applying to the Office of Passenger Rail Franchising.

More significantly, the mayor has a statutory duty to create a transport strategy for his whole region, yet the SRA invited proposals on refranchising from the private sector and announced some outcomes before the mayor had the chance to complete consultation on his statutory transport strategy (the final version of which was published in July 2001).

Nor has there been adequate consultation with the newly elected mayor of London or his TfL Board. Further, the SRA needs to develop its relationship with those parts of the GLA that have interests in land use planning and regional development issues, including the Regional Development Agencies and the Greater London Assembly. Only now are TfL and the SRA setting up a more systematic arrangement for consultation.

The need both fully to consult the London authorities and publish criteria is urgent. The commuter railway is fundamental to the long-term strategy of the London economy and to the strategy for the transport system that is to serve it. It is also fundamental to regional planning in the area.

Declining subsidies to London commuter services

Figure 1.16 shows the decline in subsidies to the London-based rail services enshrined in the franchise contracts, a situation unchanged by the Labour government.

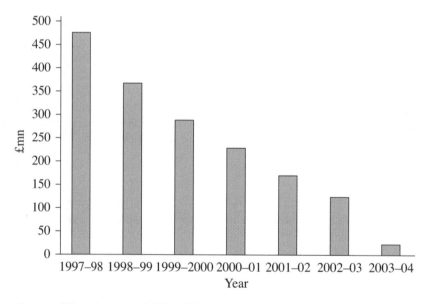

Source: Office of passenger Rail Franchising.

Figure 1.16   Total subsidies to London commuter railways, 1997–2004 (1998 prices)

London Underground

The row about who should own and control the London Underground has gone to the heart of a constitutional issue that affects the whole country: devolution of control and accountability for public services to local authorities versus Treasury centralization.

The government's public–private partnership for the Tube – promoted and controlled from the heart of Whitehall – has not been made to work as envisaged. The government has steadfastly refused to discuss a fallback should their partial, 30-year privatization of the Underground – the PPP – fail. It was originally intended that the privatization be completed by spring 2000, so it is at the time of writing already 18 months behind that schedule. This delay is symptomatic of the magnitude and complexity of what is proposed and it is likely that the process will fail to reach a resolution because the contracts, when eventually negotiated, will be seen not to offer good value for money. High annual payments by central government are now inevitable whatever the outcome – so the Treasury ought to consider how such resources can be most effectively used. Prudent, locally accountable revenue bond finance does have a proven track record and would facilitate devolution.

The origins of the London Underground public–private partnership
The 1997 Labour government had a commitment to resolve the London Underground's long-term funding and financing problems. These were threefold. First, there is hopeless variability year by year in the funds made available to the Underground by the Exchequer. This is apparent in Figure 1.17. Second, a backlog of under-investment: at the time between £1 bn and £1.5 bn was needed to restore the system to a reasonable state of repair. Third, the Underground is crowded and there is a pressing need for increased capacity.

There were several options. One possibility would have been simply to carry on with state ownership and direct grants, and to improve on the management. Another would have been a return to the situation when the Greater London Council ran the Tube: to hand it over to the mayor and TfL as a job lot, together with some kind of promise (hard to believe and unenforceable in practice) of year-by-year cash grants.

The Treasury was unwilling to continue to provide cash grants without fundamental reform of the Underground, including replacement of the (government-appointed) public sector management by private sector management. After nine months' gestation the government proposed a solution that would be a curious mixture of: full-blown, 'conventional' utility privatization; the Private Finance Initiative (PFI); competitive procurement from the private sector; and operation by the public sector.[8] The principal features were a horizontal split between day-to-day operations by the public sector and infrastructure provision by the private sector. There would be a further, vertical split of the private infrastructure provision into three distinct groups of lines. Crucially, this was all to be glued together by commercial contracts lasting for all of *30 years*. These contracts were both to procure the physical work to be

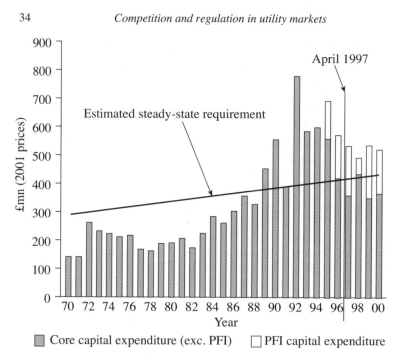

Source: *London Underground PPP: the Offer to Londoners*, London Underground, undated.

*Figure 1.17   Historic under-investment in the Underground, 1970–2000
            (2001 prices)*

done and to secure the finance necessary. They would enable payment for heavy investment in the early years to be repaid out of forecast overall profits in the later years. Arguably, the consequence would have been to achieve the worst of all worlds.

The original intention was that the contracts would be negotiated and completed by April 2000, and immediately transferred to the Greater London Authority, which would come into existence a few months later. Therefore, an important feature of the scheme is that it would greatly fetter the freedom of the new mayor of London to run the Underground in the way that he or she saw fit. The government did not seem to regard this feature as a disadvantage. A better alternative would have been to follow through the logic of the creation of proper, devolved government for London: hand the Underground over to the Greater London Authority and allow the capital to take responsibility for its financing.

The regulatory regime?
The experience with the UK telecommunications, energy, water and railway privatizations showed the vital importance of having a carefully designed and

clear economic regulatory regime. The proposals under the PPP for the Underground were different, but far from clear. Denying that they were following the 'Conservative' model of privatization, the Labour government legislated to create the post of PPP contract arbiter. This official was to adjudicate disputes about the operation and terms of the contracts and carry out reviews at fixed seven and a half year intervals to ensure that the contractors, if efficient, were able to achieve the rate of return they had originally bid.

The presence of an independent *regulator*, bound by powers and duties set out in legislation in advance, can reduce the regulatory risks perceived by the private sector, thereby easing the way to the creation of the new arrangements. But when discretion has to be exercised against a set of public interest criteria, this constitutes economic regulation, which is not the normal job of an independent *arbitrator*.

A central question is the extent to which everything can and should be tied up in a binding contract with a term as long as 30 years. An independent arbitrator and the courts could be used to settle contractual disputes. But there are complications which mean that it may not be sensible to attempt to write fully determinate contracts.

Partnership?

The government have emphasized their view that a spirit of 'partnership' would obviate a reliance on formal contract or rigorous independent utility regulation. However, this appeal to a spirit of partnership is unrealistic in the context of contracts lasting for decades, where the amounts of money involved are so large. Companies will owe a duty to their shareholders to employ the best legal expertise available in order to make the strongest possible case for favourable financial settlement.

The Failure to Invest in the Underground

The failure to deliver a practical and long-term solution to the future ownership and control of the Underground caused the 1997 government to fail to provide the financial stability it had promised.

Figure 1.17 displays the history of investment in the core Underground, excluding the building of the Jubilee Line Extension, but including an estimate of the capital expenditure on assets procured under the Private Finance Initiative (principally new trains for the Northern Line). It shows that there was more than enough investment to maintain the system in its current condition and to make a contribution towards the backlog (but note that the PFI investment will actually be paid for over the decades of life of the contracts).

However, crucially, the total investment under the Labour government was never as high as during any of the five years of the previous, Conservative, government.

London Underground Performance

A combination of continued irregular funding and the detriment to morale of the Underground staff caused by uncertainty about their future has conspired to cause a serious decline in the quality of service delivered by the Underground. Aspects of this are documented in Figures 1.18 and 1.19. Equipment failures together with periodic problems of staff absence have conspired to cause a steady deterioration in the service experienced by the public, which is represented by the increasing 'excess journey time' above what it should be if all ran smoothly to its specification.

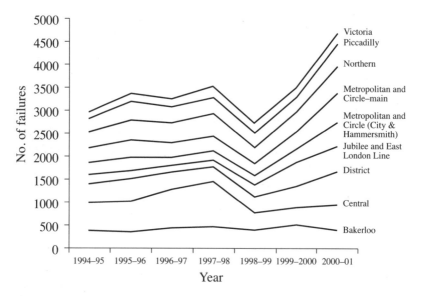

Source: Performance reports to the TfL Board.

Figure 1.18   London Underground: track and signalling failures (cumulative), 1994–2001

The Proposal for Railtrack to Take Over Part of the Underground

One of the three proposed infrastructure companies comprises the 'subsurface lines' (SSL) – the lines originally built by cut-and-cover, as distinct from the deep

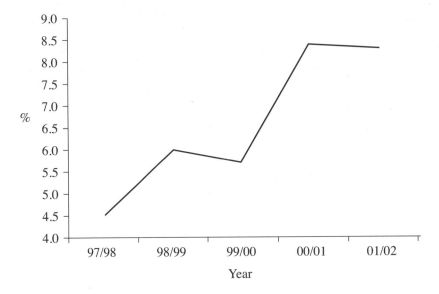

Source: Performance reports to the TfL Board.

Figure 1.19   *London Underground: percentage of scheduled kilometres not operated, 1997–2002*

tubes. In December 1998 the Secretary of State proposed that the SSL be taken over by Railtrack, in the hope that they could then provide for various commuter services to run over the SSL tracks, making through, cross-London journeys.

This was always going to be an unfortunate diversion of effort away from finding a practical solution. The idea was technically almost infeasible, and no provision was offered for the considerable capital cost. Even then it was clear that Railtrack would have neither the capacity nor the incentive to fund this fundamentally unviable scheme. In any case there was insufficient track capacity available on the crowded SSL.

This was an example of a proposal made for reasons of political expediency that an appreciation of the facts of the matter would have immediately shown to be impractical.

INVESTMENT IN TRANSPORT INFRASTRUCTURE

The July 1998 *Comprehensive Spending Review* declared the government's intention of 'investing in reform'. The theme was amplified in the case of transport in the *Ten Year Plan*: 'Transforming our transport networks and tackling the legacy of under investment is vital for this country's economic prosperity' (paragraph 1.7).

Figure 1.20 indicates that the attempt was unsuccessful at the national level. Transport infrastructure is a significant portion of investment in national infra-structure, some of it public, as in roads and the Underground, some of it private but partly funded by government subventions, as in buses and the railways.

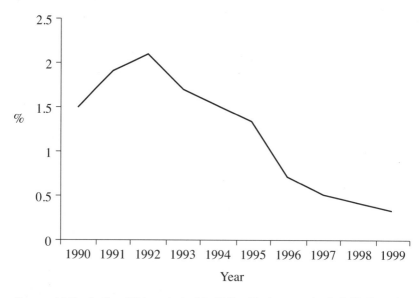

Source: 'A Plan for Growth? An analysis of the 10 Year Plan's prospective for Rail', *The Railway Forum*, March 2001.

Figure 1.20   Public sector net investment as a percentage of GDP, 1990–99

The Need to Provide for Some Traffic Growth

I have argued that it is unlikely that taxation policy and congestion charging alone will achieve the current overall transport policies. The policies themselves will have to be adjusted. Favourable treatment for public transport is desirable on its own terms but it will do little to stem the long-term growth in car ownership and use.

The reality is that traffic will continue to grow under any likely set of policies. It is therefore inconsistent to have cut the scale of roads investment to the extent that successive governments have. Figure 1.21 shows the extent of the previous, Conservative government's cut in expenditure on trunk roads and motorways, and how the Labour government carried this forward.

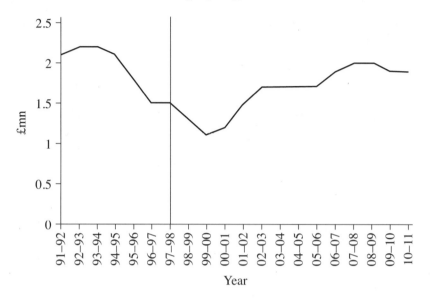

Source: DETR (2000).

Figure 1.21 Strategic roads: public expenditure, 1991–2011 (1999–2000 prices)

Appraisal of the benefits of roads

To establish that more spending would be justified it is necessary to estimate the benefits of new investment. It is possible to over-invest in infrastructure.

Over the decades the UK has been at the forefront of development and application of techniques for the assessment of the economic costs and benefits of road investments. They are under continuous review and improvement and nobody would claim that they are perfect. However, they are some of the best-established techniques for measuring value for money in use in the public sector. The Consultation Document endorsed this approach: 'Appraisal of policy options and investment proposals in terms of their costs and benefits will therefore remain at the heart of decision making and central to the review process.'

Early on the Labour government reviewed and modified the standard appraisal methodology for roads (DETR, 1998c). I believe that the results they produce do represent genuine effects. *A New Deal For Trunk Roads in England: Understanding the New Approach to Appraisal* reproduces the summary Appraisal Summary Tables for 68 trunk road schemes. On the basis of their ratios of benefit to cost as measured by COBA, the standard cost–benefit analysis technique for roads, many of them display attractive rates of economic return. In 53 cases benefits are more than twice the costs, in 36 cases benefits are more than three times the costs and in 18 cases benefits are more than four times the costs.

However, the government removed a number of schemes from the Trunk Roads Programme in spite of having very high estimated economic rates of return: ten of the 68 schemes that were not scheduled to be built had a weighted average of benefits a factor of 4.3 higher than costs, whereas the remainder had a weighted average of benefits a factor of 3.1 higher than costs. The fact that excluded schemes had a better economic performance than the included ones is not necessarily a reason for criticism because the whole point of the new appraisal method is to give due weight to considerations other than those accounted for in the economic appraisal. Even so, it is hard to think of alternative ways of spending resources in the public sector that would show such high measured economic returns. (See Shaw and Walton, 2001 and Docherty, 2001 for detailed accounts and analysis of the strategic roads policy.)

As traffic continued to grow and congestion worsened, it gradually became apparent that the policy of reducing the Trunk Roads Programme was not tenable. The July 2000 *Ten Year Plan* marked a major reversal of policy, with expenditure rates returning towards those of the early 1990s by the end of the ten years.

As the *Ten Year Plan* points out, this additional capacity is carefully targeted to accommodate traffic growth at places where congestion is a particular problem. In this way the plan is able to forecast increased traffic, but reduced congestion.

However, this attractive scenario can only be delivered if the new road capacity is indeed delivered as planned. That will require determination to persuade those who are opposed to new road building to accept the case. The best objective measures we have are saying clearly that decisions not to increase spending on highway investments have a high penalty attached to them, so we must be clear about the severity and nature of the unmeasured disbenefits that would justify such a decision.

LOCAL TRANSPORT

Figure 1.22 shows the decline in funding for local transport under the Conservatives that was a source of bitter complaint from local authorities. There was some recovery under the Labour government. However, the *Ten Year Plan* shows promise of a substantial increase in the future.

This was generally welcomed. Table 1.2 is taken from an assessment made by the British Roads Federation of needs over the next ten years. It suggests that an extra £4 bn per year could be justified. Note that of this, £0.6 bn relates to Wales and Scotland. Bearing in mind that the *Ten Year Plan* figures relate to England,

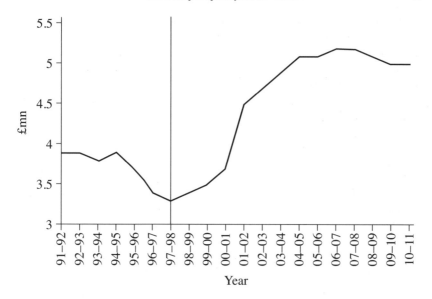

Source: DETR (2000).

Figure 1.22   Local transport: public expenditure and private investment,
1991–2011 (1999–2000 prices)

but also include some allowance for local public transport schemes, it seems that
the *Ten Year Plan* increases are probably of the right order of magnitude.

Table 1.2   Expenditure 1999–2000 and needs for next ten years

	Expenditure 1999–2000 (£bn)	Average annual need for ten years (£bn)
Local – maintenance	2.8	4.3
Local – bypasses	0.15	0.625
Local – traffic management	0.14	0.66
National – maintenance	0.955	1.7
National – new roads	0.52	0.92
National – making better use	0.215	0.5
Other expenditure	0.35	0.45
Total	5.1	9.15

Source: British Roads Federation (2000).

In its appraisal of *The State of the Nation* (summer 2001) the Institution of Civil Engineers said that it was generally satisfied about the new levels of funding on trunk road and motorway maintenance. It was also happier than in the past about local roads, though it noted the government's caution over new highways, and warned about unusual winter damage to road infrastructure. The Institution repeated its earlier call for a unified set of standards and perfor-mance indicators to help monitor the standard of all roads across the UK.

THE *TEN YEAR PLAN* AND THE RAILWAYS

Expansion of capacity for both freight and passengers is a central part of the government's integrated transport policy. Yet the railway is already congested, which is one of the reasons that the quality of service is not as good as it should be.

The *Ten Year Plan* without Inflation: the Real Picture

Working in constant prices puts the plan in a somewhat different perspective from that used in much of the document *Transport 2010* itself and the press comment. The total spend over the next ten years is £152 bn, compared with £108 bn over the previous ten years. This is a substantial increase, but it is more modest than the headline '£180 bn. Ten year investment plan to deliver top class transport system', compared to £99 bn over the previous ten years (at current prices; press notice, 20 July 2000). Further, the commitment of *public* money represents quite a modest increase in real terms: it is £111 bn over the next ten years compared to £91 bn over the previous ten. The government's aspiration is that private finance will provide the remainder.

We have noted that spending on strategic roads is increased, returning it to a similar level to ten years ago. But this is dwarfed by spending on railways. Public investment in strategic roads is to be less than either public or private investment in railways. Total rail investment is to be about three times that on strategic roads.

Risky Assumptions behind the Plan

The ten-year planning process should be used to assess the implications of non-delivery of a number of assumptions that underlie the plan, many of them far from certain. They include:

- the assumption of falling costs of motoring;
- successful implementation of congestion charging in London and eight other cities, and 12 workplace parking levy schemes;

- adoption of restrictive land use policies 'directed at increasing the attractiveness of public transport, walking and cycling';
- local parking restraint policies;
- a 'sustainable distribution strategy';
- local authorities implementing the Local Transport Plans, including 'up to 25 new light rail lines';
- significant rail service quality improvements due to refranchising, speed improvement, punctuality, reliability.

No criticism is implied in drawing attention to the assumptions that have had to be made. The point is that it is reasonable to anticipate that they will not all be realized. The government's own strategic transport planning process provides a framework for exploring and debating alternative assumptions in a consistent manner.

Balance between Modes and the Economic Rates of Return?

The *Ten Year Plan* makes no explicit statement of any criteria used to construct it. However, by inference, it seems clear that the overriding intention was to reduce road congestion and to reduce emissions of carbon dioxide. This, of course, is quite different from either an economic efficiency (or economic benefit) or an equity criterion.

Figures 1.1 and 1.9 suggest a peculiarity of the *Ten Year Plan*. Relatively few people use railways but almost everybody has daily experience of worsening congestion on the roads. The *Ten Year Plan* shows sustained increase in public expenditure on local transport, which includes local roads. This is welcome. Even so, the investment in rail looks out of scale relative to local transport. It looks even more out of kilter with the public spending on strategic roads.

The public expenditure figures shown in the *Ten Year Plan* are only 'in principle' promises on the part of the government. There is no 'bankable' commitment beyond the first three years of the plan. In any case, the need to assuage the new surge of power by the motorist, together with a fading of the current fashion for 'integration' and public transport, and the pressures to find funding for other areas of public policy, could cause the new government to look very hard at the huge sums promised for the railways by an earlier government.

In such circumstances the Treasury will once again examine the relative value for money of the various components in the *Ten Year Plan*. The supporting paper to the plan states

> All rail expenditure will be appraised in line with [the New Approach to Appraisal] against the sSRA's Planning Criteria. Expenditure will be targeted on those areas

where the greatest returns in terms of impacts on the environment, economy, safety, accessibility and integration are expected to be found ... (Annex E, paragraph 9)

Thameslink 2000 is cited as a rail scheme that 'would generate benefits 60% greater than the costs'. Four examples are sketched in Railtrack's 1999 and 2000 *Network Management Statements*. However, there has been no comprehensive publication of the economic rates of return expected to be achieved by the rail investment presaged in the *Ten Year Plan*.

One of the arguments made in favour of investing in railways is that they will relieve congestion on the roads. As Affuso, Masson and Newbery have pointed out (Affuso et al., 2000), this is a convoluted argument to the extent that the road congestion is a consequence of under-investment in roads in the first place. Ironically, as the plan demonstrates, should the cost of motoring not fall as rapidly as the plan assumes, then congestion on the roads will improve more than expected. Then, in turn, the benefits to rail investment will themselves fall.

None of this is to deny that investment in renewal and enhancement of the railway is worthwhile.

The issue is whether the balance between road and rail investment set out in the *Ten Year Plan* is the best one, especially in the light of events since its publication. Railway investment is not the panacea for all transport problems that the government sometimes appear to claim. As long-term strategy matures it will be necessary to become much more explicit about the precise objectives that public spending on specific rail projects are supposed to meet – and to verify objectively that they can reasonably be expected to perform that function.

Problems with the *Ten Year Plan* for the Railway

Unrealistic ambitions for growth
The recent accidents on the railway and the disruption caused by Railtrack's cautious response and the remedial maintenance work can only have damaged the travelling public's confidence in the quality of service railways can deliver. More fundamentally, the accidents, together with the difficulty that Railtrack has had in meeting its performance standards, may be symptomatic that an attempt is being made to run too many trains on the existing infrastructure. The *Ten Year Plan*'s aspirations for 50 per cent passenger growth and 80 per cent freight growth already looked extremely ambitious in the context of a century of experience shown in Figure 1.12. It now seems unrealistic.

In the longer term capacity enhancements are planned, as noted in the rail regulator's October 2000 *Periodic Review*. Some of these are sketched out in the chairman of the Strategic Rail Authority's March 2001 *Strategic Agenda*.[9] It will be difficult to deliver these, on top of a large volume of maintenance and renewal, while preserving the quality of service assumed in the Plan and required to generate the revenues necessary to fund the enhancements.

The physical problems

There is the further question of whether the industry is *physically* capable of delivering an investment programme of this magnitude. The whole industry was valued by the markets at £4.4 billion in 1996 at privatization. The *Periodic Review* determined the value of the Regulatory Asset Base for Railtrack at about £5.5 billion at March 2001 (in 1998–99 prices). The *Ten Year Plan* envisages maintenance, renewal and enhancement spending sustained at about this level *every year for ten years*. To deliver this scale of activity would be a major challenge in both financial and physical engineering, and in management of a business that is already under pressure to reform its safety management and under threat of more fundamental regulatory reform.

In his *Agenda* the chairman of the SRA has recently expressed the view that Railtrack is not capable of delivering the enormous investment programme that he envisages. He therefore proposed that Railtrack should become a steward of existing assets and that new ventures should be promoted, financed, designed and built by new joint ventures, before being transferred to Railtrack as working infrastructure. It is far from clear how these ideas will work in practice given the regulatory problems, the highly complex contractual matrix relating to the existing assets and the tendency of financial and other benefits of investments in parts of the railway network to accrue in places remote from the site of the investment.

The disruptions to passengers on the West Coast Main Line caused by the rebuilding of that line and the chaos on the whole network due to the repair work following the Hatfield accident point to the further question as to whether the rail plans are internally consistent. Is it possible to sustain the growth in passengers and freight volumes required to fund the plan while carrying out the disruptive work that it implies?

Prospects for rail freight

The prospects for freight on the railway depend upon the costs relative to those by road. Road freight operators have already been granted concessions. The government made concessions on fuel, licensing and other costs faced by the road haulage industry, so the competitive position of rail has been adversely affected in a way not envisaged in the *Ten Year Plan*. Similar implications would follow if rail freight access charges were to be increased because of an increase in Railtrack's cost base implied by new safety-related investments on the railway.

Such changes would inevitably affect the competitive position of rail freight, making the ambitious rail freight projections in the *Ten Year Plan* even harder to fulfil. Again, this is a reason to revisit the plan.

Security of future funding
The intended large increase in spending of the railways also raises questions about the security of the funding. It is apparent that over half of the rail total – over £30 bn – is to come from private investment, to be funded out of increased passenger and freight revenues. At an average rate of over £3 bn every year for ten years, that is a great deal to expect from the private sector. The investment carries a risk of non-delivery, as does any private sector investment programme. It relies on continuing confidence on the part of the financial markets. In particular, the supporting documents for the *Ten Year Plan* recognize quite correctly that the volume of rail travel is extremely sensitive to the overall level of activity in the economy. So, unless the historical cycle has somehow been halted, there must be a significant risk that there will be a general economic recession within the horizon of the plan. In turn, that must threaten the assumption that usage and revenues will grow at the rates specified in the plan.

The burden on the Treasury
The government has claimed that an important feature of the *Ten Year Plan* is that the Treasury is committed to the spending it implies. However, it could be hard to hold the Treasury to a commitment made by a previous government, especially if the tax take from the transport sector were to be less than antici-pated and there were pressing spending commitments in such fields as health, education, social security and pensions.

Railtrack's *Periodic Review* makes adequate provision for maintenance of the existing system to a safe standard. But committees of inquiry into recent rail accidents and the government may, between them, make unanticipated com-mitments to expensive enhancements to safety equipment on the railway. Indeed, the chairman of the SRA in his *Agenda* says 'SRA will ensure Uff–Cullen recommendations on train protection systems are taken forward and implemented ... Infrastructure investment in addition to enhanced train protection may be needed to fulfil [Railway Group] Safety Plan targets' (p. 58).

The government may well promise that they will meet the full cost of these safety enhancements. However, experience of similar situations in the past suggests that there would be a risk that, in practice, the Treasury would seek to limit the total public expenditure on the railways to previously agreed limits. The consequence could be that the mandatory safety expenditures are partially funded at the expense of the monies shown in Figure 1.23 as having been promised for capacity and other enhancements.

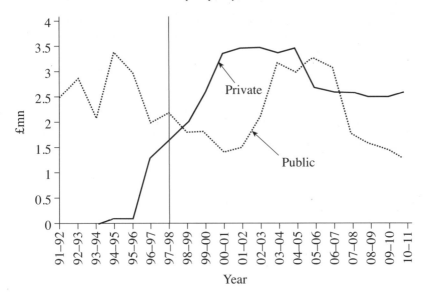

Source: DETR (2000).

Figure 1.23   Rail: public expenditure and private investment, 1991–2011 (1999–2000 prices)

THE *TEN YEAR PLAN*, FINANCE AND FUNDING

Procurement or Financing?

The transport White Paper promulgates a fallacy that has served to impede investment in transport infrastructure. It speaks of 'new sources of finance to relieve the burden on the taxpayer ...' (paragraph 4.11). Another example of the confusion was to be found in a speech by Geoffrey Robinson, then Paymaster-General, to a Private Finance Initiative conference in 1998: 'Against ... the necessity for tight control of public spending, PFI is enabling Government to support a significant number of additional projects beyond what can be provided through the public purse.' The error is to confuse financing with funding, and thereby to risk obfuscating the fundamental truth that public infrastructure must be paid for sooner or later by the taxpayer, to the extent that it is not commercially viable.

The government were particularly unrealistic to believe that the private sector would take over the London Underground infrastructure and the liability to invest on a large scale for a zero sum (*Comprehensive Spending Review*, July

1998, paragraph 8.4). The proposition must have seemed seductive in the light of the then-current commitment not to increase public expenditure.

One of the government's other reasons for proceeding with the PPP approach has been to achieve 'private sector efficiencies' by having private sector companies handle all contracting, engineering and construction, rather than these being administered by the public sector. However, this approach risks confusing the handling of capital needs with the handling of operating budgets. Public sector operating agencies can (and do) achieve operating efficiencies, if given the appropriate targets and incentives, as well as the leeway to achieve these targets. What is more, it is entirely feasible for public sector agencies to hire private sector construction managers for major projects, as was the case with the Channel Tunnel, and was finally adopted for completion of the Jubilee Line Extension.

Beyond the Underground

The existing, core reinvestment needs of the Underground is but one of many transport infrastructure needs for the future of London. It is possible that Transport for London (TfL) could be authorized to establish a structure such as a trust company with the capacity to issue its own revenue bonds. This financing could then be used for all Underground, bus or other transport needs such as purchasing the capital investment to implement congestion charging.

Figure 1.24 shows an intention substantially to increase the funds available to London in a few years' time (especially beyond the term of the 2001 government). The public trust/revenue bond structure, if established for the entire scope of TfL, would enable the Mayor to use available transport funds and grants flexibly, including the dedication of a portion of general transport funds toward underpinning bond capacity. What is more, the establishment of this type of financing structure could provide the flexibility to accommodate investment in areas other than transport, as the process of local government for London develops. Clearly, the Treasury would have to agree that this type of financing would be genuinely self-sufficient, and that the trust form of organization would pose little or no risk to the government. This approach would also demand good management of the link between raising the required capital and managing the actual investment. In addition, annual debt service on bonds could place demands on the GLA's revenue capacity in the initial years, if new revenue resources are limited or constrained.

Beyond London

London is not the only city or town in Britain that will need significant investment in its public transport system in the years ahead. If and when other

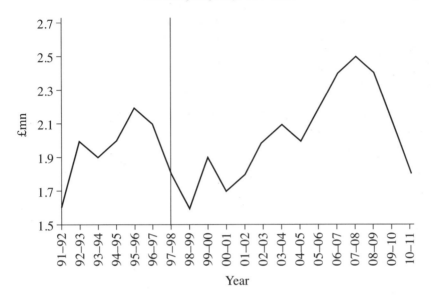

Source: DETR (2000).

Figure 1.24   *London: public expenditure and private investment, 1991–2011 (1999–2000 prices)*

urban areas adopt congestion charging (in line with government policy) there will be a need for transport infrastructure investment so that car users can find alternative ways of travelling. In accordance with the *Ten Year Plan* local authorities will have to increase bus services, build tramways and institute other transport improvements before the congestion charges are first levied. At the moment there is no way (apart from conventional local government spending) of financing public transport improvements of this kind. It would be possible to use a PPP-type arrangement to fund public transport schemes in towns and cities outside London. But the kind of infrastructure that might be needed in these centres would be very different from the kinds of investments envisaged for the Tube. In these circumstances, a bond issue by a local authority (or by some other organization) could be used as a way of raising resources for public transport investment in advance of income from congestion charges becoming available. As in London, this would almost certainly be a less expensive way of raising money than by the private sector.

The issuance of a bond imposes a healthy discipline: a clearly defined and distinct legal structure which has separate accounts, transparent statements of assets and liabilities, clear and enforceable objectives, a long-term capital plan with long-term financing commitments and a degree of isolation from day-today politics for the directors. It separates good management and procurement from efficient financing.

Treasury Consent

In the UK the Treasury would have to give general consent to this type of financing if it were to proceed. But Britain will need significant investment in the years ahead given the obvious need to rebuild its crumbling infrastructure. Scrutiny arrangements and the discipline demanded by bond-holders would give the Chancellor comfort as he let go of the purse-strings. Moreover, he would please the financial markets, which are hungry for bond issues.

The long-running débâcle over the funding of the London Underground is simply a visible manifestation of a struggle between central and local government over who should decide how best to reinvest in the nation's capital stock. The present system has a handful of civil servants and ministers in Whitehall making all the decisions for the whole country. Revenue bonds, possibly subject to local referenda, offer a responsible localist solution to a major problem.

CONCLUSION

The 1997 Labour government declared transport to be an important policy area. They created a large and powerful new department of state to integrate policy on transport, the environment and land use planning. They appointed a senior member of the government – the Deputy Prime Minister – to be its Secretary of State.

In law and administration there were successes, such as the introduction of powers to levy hypothecated congestion charges, developments in transport investment appraisal methods, the principle of a ten-year transport planning process and the creation of a devolved London government with its own transport planning powers.

However, the record shows that there was little success in delivery of policy. Such as there was largely resulted from continuation of trends set under the previous, Conservative, administration.

Traffic growth continued, but it was successfully tamed by a combination of continuing with the fuel price escalator (slightly increased from the Conservative rate) and an increase in the price of crude oil. Thus it was a result of passive fiscal policy rather than any radical transport policy. Air quality and safety on the roads continued to improve. Carbon dioxide emissions from transport grew less rapidly than they might have done because of continuation of technological improvements.

The funding for the programme for building major roads continued to be cut in line with Conservative policies and, unwisely, some schemes were withdrawn. Three years later this policy had to be reversed as the reality of the need to provide more road capacity asserted itself. In future years the nation will regret this lost time because lead times on road investment are so long and the proportion of the system that can be improved at any one time so limited.

The rising fuel price was, justly, claimed as a component in integrating transport, environment and land use policies. However, there was a failure to sell the policy politically, the sleeping dinosaur of the motoring majority was awoken for the first time and the policy was immediately abandoned. Thus the several strands of policy became disintegrated.

A coherent policy on fares and charges would have been an aid to integration. Congestion charging will help, but so far that remains an unused facility. Other charges have been set passively.

In practice transport policy in London became less integrated, rather than more, with the SRA, TfL and London Regional Transport each separately responsible for policy for a major sector: commuter railways, buses and roads and the London Underground.

Little freight was transferred from road to rail.

Like 'integration', 'social inclusion' was an often-used but ill-defined phrase in the transport context. It is not easy to recognize a contribution towards social inclusion by transport policy under the 1997 government. Railways were heavily promoted, even though they are used by relatively few people, typically on higher incomes. Buses were largely neglected although they are used by far more, and more lower-income, people. Buses remained privatized and largely unregulated (outside London) as they had been under the Conservatives.

Policy on the administration of the railways was, and remains confused. Having decided against radical reform, the government continued with the structure it inherited. In general, the train operating companies developed well. But, so far as Railtrack was concerned, the government was unable or unwilling to follow through the logic of that structure – that commercial incentives, set and policed by the regulator, would lead the industry towards a desired outcome. In the event, the industry, and hence the system of regulation, was revealed to be immature. Persistent government intervention slowed the process of maturing into a competent and responsible private industry. The interventions included: franchise renegotiation; public statements on performance and safety; an attempt to give Railtrack the responsibility for the subsurface lines of the London Underground; and, crucially, a failure to avoid the temptation to 'bail out' Railtrack to save it from its own commercial errors.

The metamorphosis of the Office of Passenger Rail Franchising into a Strategic Rail Authority filled a generally perceived need and it was widely welcomed. However, lack of commitment by government caused a two and a half year gestation period. And, in spite of the time this gave to develop a strategy, none has been produced.

Meanwhile, rail patronage continued its extraordinary growth, started under the Conservatives. Service quality at first improved, and then fell back, partly because of train congestion on the network and partly because of Railtrack's failure to deliver. The ultimate failure came with the accident at Hatfield and Railtrack's instant response to it (no doubt influenced by their anticipation of the line the government would take). The consequence was a loss of confidence that unravelled much of the patronage growth, destroyed investors' confidence and made the government's already over-ambitious aspirations for further growth impossible to fund or finance.

For future railways policy the new government needs to pause, to find an accurate diagnosis of what has gone wrong and to decide a realistic future scenario for the size of the railway, together with a realistic plan for its funding and financing. It must then decide whether the desired outcome can be achieved with the existing structure or a revised one. In particular, it must design an institutional framework for sponsoring large investments in new infrastructure that will prove attractive to such private investment as they hope to attract.

Policy on the London Underground has been a clear failure. The promised reform has not occurred, the backlog of investment has not been made good as promised and the government has presided over a steady decline in quality of service. The government's proposed PPP solution is impractical and, at best, some months from completion. It is also highly unpopular, not least because it involves imposing a 30-year contractual liability on London government, despite it not having negotiated the terms of that liability and despite the local electorate having explicitly rejected the scheme. There are several better ways forward.

The *Ten Year Plan* for transport, *Transport 2010,* published in July 2000, was a most welcome step forward. Until this government took the initiative, transport policy muddled through on a most unsatisfactory year-by-year basis for decades. Ten years is the minimum horizon necessary for sensible strategic transport planning: transport assets are long-lived, changes in personal behaviour take years to be realized and land use changes and the consequences of demographic change are powerful but take decades to work through.

The current *Ten Year Plan* needs to be revisited because circumstances have changed. It will also come to be called into question as fashion changes: the present plan is firmly based on delivering the particular objectives of the day, none of which is easily reconciled with facts relating to equity or value for public money. The plan does appear to favour railways over other modes that are used by a far greater number of people. There are doubts about the technical and managerial feasibility of the scale of the expansion envisaged. Also, there are doubts about whether the private sector will choose to invest the very large amounts of capital and whether the public sector will be willing to meet the full cost that the declared policies turn out to imply. Rail needs a proper strategy and plan for delivery. It also needs a secure and credible Treasury commitment.

A standard value-for-money approach is necessarily narrow in its considerations, but it is reasonably robust against changing fashion. A growing railway with increasing public support can have an objective justification, comparable with the high rates of return often found for road schemes, but only if the investments are in the right places: in particular, where passenger densities are high, as on the commuter routes to the large cities.[10] However, such investments will not necessarily be good 'social policy'. Again, the bus seems to have been given relatively little attention. Car use has spread so widely through the population that public expenditure to help the motorist may do more to help the poor than public expenditure on railways.

Now the motoring majority has established its power, it seems unlikely that motoring taxation can rise sufficiently rapidly to stop traffic growth. The implication will be either more congestion or more road capacity must be provided – as envisaged in the *Ten Year Plan*. Future governments will have to show strong leadership in order to get that new capacity delivered in the face of the strongly held beliefs of those who oppose all proposals to build new or improved roads.

The *Ten Year Plan* is essentially centralist. It chooses particular objectives on behalf of all local authorities. It potentially puts a great deal of money and therefore power in the hands of Whitehall. In turn, its agency, the equally centralist Strategic Rail Authority, is showing signs of exerting influence on the local transport plans in London and the other big cities. In parallel, the Treasury maintains a strong and direct central influence through its 'rules' and the public spending control process. In particular, the Private Finance Initiative and public–private partnership policies – also endorsed by the Strategic Rail Authority – fetter the discretion that local authorities have. The attempt to impose the PPP for the London Underground has been the leading example.

Should central governments wish to take devolution of powers to local authorities (including the GLA) more seriously, then the revenue bond mechanism, secured on revenues, central government grant and local taxes, offers a proven alternative mechanism for creating locally accountable capital financing. At the same time, considerable national tax funds will continue to be involved, so there will remain the need for central government, its agencies and local authorities to set out some objectively verifiable criteria about what constitutes good value for this money, together with a regime of local and national scrutiny against those criteria.

The last two general White Papers on transport policy – 1976 and 1997 – have both proved to be ineffectual. Actual transport policy has been made 'on the hoof'. Maybe we should give up on putting precious high-level administrative effort into top-level documents which are then overtaken by events. A few key aims may be enough. Government has failed to recognize that the capacity of the official system to handle implementation has become so limited. After the 1998 White Paper the government commissioned 'multimodal studies' in over 20 areas. It is hard to see how the vast volume of material that these may eventually produce could be digested and implemented in coherent, practical and effective policy.

Success in national transport policy in the future requires overcoming the two obstacles that defeated it during the 1997 Labour administration: first, a need to put an objective analysis of the facts above fashion and rhetoric; and second, a need to create a funding regime which is realistic and has an adequate contribution from the national or local taxpayer. That implies a need for realism about private sector contribution, realism about what it is worthwhile investing in and willingness to commit public money.

NOTES

1. Many of the data are to be found in the 2001 edition of *Transport Trends* published by the Department of Environment, Transport and the Regions (DETR), though a number of other official sources are also used.
2. *The Guardian*, 6 June 1997.
3. This work is currently being extended and refined.
4. These figures are derived from information at www.aeat.co.uk/netcen/airqual/statbase/
5. I am grateful to Professor Andrew Evans of University College London for providing these data.
6. *The Strategic Plan* in January 2002.
7. Sir Alastair Morton, *A Strategic Agenda*, SRA, 13 March 2001.
8. For a fuller description and critique see S. Glaister, R. Scanlon and T. Travers, *A Fourth Way for the Underground?*, Greater London Group, June 1998; *The Way Out: An alternative approach to the future of the Underground*, LSE London discussion paper no. 1, 20 March 1999; *Getting Partnerships Going: public private partnerships in transport*, Institute for Public Policy Research, April 2000.
9. Morton, *Strategic Agenda*.
10. For a cost–benefit appraisal see Glaister (2001).

REFERENCES

Affuso, L., J. Masson and D. Newbery (2000), 'Comparing investments in new transport infrastructure: Roads vs. Railways?', Department of Applied Economics, Cambridge, Working Paper 0021.
British Roads Federation (2000), *Roads – Investing in Britain's Prosperity*, April.
Coates, J. (1999), *Roads to accountability*, AA Policy, April.
DETR (1997a), *Developing an Integrated Transport Policy*, August 1997.
DETR (1997b), *National Road Traffic Forecasts (Great Britain)*.
DETR (1998a), *A Mayor and Assembly for London*, Cm 3897, March.

DETR (1998b), *A New Deal for Transport: Better For Everyone*. Government's White Paper on the Future of Transport. Cm 3950, July.

DETR (1998c), *A New Deal For Trunk Roads in England: Understanding the New Approach to Appraisal*, July.

DETR (2000), *Transport 2010: The Ten Year Plan*, July.

DETR (2001a), *Transport Statistics Bulletin: Traffic in Great Britain*, August.

DETR (2001b), *Transport Trends*, National Statistics publication.

Docherty, I. (2001), 'Interrogating the ten-year transport plan', *Area*.

Evans, A.E. (2002), Fatal Train Accidents on Britain's Main Line Railways: End of 2001 Analysis, University College London, mimeo, March.

Foster, C.D. (2001), in A. Seldon (ed.), *The Blair Effect*, London: Little Brown.

Glaister, S. (1999), 'Integrated Transport: a future for Rail?', in Beesley (ed.), *Regulating Utilities: A New Era?*, IEA, Readings 49.

Glaister, S. (2001), 'The Economic Assessment of Local Transport Subsidies in Large Cities', in T. Grayling (ed.), *Any More Fares?*, Institute for Public Policy Research, February.

Glaister, S. and D. Graham (1996), 'Who spends what on motoring in the UK?', Automobile Association, December.

Glaister, S. and D. Graham (2002), 'The demand for automobile fuel: a survey of elasticities', in *Journal of Transport Economics and Policy*, **32**, part 1, 1–25.

HM Treasury (1998), *Comprehensive Spending Review: New Public Spending Plans 1999 – 2002. Modern Public Services for Britain investing in Reform*, July.

Institution of Civil Engineers and *New Civil Engineer* magazine (2001), *The State of the Nation: measuring the quality of the UK's infrastructure*, summer.

Railtrack (2000), 2000 Network Management Statement for Great Britain.

Sansom, T. et al. (2001), *Surface Transport Costs and Charges, Great Britain 1998*, University of Leeds.

Shaw, J. and W. Walton (2001), 'Labour's new trunk-roads policy for England: an emerging pragmatic multimodalism?', *Environment and Planning*.

Strategic Rail Authority (2001), *On Track. Rail performance trends 15 Oct 2000 to 31 March 2001*, June.

CHAIRMAN'S COMMENTS

Tom Winsor

Stephen Glaister gives an extremely lucid treatment of his subject – a significant critique and a clear exposition of the reasons for his severe criticism of the record of the present government in transport policy in 1997–2001 and of the *Ten Year Plan*.

He mentions the difficulties with roads, the spending on roads, the efforts to deal with congestion and issues of environmental air quality and so on. London Underground has some very interesting regulatory issues with the 30-year contracts that will come into force, and these need to be discussed. Buses, although they are the workhorse of the transport industry, have had hardly anything in four years. And then there are the railways. When I took the job of Rail Regulator just over two years ago, I had not expected to face three very serious fatal accidents, two of them the fault of the railway (Paddington and Hatfield), a complete disintegration of the integrity of the network in the aftermath of Hatfield, and the severe financial difficulties which Railtrack has experienced since then.

The railways have many problems. These don't deter me from the job I must do. However, the picture that presented itself to me two years ago was decidedly different.

Stephen Glaister has explained that we have heard and had from the government a lot of legislation and a lot of paper, but he asks: where's the delivery? And if things go on the way they are, will the situation get worse rather than better? What is the money best spent on? Is there the political will to put the money into the industries – at least into the core networks?

I want to deal with two issues here. One is the regulatory issue in relation to the London Underground. The government, for reasons that are unclear, has decided that the relationships between the public sector and the infrastructure companies will be by way of contract rather than licence regulation. This is the decision taken with the passenger rail franchisees. The vast majority of consumer protection and other economic regulatory measures between the state and the private sector are established in this way. The government knew then – the then government knew then and this government certainly knows now – that contract-based regulation, which they are about to repeat with the Underground, has much less flexibility than licence-based regulation. The mechanisms for change are harder to establish and they will be negotiated perhaps more closely. And once those contracts are established, it is only through the mechanisms for change established within the contracts themselves that they can be changed without the agreement of both parties. Anything is possible with agreement, but we are talking about a case where the other party doesn't want to agree. That is true of the passenger rail franchises. In those cases, it is perhaps not quite such a severe problem because most of the passenger rail franchises were for only seven years, a couple were for ten, and only two or three are 15-year franchises. Those 15-year contracts are causing problems now because they are here to stay. What are the implications of that for investor confidence? If you have a licence-based system, as I have been putting in place with my colleagues at the Office of the Rail Regulator for the last two years, you can change the deal between the state and the private sector if necessary against the will of the private sector party without paying for it, if it is in the public interest to do so. And if the private sector party doesn't like it, then it has a right to appeal to the Competition Commission which will operate according to the same criteria as the regulator. But once they've made their decision, unless it is illegal, irrational or has been arrived at in the wrong way (in other words the classic grounds of judicial review), the private sector party can't do anything about it. Why reject a system of considerable flexibility like that, which has been used to enormous advantage in other industries? (I've used it seven times since I took over as Regulator – in every case Railtrack agreed to the changes to their network licence rather than making me send it to the Competition Commission.) The change mechanisms are in place, they've been used to good advantage and they haven't cost any money. That would not be the case if you wanted to change a contract.

So the regulatory system which has been established for the railways is both contract regulation between the SRA and the franchisees and licence regulation between the Regulator and Railtrack. The strengths and weaknesses of the two systems are clear.

The second issue I want to discuss is investor confidence. Again, I give the railway example because it's the one I know best. How do we bring private money into the railways? How do we look after and intensify the confidence of private sector investors, especially after the events since 17 October 2000, the Hatfield accident, which has apparently caused such very severe difficulties for Railtrack? One suggestion is that there are too many regulators and we must improve investor confidence by getting rid of one of them (me). That doesn't mean to say they want to sack me – I don't know if they want to sack me or not. I'm independent, and I think the independence of regulation is absolutely fundamental to investor confidence.

The Secretary of State is reported as saying that he will consider, after the end of my term of office in 2004, merging the Office of the Rail Regulator with the Strategic Rail Authority. I don't think that is likely to happen. It would mean taking an independent body and merging it with a non-independent body. This is so because the Strategic Rail Authority is, and OPRAF was before it, an instrument of government which can be given instructions by the Secretary of State. He can tell them what to do. So how do you merge a non-independent body with an independent body and preserve the independence? Is it the case that, in relation to those functions formerly held by the regulator, he should remain independent? It's a bit like being independent in the afternoons, or the referee playing for one side for half the game. It just doesn't work. I believe that other countries have a system whereby independent arbiters do the will of the government. That's unlikely to happen in Britain. It would hardly be conducive to investor confidence for the purchaser of the service, the state, unilaterally to determine the price and to be able to compel the seller to deliver it at the quality stated by the state and at the price stated by the state, with no right of appeal, no independence of arbitration.

Railtrack's share price has fluctuated widely for a long time. This is sometimes, by the less skilful commentators, all attributed to me. They say that if the regulator didn't give them such a hard time, their share price would have improved steadily. In the months before I took over, the Railtrack share price was at £17 or thereabouts; the Railtrack share price is now at £2½. But if you track the share price of Railtrack and the share price of other utilities on a graph, you will find that until the back end of 2000, the lines were pretty much in parallel; there was hardly any difference at all. And then, utilities prices rose sharply and the Railtrack share price fell very sharply indeed. That was attributable to two things, both of which Stephen Glaister mentioned. One was a perception of excessive government interference in the affairs of the company. It was reported that the chairman of the Strategic Rail Authority was interviewing the members of the board of Railtrack and letting each of them know whether he had a job – this was after Hatfield – and the share price fell like a stone. This wasn't quite accurate, but nevertheless investor confidence was seriously harmed because investors thought the government were going to get more involved in the sustained network. Enhancements are different, but the sustained network was at risk in that respect. But the real reason why the share price of Railtrack fell and fell so hard was that investors realized that the competence of the management of the company was seriously in doubt. The West Coast Main Line project was one that Railtrack signed up to in 1998, at a price of £2.2 billion. It's now at £6.8 billion. You can't sign a fixed-price contract like that with those kind of magnitudes and expect to walk away unscathed. The contract wasn't actually fixed price in all respects: it was partly fixed price and partly non-fixed price. Railtrack have been held to the fixed-price elements and they've eaten up £800 million so far, all overshoot. In relation to the non-fixed-price elements, it's my job to determine what is a fair price for that part of the upgrading of the West Coast Main Line. The problem is that Railtrack can't tell me what they think it is, and my consultants have had difficulty in determining the adequacy of Railtrack's plans. However, we are making progress and we will be making announcements soon.

Glaister made the point well – will the Treasury sign up to all this? Will they sign up to Railtrack's continuous pleas for relief from poverty? Railtrack announced on 27 May 2001 that, now that they understood more about the condition of their own assets since the periodic review (which increased their revenue by 50 per cent), they believed that the amount of money that they got in that review was short by about £3.5 billion, and they allowed investors and others to know that they were reasonably confident that, of that £3.5 billion, the regulator would hand them another £2.5 billion. The formal position is that there is provision for interim reviews in the periodic review, and Railtrack have two hoops to clear to get relief. They must make a sufficiently strong case for a reopener. They haven't made that case yet. And if they do so, they must then make another case, which is to answer the question, how much money should they have and why is the original settlement not enough? Neither question has been answered and it is unlikely to be answered for some months to come. No application to me has been made.

However, the main question is, will the Treasury sign up to all this? In relation to the sustained network (and this is absolutely essential for investor confidence), it's not the Treasury's decision. If it were, we might as well go back to the days of nationalization. When I first became involved with the railways in 1993 (as chief legal adviser to the first regulator), I was amazed that the BR managers of the time could run a railway that well for so little money. They were very good at making ends meet, patching and mending, and their coat was very threadbare, but they kept it going through many frustrations and many difficulties. That was a function of the stop–go Treasury policy. On many occasions BR did not know until some time after the beginning of the financial year in question how much money they were going to have. You can't run a business like that. And therefore it was one of the fundamental planks of privatization that there should be an independent economic regulator who would, according to public interest criteria, take a decision as to what a competent and efficient company would need to spend in order to look after the assets. That is absolutely the same for railways as it is for gas, water, electricity and telecommunications.

One final example: Virgin Rail Group have invested well over £1 billion in the new tilting trains, which it is hoped will go very fast when Railtrack look after the infrastructure and upgrade it. The group put in that money in conjunction with some very nervous bankers. The bankers took into account the strength and stability of the contract with Railtrack, but also the strength and stability of the regulatory regime. This is because all the new trains in the world – with whatever bells and whistles and whatever speed capabilities and other sophisticated things they may have – are useless if the track on which they will run is being allowed to rot because the Treasury on a year-by-year stop–go basis have decided to cut off the money supply. They would simply not have invested if they did not have the assurance (a) of the firm contract with Railtrack and (b) of an independent regulatory regime so that they know that every five years the regulator will reset Railtrack's access charges so as to ensure that Railtrack had enough money as a competent and efficient company to look after the track. If they thought that the track might be allowed to rot for whatever reason, political or other, they would not have made the investment. This is therefore another reason why taking away the independence of the rail regulator is simply a non-starter, and I don't think the Treasury will entertain the idea for a moment. Indeed, the Chancellor has made the point that the independence of the competition authorities – and the regulator is one of those – should actually be intensified, and the Enterprise Bill, to be introduced in Parliament in March 2002, will do that. I do not see the government looking both ways on the same issue; they understand the importance of independence, so I think that investors can be confident that they won't jeopardize it. Let us be vigilant.

Regulatory risk is sometimes given as an argument against there being regulators at all. I fundamentally disagree with that for the reasons I've just given and for one more reason: regulatory risk is not the risk that the regulator will be firm, it is the risk that the regulator's decisions may be uncertain, unpredictable and arbitrary. The existence of a regulator is not a matter of risk. It is a matter of investor confidence if the regulator is doing his job properly. So it is *uncertainty* of regulation which is anathema to investor confidence, not *firm* regulation.

Indeed, in the aftermath of the Hatfield accident, the train operators, with one voice, applied for regulatory remedies against Railtrack because they realized that their contracts with Railtrack were too weak. They didn't have a strong one like Virgin (but they soon will). Their contracts were too weak and they had no other than regulatory remedies. Thus it was essential that the regulator took action. So the presence of regulation, as an instrument to deal with the bad boy in the playground, is also fundamental to investor confidence.

These issues are highly relevant to Stephen Glaister's discussion in relation to the future of London Underground and what is the best flavour of regulation, and also in relation to the future of the railway, which I think is far brighter than many commentators believe.

2. Electricity: regulatory developments around the world

Stephen Littlechild[1]

With hindsight I now realize that the title for this chapter is over-optimistic: privatization, liberalization and regulation of the electricity industry are now very widespread phenomena, and it is totally impracticable to try to give an account of developments around the world that is comprehensive, accurate and up to date.

I therefore focus on a few common themes, and explore some issues that are presently stimulating debate or causing concern in a number of countries, not least the UK. Not surprisingly, the themes are familiar: the nature of regulation, competition in generation and retail supply, and wholesale trading arrangements and Pools.

Unfortunately, space precludes discussing regulation of the monopoly networks. Briefly, some other countries, such as Australia, Norway and the Netherlands have been following a similar policy to the UK, but other countries, such as the USA and New Zealand, have done relatively little in this area. Developments in the competitive markets overseas rather than in network regulation are probably of most interest at present.

OVERALL TRENDS

Before we get to the detail, are there any worldwide trends in electricity regulation? Over the last decade or so, variants of what might be called the 'standard model' have gradually been implemented around the world. This standard model includes a separate transmission company, privately owned and competing generation companies bidding into a Pool, all or part of the retail market open to competition, privately owned transmission and distribution networks with third-party access on published and non-discriminatory terms, and an independent regulatory body. This type of model has been implemented in developing as well as developed countries. Not all the components are always there in full. For example, two countries have sought to avoid regulation, while in other countries regulation has arrived before there is much to regulate.

My impression is that there have been two broad streams of thought and activity over the last couple of years. The first has been to extend, implement and refine the standard model. For example, the model is under active consideration in several countries at present, including Mexico, the Philippines, India and Thailand. The international development banks are considering how to apply the model in very small countries – for example, with a total generation requirement of about 1000 MW or even less – where extensive competition might seem impracticable.

Some countries that have already implemented elements of the standard model are implementing or strengthening other elements of it – for example, dominant incumbent generators are being required to divest, retail competition is being extended, the scope of regulatory authority is being clarified, and so on. There are several examples of this in the European Community, following the policy suggested by the European Commission itself, though that policy is silent on ownership and restructuring.

Finally, those countries that were first to implement the standard model are now refining their arrangements in the light of considerable experience, to make the competitive market as effective as possible. Examples here are Australia, particularly at the national level, the eastern jurisdictions in the USA, and of course England and Wales.

But in parallel with these developments, there has also been a reaction against the concept of privatization and competition in the electricity sector. California is the standard example cited as the justification for this stance, though this may often be just a convenient peg on which to hang an argument – and not really a convincing one, since privatization was never an issue in California, and the difficulties experienced arguably reflected regulatory limitations on the competitive market rather than limitations of competition *per se*. Nevertheless, in some countries this attitude has stopped privatization and competition; in others it has delayed it.

In some countries that have implemented some variant of the standard model – Australia, New Zealand, California and the UK, for example – there is much soul-searching and questioning of the benefits of privatization and competition. There are numerous official and unofficial reviews of the regulatory framework. The decisions of the companies, the competitive market, the regulator and indeed the customers are all under scrutiny. There are proposals to supplement, influence or replace these decisions by the decisions of government. In many ways this is a pity, and likely to be counterproductive. One of the aims of the original policy was to get the government out of the market, precisely because of the problems caused by its involvement in that sphere.

But the concerns about the competitive market need to be assuaged. Rather than addressing this issue directly, for the most part I shall concentrate here on what might be called the refinements to the competitive market approach. This is not because the other issues are unimportant – quite the contrary – but because the most effective way to assess and justify the competitive market approach is to make it work as well as possible. If we can debate and clarify our ideas and policies in that area, that will facilitate the implementation of sensible policies elsewhere.

THE NATURE OF REGULATION

If we ask, 'Is electricity regulation really needed?', most would answer, 'Yes, of course.' This was not always the case. Around the middle of the last century, several respected economists challenged the need for regulation of monopolies, on the grounds that it might put unnecessary obstacles in the way of innovation and competition.[2]

My answer to those concerned about this aspect of regulation is threefold. First, their suggested alternative of an unregulated private monopoly is typically not available. It is generally not politically possible to introduce competition and private ownership without regulation. Second, the modern regulatory framework typically gives the utility regulator a duty to promote competition and encourage new entry, in contrast to traditional regulatory frameworks that sought to replace competition. Third, where competition is not feasible, incentive regulation rather than traditional cost of service regulation has sought to promote the kinds of efficiency improvements associated with competitive markets.

Nowadays, there is concern about the extent and cost of regulation rather than the principle.[3] One issue is whether a sector regulator able to act *ex ante* is preferable to reliance on a competition authority acting *ex post*. In March 2001 the European Commission proposed a directive declaring that 'independent national regulation is pivotal'. It said that such regulation should secure non-discriminatory access to transmission and distribution networks, fix or approve the network tariffs, act *ex ante* rather than *ex post*, facilitate cross-border trade, and generally bring continuity and transparency to the market.

Two countries have resisted this approach: Germany and New Zealand. Both countries set their faces against it as a result of unfortunate previous experiences with regulation. But what of their more recent experiences of not having an *ex ante* sector regulator?

Germany

Private ownership and competition are not at issue in Germany. Indeed, in 1998 Germany suddenly declared that all customers could choose their retail supplier, with immediate effect. Retail competition has already led to significant price reductions to some large industrial customers, who previously had been paying high prices, in part because of the high costs of the domestic coal industry.

However, a problem has now arisen as competing suppliers have tried to access smaller industrial, commercial and residential customers. There are no published non-discriminatory terms of access to the networks. Each potential third-party user has to negotiate these with each incumbent network operator. There have been increasing concerns that the vertically integrated incumbents are charging excessive prices and delaying access so as to increase their own profits and protect their own retail supply businesses. It is feared that the utilities are cross-subsidizing their larger industrial customers, and facilitating the expansion of their own businesses elsewhere in the world.

Whether or not these accusations are true is unclear, but they are widely believed. Quite apart from the precise level of the charges, the unbundling and lack of transparency are increasingly problematic. But there is no sector regulator to deal with these problems *ex ante*. In principle complainants may take their case to the competition authorities. The Federal Cartel Office (Bundeskartellamt, BKA) is said to be sympathetic, but to have too few resources to deal with many complaints. The state-based structure is not conducive to one decision setting a precedent for others. Decisions by the competition authorities can be appealed, and may take several years to implement.

In September 2001 the Federal Cartel Office announced that it was investigating the network charges.[4] Significant differences between network operators suggested that some companies were abusing their monopoly position to charge discriminatory prices. The Office was also looking at whether some network operators cross-subsidize other parts of their business. In some cases, vertically integrated grid operators have set end-user prices below the tariffs charged for third-party network access. What this investigation will find, and how soon, and what it will do to remedy the situation, all remain to be seen.[5]

New Zealand

The electricity industry in New Zealand was liberalized but only partially privatized in several steps over the period since 1994, without the creation of a regulator other than the Commerce Commission. I happened to arrive there one day in 1999 when several of the companies put up their prices significantly, and the then minister immediately announced that he would have to consider regulation. There was a general election soon after, and the incoming minister launched an Inquiry in February 2000 as to whether the current regulatory arrangements were best suited to achieving the government's objective of (in brief) efficiently delivering electricity to all consumers.

The Inquiry reported in June 2000.[6] It recommended no less than four different kinds of regulation: multilateral industry agreements subject to endorsement by the government; the influence of ownership by public bodies; comparative competition by peer pressure and public opinion based on performance indicators; and targeted price control via the Commerce Act. But not a traditional sector regulator.

In December 2000 the government confirmed that it wanted an Electricity Governance Board to consolidate, replace and extend the powers of three existing industry boards. Amongst other things this new board would be responsible for:

- developing the rules of the wholesale markets;
- transmission pricing methodology and security standards;
- system expansion and replacement;
- terms and conditions for connection of distributed generation to the distribution systems;
- retail switching and customer complaint procedures;
- dispute resolution procedures;
- model arrangements for use of system charges and distribution pricing;
- model arrangements for domestic customer contracts.

The board would be required to ensure that rules were developed consistent with Guiding Principles laid down by the government. The board was to have a majority of independent members, who would be appointed after consultation with the Minister of Energy. Their prime obligation should be to develop and enforce rules consistent with the government's Guiding Principles. The industry was invited to move quickly to set up this board, and to report on progress by 28 February 2001. If there was insufficient progress, the government would regulate to establish the board.

As regards the monopoly networks, the government said that its policy objectives would be embodied in the statement of corporate intent of the publicly owned transmission company Transpower. The government expected the distribution companies, the majority of which were owned by trusts, to keep changes to their rural-line charges in line with their urban-line charges. In addition, they would have to set at least one tariff to domestic customers with a fixed charge less than 10 per cent of the average bill. This tariff would have to give the same total bill as at present at the average level of usage, so as to benefit those using small amounts of electricity.[7]

If this is New Zealand's idea of avoiding government regulation, some might wonder what the solution would have been like if it did wish to use this approach. More seriously, it seems that the now-standard job of the sector regulator is being split between an all-singing, all-dancing governance board, which also carries out the function of a market operator, and the government itself. It remains to be seen whether this allocation of governance responsibilities is as responsive to change and to problems, and as able to implement necessary modifications in a timely way, as a typical sector regulator, imperfect though the latter may be. It is also unclear what effect such explicit involvement of the government will have. In general, experience with industry boards and government stewardship is not particularly encouraging when it comes to regulatory matters.[8]

The timetable for forming the new governance board already seems to have been put back somewhat. The chairman of the Inquiry panel was appointed to chair a process to set up the board. On 7 September 2001 he noted that several market participants were not minded to sign unless their concerns about generator market power and vertical integration were addressed, but that these were beyond the scope of the board. He envisaged that the board could come into effect in 2002.

Meanwhile the New Zealand government has announced another review of the industry. During early 2001 there was a period of low rainfall, shortage of water for hydroelectricity, high electricity prices, and customer complaints. A large retail supplier had to exit from the market with large losses, having been unable to purchase electricity within the price at which it had sold. The government announced in September that it was reviewing the events of the year.[9] Both these are of course matters that would normally fall to a sector regulator to deal with.

Conclusion on Regulation

I have no desire to introduce or perpetuate sector-specific utility regulation where it is unnecessary, and I am sympathetic to proposals to transfer the regulation of competitive parts of the industry to the competition authorities. However, the countries where sector-specific regulation has so far been resisted do not present appealing pictures of more efficient and innovative electricity sectors that are more responsive to the need to change. Nor are they independent of the government – if anything, the opposite. There is a question whether independent sector-specific regulation can be more actively reduced as competition develops, but these examples do not suggest that it should be eliminated altogether.

COMPETITION IN GENERATION: INITIAL RESTRUCTURING

How important is it to restructure the generation sector of an industry? When the government privatized the electricity industry in England and Wales, it initially planned to create just two successor companies to the Central

Electricity Generating Board (CEGB). One company (Big G) would provide nearly two thirds of the output, including all the nuclear; the other (Little G) would provide nearly the other third. In the event, the nuclear stations were deemed not saleable at the time. National Power ended up with just under half the total output, PowerGen 30 per cent, and Nuclear Electric 15 per cent. So the largest two companies had nearly 80 per cent and the largest three had 94 per cent. Interconnectors and others provided the remaining 6 per cent. By today's standards, the degree of concentration of output in two or three incumbent companies would be unacceptable.

The implicit assumption was that customers would be protected by the ability of other generators to enter the market and construct new plant if these three incumbents were able and willing to exercise market power. In the event, entry took place on a larger scale than anyone had foreseen. Nevertheless, this was not sufficient to prevent the incumbents from increasing prices above the new entry level. As regulator, I had to take steps to require the two largest incumbents to divest some price-setting mid-merit plant to a new competitor. Since then there has been further divestment, partly in the context of merger clearance and partly on a more voluntary basis. Now the largest company, which is neither of the two former duopolists, has less than 20 per cent of total output. PowerGen and the successor to National Power each have less than 10 per cent. It is now generally agreed that three successor companies were by no means enough.

New Zealand had a similar problem. When it originally separated off transmission as Transpower in 1994 it left Electricity Corporation of New Zealand (ECNZ) as a single successor generator. It assumed that new entry would suffice to protect customers. But this was untenable. In 1996 it had to split off Contact Energy, which was privatized, and in 1999 it split the remainder of ECNZ into three state-owned enterprises.[10]

This is not to argue that the number of competitors is the only criterion for a competitive market, and that conditions of entry are of no importance. On the contrary. Michael Beesley always used to argue that, however many competitors there were in a market, they would seek to exercise market power unless others could enter the market and upset their plans. Events in California have demonstrated the terrible consequences of preventing or delaying new entry. Initially there were higher prices; later there was inadequate capacity to meet demand.

The number of competitors and the ease of entry are more closely related than is generally appreciated. Building new plant is one way of entering the market, but it is time-consuming and expensive. Another way is to buy an existing plant, or even an existing company. Sites alone have value, even if the plant is worn out, by virtue of their planning permission and existing grid connection. All these means of entry are normally available in competitive markets for other products, but until recently they were not available in the electricity markets of most countries in the world. Opening the market with only one or a few successor companies therefore restricts the options available to entrants, and thereby deters entry. This is particularly the case if some of the companies are not for sale because they are government-owned.

Now, however, generating plants, sites and companies are increasingly freely bought and sold, at least in England and Wales and to some extent in Europe, Australia and the USA. The ability of potential competitors to enter the market quickly, at whatever scale suits them, will enhance competition. So too will the ability of existing players to exit the market equally quickly if they feel they are not as well placed as others to compete.

The need for an adequate number of competitors in the market is increasingly appreciated. Argentina even sold each generating station separately, and as far as I know has not regretted this. Scandinavia and most of the US and Australian states that have embraced competition have a significant number of competitors, in some cases as a result of divestiture. Spain and Italy are presently requiring their incumbent utilities to divest some plant, though they will need to go further to achieve an adequate degree of competition in the market.

Some countries and companies have resisted. Electricité de France has offered to sell some output to competitors, but not some plants. France has created a regulator, but it stands out as the country that has refused to take the necessary steps to create a competitive generation market, and a fully competitive retail market is not possible without adequate competition in generation. Germany has precluded a fully competitive retail market by a different route, as explained earlier. It is unfortunate that two of the leading countries in Europe have so far set the worst examples in terms of liberalizing the electricity market.

COMPETITION IN GENERATION: CONDUCT AND STRUCTURE

Despite restructuring and new entry, actual or potential generator market power remains an issue that concerns market participants, customers and regulators in many countries. How significant is it, and what steps should be taken to deal with it?

I leave aside discussion of the Market Abuse Licence Condition (MALC), where the Department of Trade and Industry's (DTI) present consultation nears a conclusion. But there are similar concerns elsewhere. In Australia the National Electricity Code Administrator (NECA) recently issued draft guidelines to prevent the withholding of capacity artificially to increase prices, the exploiting of network constraints, and the practice of rebidding following reductions in transmission capacity.[11] The statement explicitly made reference to the MALC in the UK.

In the USA, market monitoring has become standard practice. Events in California have put this issue at centre stage. There were undoubtedly very high generation prices there at some times over the last two years. But how far were these the natural result of increased costs and market-clearing prices in a situation where demand had outstripped capacity, and how far the result of generators exploiting market power?

It has been fascinating to follow the debate between some of the leading energy economists in the USA. Joskow and Kahn[12] have argued that there is evidence of withholding behaviour by generators in California, and that 'about a third of wholesale price can be attributed to market power during June, July, August and September 2000, after accounting for changes in fundamental supply and demand conditions'. Harvey and Hogan[13] have challenged this, suggesting that market structure inefficiencies and resulting uncertainties could explain this behaviour.

In terms of economic and engineering expertise, and use of empirical evidence, it would be difficult to match the quality of these analyses. Perhaps Joskow and Kahn have the edge at present, so that on the balance of the evidence the generators may have restricted output in order to raise prices in the market. However, my concern here is not to pass judgement on that issue, but to examine what the implications are for policy. Are we to conclude that regulators should carry out studies of this kind when market abuse is suspected, and on the basis of those studies should penalize the offenders in some way, for example by fines?

There are at least two difficulties with such an approach. First, despite the enormous and focused intellectual input over nearly a year, I am not sure that the incidents in California have been conclusively resolved. Contrast the situation of the average regulatory office, with the average amount of expertise and time and resources at its disposal, subject to the pressure of other regulatory business, and faced by well-resourced experts acting on behalf of the parties whose conduct is at stake. Is it realistic to expect that such an office could discover, analyse and resolve any such controversial issue within a reasonable time, to the satisfaction of whatever court might ultimately be called upon to adjudicate?

It might be counter-argued that, although the techniques, arguments and evidence deployed by the economists I have cited were in this case relatively novel, once this immediate issue has been resolved it would be relatively straightforward for a regulatory office to identify and analyse the evidence in a future instance. However, such a response would underestimate the variety of circumstances likely to arise in practice, and the ability of interested parties to find ways around any specified set of criteria.

The second difficulty has to do with the economic analysis of competition. Given that a particular type of conduct has been identified, how are we to interpret and treat it? Underlying the analyses just referred to, and many more, is the proposition that in a competitive market, price should equal marginal cost. If price is systematically above marginal cost, this indicates market power.[14] The most familiar derivation of the optimality of marginal cost pricing is within the models of theoretical welfare economics, in which the market and all firms within it are assumed to be in equilibrium. Typically there is perfect knowledge, and the firms have made optimal decisions about technology, scale of output, and so on.

It is fair to say that no one assumes that this is really the world we live in, and the authors cited do not assume that. It is surely more realistic to assume that we live in a world of constant and more or less unexpected change. Neither the generation market nor any other is ever actually in equilibrium. Certainly there may be equilibrating tendencies – an increase in price will stimulate existing generators to try to produce more, and (depending on their estimates of future prices) generators will be more inclined to enter the market, including by building plant. But equally there are disequilibrating tendencies – an explosion at a plant, unexpected movements in gas prices, levels of rainfall affecting hydro capacity, changes in the growth of consumer demand, events in the macro-economy (no small factor after 11 September) and not least intervention and changes in policy by regulatory and government authorities.

In such a world, it would be commercial suicide for a generator to assume that the market will always be in equilibrium and that it should price at marginal cost. The world is too risky for that. Investment in new plant is very expensive and typically takes a long time to recover. The entrant must reduce its risks and plan to get its investment back as soon as possible. It will do this by a variety of long-term and short-term contracts to allocate risk to those parties best able to control them – which will typically include fuel suppliers and equipment manufacturers as well as retailers and customers. In the absence of regulatory or other constraints, there is a continual process of trading and re-trading such contracts in the face of ever-changing market conditions. The bid that a generator makes in the spot market, if indeed it chooses or is forced to be in the spot market, is thus just a small part of its whole strategy for coping with the substantial risks of a generation business.

This is not to argue that the generation market is different from other markets. I am arguing that, in the real world, competitive markets generally are not characterized by price equal to marginal cost. That is the wrong benchmark for judging possibly anti-competitive behaviour. Life is more complex and in particular more risky than the marginal cost criterion recognizes. In a competitive market each participant will seek to reduce its risks and cover its investment whenever and wherever it can. It cannot price at any time on the basis that each of its assets will earn an equilibrium return for the rest of its life.

What does this more Schumpeterian approach imply for regulatory policy? A need to consider the long-run as well as the short-run consequences of any policy. If there is a substantial penalty for alleged withholding of output, an existing generator may well be more inclined not to do this. But a potential new generator might also be less inclined to enter the market. Ameliorating today's problem may thus be at the expense of exacerbating tomorrow's.

This is obviously not an easy balance to strike. Given the difficulties of satisfactorily defining and proving anti-competitive conduct, my own inclination would be to focus where possible on structure and incentives when designing remedies, rather than on conduct. Protection for customers can be provided in a number of ways. These include promoting new entry, and enforcing divestment where necessary and practicable, taking into account local as well as market-wide monopoly positions. Wholesale trading should allow suppliers to contract ahead rather than force them to trade only in the spot market. Retail competition should give suppliers incentive to protect themselves and customers. The system operator should have flexibility to contract ahead so as to avoid or minimize market power, and there should be incentives to remove network bottlenecks where it is economic to do so.[15]

These are almost the opposite of the policies followed in California. As I indicate later, regulatory restrictions there left utilities and customers needlessly exposed to generator market power. But the experience of California should not be typical.

COMPETITION IN RETAIL SUPPLY

Allowing competitive suppliers access to the wires of the local distribution companies, and thereby allowing all customers a choice of supplier, was one of the more innovative aspects of the privatization in England and Wales. My own thinking was that it would provide more effective protection for customers, and a more efficient and innovative market, than regulation of monopoly distribution companies. Introduction of retail competition had to be phased in over eight years in order to provide transitional protection to the coal industry. But no one knew whether the concept would succeed.

In the event, it has done so. Over 80 per cent of large customer demand is now met by so-called second-tier suppliers rather than the local utility, and over two thirds of medium-sized customer demand. In the less than three years since the residential market has been open, about 27 per cent of such customers have moved to a second-tier supplier, and present rate of change is about 100 000 customers per week.[16]

Other countries have opened the market for larger customers. A smaller but increasing number is opening the market to residential customers. The take-up here is more mixed, and the data less up to date. In Norway, the number of households that had switched to another supplier rose steadily to 7 per cent by the end of 1999.[17] At the same rate of increase the proportion might be nearly double that by now. In New Zealand some 5 per cent of residential customers had switched within a year of the market opening in 1999.[18] It has been suggested to me that this proportion may have increased to between 20 and 25 per cent by 2000, but with the problems of higher generation prices in New Zealand the proportion switching back to incumbent suppliers may also have increased. One of the largest retail suppliers recently pulled out of the market having made serious losses.[19]

In the USA the situation is mixed and reportedly volatile. One report with figures for the end of 1999 and early 2000 shows between 1.5 and 17.5 per cent of residential customers switching in five different companies in Pennsylvania, 2 per cent in California and under 1 per cent in Massachusetts.[20] In California and perhaps elsewhere the proportion subsequently declined as generation prices rose or fluctuated.[21] Few retailers entered the market, and many have now left it.

Looking forward, the Netherlands is scheduled to open its residential market in 2004. Texas has just begun the pilot stage with a view to full opening next year. The state of Victoria in Australia is scheduled to open its market in January 2002 (deferred from January 2001). The European Council recently recommended that all member states open their markets completely by 2005.

There have been some backward steps, however. France vetoed the EC recommendation in March. And very recently, the State Government of California proposed to repeal retail competition.[22]

Here, I want to look at four topics: the doubts that some economists have expressed as to whether retail competition is worthwhile; the policy of direct wholesale access in California; the subsequent suppression of retail competition in California; and the alternative policy of transitional price caps adopted in Britain and elsewhere.

Costs and Benefits of Retail Competition

In 2001 the National Audit Office (NAO) published an assessment showing that the price reductions to customers who changed supplier outweighed the total costs of implementing retail competition.[23] There have also been a number of innovations such as green electricity, tariffs with no standing charge, the convenience of buying electricity and gas from the same supplier, price reductions for dual fuels and prompt payment, guaranteed fixed charges for the year independent of consumption, and so on.

Gordon MacKerron of National Economic Research Associates (NERA) challenged the NAO's assessment.[24] He argued that the benefits of competition were less than they seemed, and that those who did not change supplier were worse off, because they paid the cost without receiving any benefit. Moreover, some of the benefits like prompt payment discounts could have been secured without competition. He suggested that the benefits of full retail competition may have been less than the costs, and that the policy probably made customers worse off. He implied that France might be justified in not opening its market.

I argued that his assessment undervalued the contribution of competition to reducing the costs of generation through sharper purchasing by competing retailers, and through the reduction in coal and nuclear costs now that these fuels were no longer protected by a monopoly buyer. [25] There was increased knowledge about distribution costs as a result of the pressures to ensure a competitive and undistorted retail market. There was greater incentive for retailers to discover and provide the kinds of terms that customers wanted. All these factors meant that the benefits of retail competition were greater than the critics allowed. In fact, many of these benefits had already been factored into the tighter transitional price cap that was set when the residential market opened. So measuring the benefits of competition against that price cap was already to undervalue them.

Graham Shuttleworth of NERA reaffirmed Gordon's argument in the phrase 'if you can do it under monopoly, it isn't a benefit of competition'. He suggested that appropriate action by government and/or regulator could have achieved some of those benefits.[26]

The extent of this is what I dispute. Austrian and public choice economists have been arguing over the last quarter of a century that governments and regulators typically do not have either the knowledge or incentive to do all these things. Competition is precisely a way of providing the relevant information and incentivizing the market participants to use it to benefit customers. Most economists have now accepted these arguments, at least in principle. Putting the arguments into practice seems to be more difficult.

Direct Access to Wholesale Spot Price in California

The problem in California was not a lack of faith in the benefits of a competitive retail market, nor the failure of that market *per se*. It is often said that California's experience reflected a mixture of bad luck and bad judgement. The bad luck was the upturn in demand coinciding with the reduced availability of hydro capacity. The bad judgements included the undue restrictions on construction of new capacity, the regulatory insistence that utilities purchase generation only in the spot market, even though subject to a fixed retail price cap, the inadequate consideration of the feasible level of that cap, and the reluctance to increase it when it was plainly untenable. The list should probably also include undue restrictions on the ability of the system operator to contract ahead to minimize vulnerability to the market power of generators.

There have been several excellent papers on the experience in California.[27] Less well appreciated is an aspect of the regulatory policy that was advocated by several leading economists, yet in my view hindered rather than facilitated the transition to a competitive retail market. This was the policy of direct retail access to the wholesale spot market that was briefly implemented in San Diego. It too reflected a failure to appreciate the importance of forward contracts in minimizing risk in a competitive market.

After a utility's stranded costs were paid off, it was effectively required to exit the retail supply business and concentrate on distribution. Customers could choose another supplier, from whom they could purchase at fixed prices or on whatever other terms were on offer. If they failed to do so, the utility was required to pass through the wholesale spot market price. Supporters of this policy argued that it gave all customers the benefit of direct access to the competitive wholesale market, without the need for retailers. Retailers would survive and prosper only if they added value to this service – for example by providing fixed price hedges that customers were willing to pay for.

San Diego was first to pay off its stranded costs, and it moved to this policy. At the time, spot market prices had not increased, and customers did not switch supplier or arrange hedges. When spot prices did increase, customer bills rose sharply, doubling or even trebling. There was public outrage and demands that something be done.

The California State government decided to intervene in the process. It argued in favour of generation price caps and against increasing retail price caps. It spent about $11 billion on large-scale long-term purchases of high-priced generation output, some of which it subsequently had to sell at an enormous loss. It is still trying to find a way to fund this. It proposed to take one of the transmission networks into public ownership. Most recently it has proposed to repeal the ability of residential customers to choose their own supplier. It is difficult to imagine a more counterproductive set of measures.

A better approach than direct retail access would have been to leave alone the customers that did not switch supplier. They would continue to be supplied by the utility's retail supply business under a regulated tariff. UK experience is that customers both large and small have generally rejected the opportunity to buy on spot-price terms. They prefer fixed prices, or limited and well-specified demand management terms. I am not aware of any country other than Norway where any residential customers have chosen wholesale spot prices. Even in

Norway that proportion seems to be small. At the end of 1999, 85 per cent of households had chosen variable price terms where the price is fixed at any time with the supplier able to give notice of change. Of the remaining customers, some were on a fixed-price tariff. An unspecified proportion, but evidently less than 15 per cent, had chosen to pay a markup on spot price.[28] I understand that even here a maximum price 'insurance policy' was typically offered.

Regulatory policy thus forced customers in San Diego on to an unfamiliar and inappropriate tariff. Many may not have been aware of what was happening. In effect it forced them to incur a further cost of choosing and purchasing a hedge from a new retail supplier. It would have been less disruptive and less costly to let customers stay with their existing supplier. They could then switch supplier if and when they saw it as advantageous to do so. A transitional price cap implemented as in the UK would have seen customers, and the industry as a whole, through the turbulent events of 2000 to 2001.[29] No doubt there would still have been some complaints, but there would have been many fewer than were actually made. It is questionable whether they would have triggered the unhelpful series of government interventions.

Suspending Retail Competition in California

These government interventions are increasingly serious. On 20 September 2001 the California PUC voted to suspend the right of customers of any size to enter into direct access contracts or agreements, with immediate effect.[30] Direct access is what we would call second-tier supply in the UK.[31] The reasoning was as follows.

> Recent events in the California electric market have caused a radical change in the area of direct access. First the Governor's Proclamation of January 17, 2001, found that an emergency situation exists in the electricity market in California threatening 'the solvency of California's major public utilities, ...' Second, on February 1, 2001, Assembly Bill No. 1 from the First Extraordinary Session ... (AB 1X) was signed into law which, among other things, requires that the Department of Water Resources (DWR) purchase electricity on behalf of the customers of the California utilities.

This bill, called AB 1X, provides that the right of retail end-use customers to acquire service from other providers shall be suspended until the DWR no longer supplies power. The PUC took the view that

> In order to address the rapid, unforeseen shortage of electric power and energy available in the state and rapid and substantial increases in wholesale energy costs and retail energy rates, that endanger the health, welfare and safety of the people of this state, it is necessary for this act to take effect immediately.

It noted that

> Currently, the State of California through the DWR is purchasing electric energy on behalf of the utilities' existing ratepayers ... with funds from the State's General Fund and an interim loan. To repay the general Fund and continue the power purchase program, state agencies are preparing to issue DWR Power Supply Revenue Bonds. We have been informed by the State Treasurer's Office [and other agencies] that 'to sell the bonds with the investment grade rating required by law, it will be necessary to control the conditions under which ratepayers (generally large users such as industrial customers) "exit the system".'

The PUC further commented: 'We note that the suspension of the ability to acquire direct access service will provide DWR with a stable customer base from which to recover the cost of the power it has purchased and continues to purchase', and continued:

> Customers might be tempted to switch from utility bundled service to electric service providers in order to avoid some of the impact of higher rates and take advantage of lower spot market prices. It is not in the public interest to permit such behavior. All ratepayers benefit from the State's actions to ensure reliable electricity service and, therefore, all ratepayers should contribute to the effort to pay down the unprecedented debt incurred by the State to help weather the energy crisis.

Two of the five PUC commissioners dissented from the majority view. They wrote:

> One could say that this order is consistent with the Administration's present third world country mentality. We are punishing the very consumers who made a commitment to ensuring electric restructuring did work by adding a demand retail component to cure the dysfunctions in the wholesale market.
>   We are not convinced that the DWR bond ratings depend on killing direct access. This notion is a scare tactic and a smoke screen. Direct access comprises such a small percentage of overall demand that it cannot reasonably be seen to be a threat to the sale of the bonds. ...
>   Something else is going on here. We think that the DWR does not want direct access because if the public is presented with alternatives, it will make the DWR's purchasing mistakes abundantly clear ...
>   DWR and the bonds should not be threatened by direct access if DWR is making prudent energy purchases. Only if DWR's contracts are too expensive, relative to the market, will customers seek shelter in lower direct access prices. Indeed, retaining direct access as a way to send price signals to consumers may be the only way to place pressure on DWR to make more prudent purchases.

The cases for preventing full retail competition and for allowing it could not have been presented more clearly. Those who doubt the case for full retail competition and argue in favour of regulated monopoly should consider these events carefully. As one of Harry Enfield's characters is fond of saying: 'Is that what you want? Cause that's what you'll get.'

A Transitional Retail Price Cap

The final question on this issue is whether California should have regulated the retail tariff charged by the incumbent utility once the retail market was open, and if so how. I can appreciate that the PUC felt that this was an unattractive prospect. Any regulator faces considerable difficulties in deciding what generation and other costs to allow and what not to allow. It was precisely because of these difficulties that I argued at the time of privatization for retail competition to obviate or at least minimize the need for such regulation.

The obligation to retain a franchise monopoly for eight years in the UK meant that we had to design and implement retail price controls for that period. We also decided to keep a transitional retail price cap on the residential market for another four years. So even though we got rid of most retail price controls, not quite all have disappeared yet. However, our experience during that period led us to a transition policy that seems to have worked well here, and could do so elsewhere.

In brief, when the residential market opened we moved from a cost pass-through control to a fixed price cap. We made sure that the level of the price cap explicitly covered the cost of entering hedging contracts for the duration of the price cap.[32] Whether each incumbent supplier chose to do so was a matter for them.

In a competitive market it was no longer necessary or desirable to ensure that price equalled cost actually incurred. We did not seek to remove all the risk and margin from the incumbent supplier. If profit was so high in relation to the risk that competitors could offer a better deal, they were free to do so. Such competition would protect customers, who were now free to go elsewhere. The purpose of a transitional price cap was primarily to ensure that things did not get worse as the market opened and as customers and suppliers each gradually came to understand an unfamiliar world. For those who chose a lower-priced supplier it would get better. Actually, things got better for all customers because in setting the level of the price cap we were able to pass on to customers the benefit of ending the high-priced coal contracts. But this was an exceptional circumstance.

This approach worked. Competitive suppliers were attracted, and customers were too. The competitive market has developed, to such an extent that Ofgem has indicated that it expects to remove the price cap in April 2002.[33] And rightly so. At the present rate of switching, about one third of residential customers will have moved from the incumbent supplier by the time the price cap ends. It is no longer needed.

I would emphasize only one further point. Setting a transitional price cap until competition is effective does not mean setting that price cap at the lowest level that price would be if competition were already effective. Nor does it mean trying to estimate what the costs of an efficient competitor would be, and periodically updating the price cap to reflect the past and/or future movements of such costs. That may well be appropriate in some form for a permanent price control on the monopoly sector of the industry. But there is a real danger that such an approach would stifle the growth of competition and undermine the criteria for removing the control. I took issue with Ofgem on this point.[34] Fortunately the danger was averted. However, I fear that the danger looms large in the recent proposals of the Office of the Regulator General for a retail electricity price cap in the Australian state of Victoria.[35] Closer to home, I fear that it is also reflected in Oftel's proposals for the mobile telecommunications market, issued very recently.[36]

WHOLESALE TRADING ARRANGEMENTS

The Pool set up in England and Wales at the time of privatization was compulsory in the sense that all generators were required to bid into it the day before 'real time' and all suppliers or retailers were required to buy out of it. The system operator scheduled plant and set market-clearing prices for each half-hour period of the next day. Market participants typically entered contracts for differences around these Pool prices, to hedge their risks.

Different countries have implemented variations on this theme, and there has been considerable refinement over time. For example, the national electricity market in Australia now has a succession of markets held every five minutes. Some countries have separated the functions of system operator, market operator and transmission operator; others have combined some of these. Among the live issues at present in the USA are the scope for regional transmission operators, the best way to deal with transmission constraints, and the externalities associated with interconnecting systems. These are important issues, perhaps more important in the USA than in England and Wales, and they have also influenced the development of US Pools, but there is unfortunately not space to deal with them here.

The compulsory nature of the Pool has naturally been questioned. Increasingly, arrangements are accommodating physical as well as financial bilateral trading outside the Pool. The PJM and New York (or Northeast) Pools are said to be explicitly designed to facilitate bilateral trading as much as possible. But these issues were not so clear some years ago. Two contrasting experiences are worth exploring.

In California there was a contentious debate between advocates of a 'Poolco model' and advocates of bilateral trading. According to Paul Joskow,

the ultimate design of the wholesale market institutions represented a series of com-
promises made by design committees including interest group representatives,
drawing on bits and pieces of alternative models for market design, congestion
management, transmission pricing, new generator interconnection rules, and locational
market power mitigation. ... The end result was the most complicated set of wholesale
electricity market institutions ever created on earth.[37]

The core of the design was an Independent System Operator (ISO) and a Power
Exchange (PX). Subsequent experience was problematic, including lack of
coordination between the two institutions.

In January 2001 the Power Exchange stopped operating and eventually filed for
bankruptcy. Since then, there has been no public organized power exchange in
California. Buyers and sellers rely either on bilateral contracts which are scheduled with
the ISO, self-supply in the case of the portion of utility load that can be served from
their remaining resources, or purchases from the ISO's real-time imbalance market.[38]

The other experience is the New Electricity Trading Arrangements that have
operated in England and Wales since the end of March 2001, in place of the Pool
established at the time of privatization. NETA was preceded by a quite
remarkable barrage of criticism, not least from commentators in the USA.
NETA has also caused consternation among countries in course of implementing electricity reform. I well remember delegates from the regulatory body
of one East European country coming to see me at Offer. They had the restructuring of their industry all planned out, including a Pool, precisely as in England
and Wales. But now we had announced that the Pool concept was all wrong.
Could I please confirm to them that at least one had to start with a Pool?

I'm not sure of the answer to this question. The Pool concept is now tried and
tested in many economically developed countries, and some developing ones.
But would it work in countries where the accurate transmission of information
and the routine enforcement of contracts cannot be relied upon? Does the logic
imply that we should be working towards a single Pool across each continent,
including the USA, Europe, India and Africa?

It might help to answer these questions if we could clarify our thinking about
NETA. Is bilateral trading with appropriate real-time balancing arrangements
the way to go, or simply misguided? Is there a real difference about the bulk
of the trading, or is the real debate limited to the precise nature of the balancing
arrangements?

Early Criticisms of NETA

The predominantly academic or professional criticisms of NETA (as opposed
to the concerns of interested market participants) seem to fall into two main

categories. The earlier criticisms focused on market power, the merits of more moderate reform, pay-as-bid, and the role of simulation models and evidence. David Currie dealt with many of these concerns,[39] and I agree with his arguments.

Briefly, Offer was not deluded into thinking that the Pool was the only source of market power. We thought it exacerbated the extent of market power, but we knew parallel action had to be taken on the structure of the generation market, and when the opportunity arose we took it. We were sympathetic to many of the particular modifications proposed to the Pool, such as firm bids and the abolition of the capacity levy. However, we doubted that they were more easily delivered or more predictable than more fundamental reform, and they did not deal with the problem of the uniform system marginal price (SMP). We thought that pay-as-bid in place of a uniform system marginal price would have a beneficial effect on the competitive process in both generation and retail supply. We were not convinced that this would increase risk, because it would apply to a voluntary mechanism covering a very small part of the market, not to compulsory bidding into the previous Pool. This was a point that our critics generally overlooked. We tried to take account of economic theory, empirical evidence and system modelling. However, we were not as convinced as some critics evidently were of the possibility of modelling a new system adequately, conclusively and in a timely way, consistent with the needs of users and the window of opportunity available.

Centralized versus Decentralized Contracting

The main issue I want to explore here is the concern succinctly expressed by Larry Ruff, but evidently shared by others, including Bill Hogan.

> The giant step back in NETA is OFGEM's outright rejection of the very concept that has made competition in electricity practical – a central spot market integrated with physical dispatch – in favour of the discredited idea of an electricity market based almost entirely on decentralized contracting.[40]

Let me first acknowledge that Ruff's contribution to designing the original England and Wales Pool was a giant step forward because it made it possible to privatize the industry in England and to introduce competition. He showed how to cut through the fruitless debates about trading contracts in the G Pool and the D Pool and the difficult issues assigned to the increasing number of 'boxes on the bridge' between them. However, whether or not that particular version of contracting is discredited, no one is advocating that earlier idea today.

The Pool and the CEGB that it replaced both involved a system of central-ized dispatch. Both assumed that it was the job of what we now call the system operator to ensure the efficient scheduling of plant. It was accepted that in a competitive market it is up to the individual market participants to choose what plant to build and how to run it and how to bid it. Nevertheless, the system operator's job was to decide what plant should be run so as to maximize system efficiency, given the bids before it, and to instruct the plant accordingly. It was also the system operator's job, or that of an associated process, to tell the buyers and sellers what price they had to pay or be paid in the first instance.

In practice (as some of my commentators have emphasized), some generators were in effect able to decide that their plant should run, by bidding zero in the knowledge that they would nevertheless get the system marginal price. They also entered bilateral contracts for differences that determined what they would be paid regardless of what Pool price was. But not everyone could do this, and it is not clear that everyone accepted zero bidding as consistent with either the ideal of the Pool or with normal competitive markets.

NETA explicitly rejected the propositions about the role of the system operator in determining prices and schedules for the bulk of electricity output. It affirmed that, within specified but minimal limitations, it is the job of electricity participants themselves to decide which plant they wish to run, and to self-dispatch that plant. It is the job of the system operator to make this possible. The system operator takes orders instead of giving them. Moreover, it is no longer any business of the system operator to dictate the terms on which the bulk of electricity output is traded.

This transformation of roles seems to me fundamental and eminently reasonable. In an increasingly competitive market, generation plant will be in many separate ownerships and there will be many competing suppliers. Constantly fluctuating market conditions, plus developments specific to each generator's plant position and each supplier's customer situation, mean that each market participant needs to engage in a continual process of contracting and possibly recontracting to minimize its risks, reduce its costs and maximize its competitive advantage. It is impractical for each generator and each supplier to keep the system operator fully informed of all the relevant considerations necessary to enable the latter to maximize the efficiency of the system as a whole.

In other words, far from being discredited, an electricity market based almost entirely on decentralized contracting seems to me the only economic way to proceed. In fact, I suspect that it will be the converse idea, of an electricity market based almost entirely on centralized contracting, that will increasingly become discredited.

I cannot believe that Ruff really disagrees with this. His earlier paper clearly spells out the role of contracts leading up to what he calls the operational 'day'.[41] I hope we are now agreed that US Pools in the Northeast and NETA (and in practice the England and Wales Pool to a significant extent) are all based almost entirely on decentralized contracting.

The qualification 'almost entirely' is important. As Ruff points out, it is not feasible to expect the system operator to feed back signals for the market participants to respond adequately in real time. At some point the system operator has to take decisions to balance the system, based on the prices bid and offered to it, and schedule changes in plant accordingly. But all this is not in dispute as between the proponents and critics of NETA. The main outstanding issue (deferring transmission constraints for the moment) is precisely how those balancing trades are paid for.

Single or Dual Cash-out Prices

Detailed proposals on cash-out prices first appeared in 1999. Ofgem argued that 'in principle, imbalance cash-out prices should reflect the full costs of imbalances having to be resolved by the System Operator over relatively short timescales'.[42] Ofgem concluded that a dual cash-out price was required. In contrast, Ruff argued that there should be a near-to-real-time spot market, with in effect a single cash-out price.

In practice, the difference between the two approaches has been very significant. In the first few days of NETA, at the end of March, System Buy Price averaged over £103/MWh while System Sell Price averaged under £3/MWh, a spread of £100/MWh, against a generation price of around £20/MWh in the bilateral markets and power exchanges.[43] Since then the spread has fallen considerably, to about £30 System Buy Price to £10 System Sell Price. None the less, the spread is still a major concern to most generators, particularly of renewable energy who cannot always easily control their level of output.

The Ofgem principle – that imbalance cash-out prices should reflect the full costs of imbalances – is surely correct. It would be inefficient to charge a single cash-out price if the costs of dealing with under- and over-contracted participants were to differ significantly. However, on the basis of my admittedly limited knowledge of the balancing mechanism, it is not clear that these costs do differ significantly in most cases. The National Grid Company (NGC) takes its decisions based on the aggregate situation, and is not aware of the contract positions of each party. In most cases, therefore, it is not clear that a dual cash-out price is called for. Here I agree with Ruff and Hogan about the potential inefficiencies that could be caused by significantly divergent prices.

The designers of NETA will no doubt have had to consider certain broader issues. For example, would the pricing principles in the balancing mechanism be consistent with changing the attitudes, awareness and opportunities of market participants so as to promote a more competitive market in both generation and supply? Would they encourage sufficiently balanced contract positions that NGC would be able to balance the remainder of the system in less than four hours compared to the previous 24? I would not underrate these considerations.

It is important to get 'the big picture' right as well as the details of price in relation to cost.

As regards that big picture, the present position seems encouraging. I understand that about 92 per cent of trades are now bilateral, about 5 per cent are in the power exchanges, and only about 3 per cent in the balancing mechanism. NGC seems to be coping well with the task of balancing the system. Indeed, it is coping increasingly well, and its costs of doing so have reduced.

Experience overseas is not inconsistent with this. Pools elsewhere in the world are increasingly moving towards facilitating bilateral markets (both physical and financial) and forward exchanges, with their own roles as crucial but relatively low-volume balancing markets or mechanisms. The use of a single balancing price does not seem to have led to undue reliance on the balancing market. For example, in Norway the proportion of trades in the so-called regulatory market has continued to be very small.[44] The National Electricity Market in Australia now sets a price (SMP) every 5 minutes, but almost all electricity is traded earlier on a bilateral basis. The proportion traded in the balancing market is similar to that in the UK. In the PJM the proportion of electricity traded on the spot market was higher, at 18 per cent in 2000.[45] The proportion traded at market-clearing price in the New Zealand Energy Market (NZEM) spot market was as high as three quarters last year, when bilateral trading accounted for only about a quarter of the total output.[46] However, since then generators have 'self-hedged' by acquiring retail customer bases, and the proportion traded in the spot market may now be down to about 20 per cent.[47]

In the light of this experience, it is appropriate to consider gradual modifications to the details of the cash-out mechanism, as David Currie himself urged. For example, the recent reclassification of shorter (under 15 minute) balancing contracts as system balancing rather than energy balancing seems more accurate, and is likely to reduce the spread of the dual cash-out prices.[48] Further modifications should be considered on their merits, but in general a reduction in the spread of cash-out prices should be welcomed, together with increasing provision for default to a single cash-out price when there are relatively few balancing trades in the opposite direction. This might be coupled with another of Currie's suggestions, namely a charge for discrepancies between a generator's final physical notification and its actual metered position. The generators' physical positions are important factors in NGC's actual operation of the system.

Changes of this kind should justifiably relieve the situation of generators in general, and of renewable generators in particular, without compromising the principle that each market participant should be charged the costs that it imposes on the system. Some of the modifications proposed to avoid the balancing mechanism may no longer be needed. And a reduction in the so-called 'beer fund' (which arises from the spread between the dual cash-out prices) would also be desirable in itself.

As a result of such modifications there may be greater use of the balancing mechanism. This is not undesirable given that the market seems now to have changed irrevocably and assuming NGC can cope. Refining the cash-out calculation will enable an increasingly efficient allocation of trades as between the bilateral markets and forward exchanges on the one hand, and the balancing mechanism on the other.

CONCLUSIONS

I hope that I have said enough to give a flavour of what is happening in electricity regulation in at least some countries around the world. A wide variety of issues is being actively debated internationally. Industry participants, customer groups, academics, consultants and not least regulators themselves are active participants in these debates. One theme emerging from analysis of experience to date is the scope for improved regulation to promote a competitive market, and not intervene unnecessarily.

I would not wish to be critical of regulators here. In addition to all the debates I have referred to, they have to cope with many official and quasi-official reviews, often trying to second-guess the regulator's decisions. Whether these reviews tend to generate heat or light is debatable, but they certainly take up considerable regulatory time and effort. Maybe those who so readily demand cost–benefit analyses of regulatory actions should consider such analyses of regulatory reviews. My own impression is that regulators are already thinking seriously about all these issues without further prompting. Electricity regulation is generally alive and well all round the world, perhaps too alive and well for some people's taste.

NOTES

1. The views expressed here are strictly my own, and should not be taken as reflecting the views of Ofgem. I am grateful to Bill Heaps, Alan Moran and Jim Wilson for guiding me to useful sources of information in New Zealand, Australia and the USA, respectively. I am also grateful to Bill Hogan, Larry Ruff and Susan Wakefield for comments.
2. For a review of these concerns see my Wincott Lecture, published as *Privatisation, Competition and Regulation*, Occasional Paper 110, Institute of Economic Affairs, London, February 2000.
3. For example, John Blundell and Colin Robinson, *Regulation Without the State …The Debate Continues*, Institute of Economic Affairs, Readings 52, London, September 2000. Better Regulation Task Force, *Economic Regulators*, London, July 2001.
4. *European Power Focus Weekly*, Issue 16, 28 September 2001.
5. But there has been a further development: 'After the recent announcement of the Federal Cartel Office to scrutinize the grid tariffs of 22 network operators, the cartel office in the state

of Baden-Württemberg has now also launched an investigation into the grid charges of 86 local and regional network operators.' *Powerfocus Europe*, 12 October 2001.

6. *Inquiry into the Electricity Industry*, Report to the Minister of Energy, June 2000. I acted as adviser to the Inquiry, but was not a member of the panel.

7. The Commerce Commission is required to publish thresholds and to investigate lines businesses (both distribution and transmission) that breach those thresholds for the purposes of price control. There is a legislative requirement for ownership separation between energy businesses (retail and generation) and lines businesses.

8. Government or non-profit ownership of transmission and distribution also restricts the scope for specialization and incentives to increased efficiency. Cf. Paul L. Joskow, 'Regional Transmission Organisations: Don't Settle for Nth Best (N>>1)', Presentation to Harvard Electricity Policy Group, 21 September 2001.

9. 'Government Policy and Statement: Further Development of New Zealand's Electricity Industry', Hon. Pete Hodgson, Minister of Energy, September 2001.

10. It is fair to acknowledge that New Zealand has a smaller population than most of the other countries considered here. This may influence the feasible depth of competition in generation, though it may also suggest the importance of securing whatever competition is possible. It should not affect the points made about regulation, except to the extent that in a smaller country informal contacts and pressures may be more significant.

11. NECA, 12 September 2001. An earlier statement (24 May) proposed to consider limiting the increase in prices from one 5-minute period to the next to A$500. It would then take about an hour for prices to reach the then-current generation cap. NECA said this would remove specious and unwarranted short-term price spikes while retaining genuine market signals about supply and demand.

12. Paul L. Joskow and Edward Kahn, 'A Quantitative Analysis of Pricing Behaviour in California's Wholesale Electricity Market During Summer 2000', NBER Working Paper 8157, March 2001 and 'Identifying the Exercise of Market Power: Refining the Estimates', 5 July 2001. Paul L. Joskow, 'California's Electricity Crisis', NBER Working Paper 8442, August 2001, © P.L. Joskow, quotation from p. 32 (subsequently published in the *Oxford Review of Economic Policy*, **17** (3), Autumn 2001, 365–88).

13. S. Harvey and W. Hogan, 'On the exercise of market power through strategic withholding in California', April 2001.

14. For example, 'The more the observed price exceeds the competitive benchmark price, the more one can presume that either market power was being exercised or some other source of market imperfection has interfered with the competitive interplay of supply and demand. The competitive benchmark that we utilize is the short run marginal cost of supplying electricity from the last unit that clears the market in each hour. Comparing realized prices with marginal supply costs in this way is a widely accepted method for measuring the presence of market power' (Joskow and Kahn, 15 January 2001, p. 9 (earlier version of their March 2001 paper)).

15. In Australia, and potentially in the USA and elsewhere, there are now entrepreneurial interconnectors that should help to reduce market power.

16. About a quarter of those seem to be moving back to the first-tier supplier, so the net movement away from first-tier suppliers may be nearer 50 000 per week. Even so, over the course of a year that represents about 10 per cent of residential customers.

17. Norwegian Water Resources and Energy Directorate (NVE) 2000.

18. Inquiry into the Electricity Industry Report 2000.

19. A colleague writes: 'customer confidence in changing supplier was hit hard as the retailers struggled to produce bills and manage customer data bases. A big lesson from the NZ experience is that data management is the most important feature of retail markets and must be in place before the market is opened;' (Bill Heaps, personal communication, 3 October 2001). This provides some justification for the thorough but time-consuming procedures adopted in the UK and probably in Australia, but I suspect not in all countries.

20. Paul L. Joskow, 'Why do we need electricity retailers? Or, can you get it cheaper wholesale?', Center for Energy and Environmental Policy Research, Massachusetts Institute of Technology, revised discussion draft, 13 January 2000. The proportion switching seems to depend on the level of so-called 'shopping credits' represented by the discount on the incumbent utility's bill

for moving to another supplier. There have been considerable concerns about cross-subsidy. My view is that the UK approach is preferable, not least because of the more explicit calculation and charging of network costs here, without using the incumbent supplier's costs as the basis for granting credits to competing suppliers.

21. The proportion of California's residential customers taking another supplier was down to 0.6 per cent as of 31 August 2001. California Public Utilities Commission (CPUC) data filed 15 September 2001.
22. Followed by Arkansas, which proposed to delay or repeal retail competition.
23. NAO, *Office of Gas and Electricity Markets: Giving Domestic Customers a Choice of Electricity Supplier*, Report by the Comptroller and Auditor General, HC 85 Session 2000–01, 5 January 2001.
24. Gordon MacKerron, *Costs and Benefits of 100% Electricity Market Opening*, NERA Energy Regulation Brief, April 2001.
25. 'Retail competition – the benefits must not be underestimated', *Power UK*, 89, July 2001, pp. 17–25.
26. Graham Shuttleworth, Letter, *Power UK*, 90, August 2001, pp. 3–4. Reply by S.C. Littlechild, *Power UK*, 91, September 2001, pp. 44–5.
27. For example, Joskow, 'California's Electricity Crisis'.
28. Norwegian Water Resources and Energy Directorate (NVE), 2 January 2000.
29. 'It was expected that most retail customers would gradually migrate to electricity service providers during the four-year transition period', (Joskow, 'California's Electricity Crisis', p. 7). A four-year price cap set before the market opened in April 1998 would have been consistent with utilities and other retail suppliers hedging at 'normal' prices. This would seem to have still been possible even if the cap had been set for two years from April 1998, and renewed in the winter of 1999–2000 for a further two years from April 2000. The relevant prices are the two-year contract prices obtaining in the forward markets in late 1999. Not having those to hand, I note that average day-ahead price in the California Power Exchange during October 1999 to March 2000 was only one third higher than in the same months of the previous year. The average price was actually lower in February 2000 than in any previous month apart from May and June 1998 (Joskow, Table 1). Moreover, 'In March 2000, the California Energy Commission continued to publish projections of wholesale market prices in the PX for 2000 and beyond which were in the $28 to $35/MWh range', (ibid., p. 24). 'It is quite clear, however, that the terms and conditions of these contracts [negotiated by DWR in early 2001] would have been much more favorable if the state had encouraged the utilities to enter into longer term contracts in 1999 or even during the summer of 2000 when they requested this authority. Moreover, earlier contracting activity likely would have mitigated some of the problems that emerged during the late fall and Winter of 2000/01', (ibid., p. 38).
30. Interim opinion suspending direct access, A.98–07–003 et al.
31. 'A direct access customer receives distribution and transmission service from the utility, but purchases its electric energy from its electric service provider', (Interim opinion, p. 2).
32. There is a legitimate concern about the cost of providing default service, for example if customers leave when prices are low and return when they are high. If the price cap is used for this service too, it must be set to include the relevant costs. Spot market prices could be an option here, without being compulsory for all customers.
33. The price cap was removed when expected.
34. 'Promoting Competition in Electricity Supply', *Power UK*, 68, 29 November 1999, pp. 12–19.
35. Office of the Regulator General, Draft Report – 'Options for the Review of Retail Electricity Tariffs', 17 September 2001.
36. Oftel, 'Review of the charge control on calls to mobiles', and 'Effective competition review: mobile', both 26 September 2001.
37. Joskow, 'California's Electricity Crisis', p. 11.
38. Ibid., fn. 15.
39. David Currie, 'The New Electricity Trading Arrangements in England and Wales: A Review', Beesley Lecture, IEA/LBS, 10 October 2000, revised version February 2001. Published as ch. 1 in Colin Robinson (ed.), *Utility Regulation and Competition Policy*, Cheltenham, UK and

Northampton, USA: Edward Elgar, in association with the Institute of Economic Affairs and the London Business School, 2002.

40. Larry E Ruff, 'The Proposed "New Electricity Trading Arrangements" for England and Wales: A Setback for Competition, Consumers and Logic', *Electricity Journal*, January/February 2000, pp. 69–72. See also W.W. Hogan, 'The Power of Competition', Cantor Lecture 2, *RSA Journal*, 2/4, 2000; W.W. Hogan, 'Electricity Market Restructuring: Reform of Reforms', 20th Annual Conference, Center for Research in Regulated Industries, Rutgers University, 25 May 2001.

41. Larry E. Ruff, 'Competitive Electricity Markets: One Size *Should* Fit All', *Electricity Journal*, November 1999, pp. 20–35.

42. Ofgem, *New Electricity Trading Arrangements*, July 1999, p. 51.

43. Ofgem, *The New Electricity Trading Arrangements: A review of the first three months*, August 2001.

44. Meanwhile, 'From 1997 to 1998 the turnover in the Elspot market [day-ahead with hourly market-clearing price] rose by 30 per cent and in the financial market [for hedges] by 70 per cent. The turnover for the clearing service [for Elspot and bilateral trades] rose by almost 200 per cent', Norwegian Water Resources and Energy Directorate (NVE), January 2000). It is not clear what happened to the proportions of bilateral and market-cleared trades.

45. Testimony of Philip G. Harris to the US House Subcommittee on Energy Policy, 2 August 2001.

46. *Inquiry into the Electricity Industry*, Report to the Minister of Energy, June 2000.

47. Personal communication.

48. Given the likely increase in system (as opposed to energy) balancing costs, it would seem desirable to find ways of relating the recovery of these costs to the rapid fluctuations in output or to demand that tend to cause them.

CHAIRMAN'S COMMENTS

Eileen Marshall

It is always much more difficult to comment on a chapter when you generally agree with it. But that is my task. Stephen Littlechild's last comment was that regulation is alive and well. It strikes me it's alive but it doesn't seem to be very well. My implicit assumption used to be that somehow there would be eventual liberalization of electricity around the world. People would learn from our lessons, the good bits and the bad bits, but liberalization would happen, and yet it hasn't proved to be quite that easy. It hasn't proved easy in Europe, in terms of both electricity and gas – a particularly important issue because we are linked with gas and electricity interconnectors. As far as the gas interconnector is concerned, our prices have sometimes been pulled up to the prices on the Continent. It hasn't happened directly with the electricity grid and the electricity interconnector, but after the events of 11 September in America there was something of a hike in oil prices, which pulled up continental gas prices. This tended to pull up UK gas prices, and with an increase in arbitrage between gas and electricity you could actually see a movement in electricity prices.

The first issue that Professor Littlechild covered was the nature of regulation in terms of two different aspects. First, should regulation be independent of government as regards day-to-day operation of the Regulatory Office? Second, should there be sector-specific regulation of an *ex ante* nature, where the regulator sets rules ahead of time rather than simply reacting to problems after they have occurred? I have two comments to make here. First, when governments want to privatize, there is more chance of getting independent regulation, because this lines up with the political imperative to get more money for the shares. Once privatization is over and done with, perhaps there is then a greater tendency to move away from independent regulation. Second, on sector-specific regulation, Littlechild said that there was a political issue. I think it is more than a political issue: there is an economic imperative as well because the electricity industry is based on a network, and access to that network is so important to fostering competition that this provides a key economic reason for specific regulation. In addition, there is often a statutory monopoly situation, which is a much more severe monopoly than you might have elsewhere in the economy. Those are economic reasons why even the most liberal of us think there should be some *ex ante* sector-specific regulation. An interesting point is, if you can't have independent regulation, is it better to have sector-specific regulation with government interference or none at all? My vote would be to go for non-sector-specific regulation, with the industry regulated through the usual competition authorities. What New Zealand seems to have is the worst of all possible worlds, regulation that is sector-specific and government-sponsored as well.

On competition in generation, perhaps the initial structure is more important, the steadier the demand. If there is a rapidly increasing demand then the structure isn't perhaps quite so important. In the UK gas industry, we did have rapidly expanding demand and to some extent competition was managed by people responding to that demand through the power sector expansion.

Professor Littlechild mentioned in passing that the forward prices of electricity must if at all possible be kept in line with planning regulations. I agree. If the markets give signals that suggest more capacity is needed, then planning regulations that are not as speedy as they might be are raising prices and reducing security unnecessarily.

On retail supply, some people unfortunately think that retail supply is only about price. It's also about methods of billing, tariff structures, dual fuel, single meter reading, and smart metering. There is plenty of value added that can be put in to retail supply packages. The idea that there is a single price product for all suppliers, who are then expected to go out to compete, is such a nonsense that it's hard to believe it has even been suggested in a competitive market.

On wholesale trading and Pools, I don't want to get into any discussions about the balancing mechanism and the imbalance settlement arrangements, not because they're not important in their own right but because they are categorically not what NETA was about. I see NETA as an absolutely massive deregulation process where everybody was freed up to the maximum possible extent to contract freely in voluntary markets. As a result, we have the commoditization of electricity within six months or so of the NETA start, which is an amazing feat for all the people who were working in the industries and in those markets. We have forward prices going out up to four years. We have power exchanges. We have price reporters. All the things that we hoped and prayed would happen actually have happened: with NETA, 97 per cent of power is being traded in those voluntary markets. You don't even have to bid into the balancing mechanism if you don't want to. You don't have to be centrally dispatched. It's a voluntary market. The only thing you have to do is pay for your electricity if you take it through the meter and you haven't had a contract for it. That seems reasonable to me. So I think that's a key message: NETA isn't about the balancing arrangements. Three per cent of trades go through there; the prices in there are not key in the way that they are if you have a central Pool.

It was necessary to start with a Pool ten years ago, because it was such a controversial issue then that things had to be kept reasonably close to what the CEGB had been doing. Perhaps with hindsight, there could have been more flexible governance of the Pool, so that things could have evolved over the years.

Finally, it's always a bit of a mystery to me that there are eminent economists around who are exceedingly free market in all other respects and yet still fervently advocate central planning of electricity. They want everybody to sell into the Pool and get the same price, and all the suppliers to buy out of the Pool at the same price. I just find it really fascinating that they don't suggest that in other sectors. I call it the 'potato marketing board' mentality.

3. Prospects for gas supply and demand and their implications with special reference to the UK[1]

Alexander G. Kemp and Linda Stephen

1. INTRODUCTION

Gas demand in Western Europe has been growing rapidly over many years. The Commission of the European Communities (2000) calculates that in the period 1990–2000 it has grown by 52 per cent for member countries. This rate of growth is much faster than for other main fuels. In the same period nuclear power consumption grew by 23 per cent and oil by only 10 per cent. It is generally agreed that substantial growth will continue. The Commission estimates that demand may grow by 19 per cent from 2000 to 2010, and by 27 per cent to 2015. Gas is already the second most important fuel in the EU, accounting for over 23 per cent of total primary energy consumption in 2000. On the Commission's forecasts its share could reach 26 per cent in 2010 and 27 per cent in 2015. The absolute amounts are 40 billion cubic feet per day (bncf/d) in 2000, rising to 47 billion in 2010, 50 billion in 2015, and 51 billion in 2020.

The high prospective growth in consumption is confirmed by other studies. The International Energy Agency (2000) estimates that primary gas demand for all OECD Europe could increase from 40 bncf/d in 1997 to 61 billion in 2010, and 77 billion in 2020, an annual average increase of 2.8 per cent over the whole period.

There are several energy policy implications of these prospective consumption trends. The source of the required gas is an obvious one. Equally important is the infrastructure network of the necessary capacity and in the appropriate location to ensure that the needs of consumers are efficiently met. This chapter provides a detailed analysis of the nature and scale of the issues as they are likely to emerge in the UK, and also examines the policy issues for the EU as a whole.

2.   THE UK GAS MARKET – BACKGROUND

The UK gas market has undergone some fundamental changes in the last few years. The emergence of a substantial excess of producing capacity above UK demand in early 1995 led to a dramatic fall in beach prices. The gas bubble continued until after the interconnector between Bacton and Zeebrugge opened in late 1998. This coincided with a period of low oil prices, and the full implications of the link with the Continent were not appreciated until some time later when the oil price recovered. Wholesale gas prices on the Continent in the long-term contracts with Norway and Russia are largely indexed to oil prices. The sustained increase in oil prices thus led to major gas price increases in 2000. In turn this led to substantial exports from the UK through the interconnector and a dramatic increase in UK wholesale prices.

In recent years UK internal gas consumption has grown substantially, fanned in particular by sharply increasing demand from the power generation sector. Uncertainty regarding market prospects was increased as a result of the moratorium on the use of gas for power generation, its subsequent removal, and the introduction of coal subsidies. On the supply side the UK Continental Shelf (UKCS) is now a mature province, characterized by declining production from older fields and generally smaller sizes of new fields. The Southern North Sea is particularly mature. New discoveries tend to be small, though the exploration success rate has kept up surprisingly well. A growing proportion of total production now comes from central and northern waters. Substantial new field developments have recently been completed in the Central North Sea in particular. In these fields gas is generally found in association with oil or condensate. A consequence of this joint product feature is a reduction in the swing factor relating to gas sales contracts compared to the position in the Southern North Sea where dry gas dominates. Since the opening of the interconnector exports in the summer months have increased substantially, reducing the importance of the seasonality of UK market demand to gas producers.

3.   POTENTIAL UK GAS PRODUCTION

3.1   Data and Methodology

Future UK gas production depends on a number of factors, such as oil and gas prices, the exploration effort and success rate, field sizes, and development and operating costs. To reflect the sensitivities three price assumptions are employed. In the medium case the oil price is $20/bbl and the gas price

18p/therm for new contracts, both in constant real terms. In the low case the prices are $12/bbl and 12p/therm, and in the high case $28/bbl and 25p/therm.

The study was conducted with the aid of a large field database. The first element contains key information on 247 sanctioned fields relating to production, and development, operating and decommissioning costs. The second element contains similar information on 97 (unsanctioned) incremental projects associated with these fields. The third element contains similar information on 65 'probable' fields and 56 'possible' fields. In all three cases the data have been supplied by the operators. A fourth database contains very summary information on 234 other fields known as 'technical reserves'.

The Monte Carlo technique was employed to estimate likely future gas discoveries. The modelling involved several steps. Historic success rates for each of the main regions of the UKCS were found from DTI (2001a). In line with experience in the 1990s it was assumed that the success rate will decline slowly over time. Details for the medium case are shown in Table 3.1.

Table 3.1   Significant exploration success rates (%), 2001–15, medium case

	2001	2005	2010	2015
Central North Sea	16.1	15.3	14.3	13.3
Northern North Sea	21.1	20.3	19.3	18.3
West of Scotland	8.3	7.5	6.5	5.5
Irish Sea	17.8	17.0	16.0	15.0
Southern North Sea	25.5	24.7	23.7	22.7

For the high case the success rates are assumed to be 5 per cent higher and for the low case 5 per cent lower than for the medium case. For each of the UKCS basins the relative chances of finding oil, gas or gas/condensate were based on experience in the 1990s.

The exploration effort is a function of a number of factors, including prospectivity, oil and gas prices, and net cash flows from ongoing activities. Distinguishing among them is complex, and for present purposes it was felt appropriate to consider three cases. In the medium case there are 30 exploration wells in 2000, falling to 18 by 2015 for the whole of the UKCS. Table 3.2 shows the numbers in the three cases.

From data relating to the 1990s the exploration effort in each region was calculated. This was used to distribute the exploration wells among the five regions.

The average size of discovery in the UKCS has been declining for some time. The average size of future discoveries in each of the UKCS regions is based on historic trends in the 1990s. The figures are shown in Table 3.3.

Table 3.2   Number of exploration wells, 2000–2015

	2000	2005	2010	2015
Whole UKCS				
Medium case	30	25	20	18
Low case	10	8	6	5
High case	50	40	30	25

Table 3.3   UKCS mean discovery size (mboe), 2000–2015*

	2000	2005	2010	2015
Central North Sea	32	28	24	20
Northern North Sea	16	14	12	10
West of Scotland	200	175	150	125
Irish Sea	42	37	32	26
Southern North Sea	21	18	16	13

Note: * Mboe = million barrels of oil equivalent.

To undertake the full financial modelling of new discoveries, information is also required on their likely development and operating costs. Examination of the development costs of the 'probable' and 'possible' fields given by the operators provided useful information to estimate the likely costs of developing new discoveries. The average development cost in the Southern North Sea was taken to be $3 per barrel of oil equivalent, for West of Scotland $5, and for the rest of the UKCS $4.

The next step in the modelling process involved the design of distributions of field size and development costs. In line with experience to date, the field size distributions were assumed to be lognormal. A standard deviation of 50 per cent of the mean value was used. The development cost distributions were assumed to be normal, with a standard deviation of 20 per cent of the mean value. The annual operating costs were set at 5–15 per cent of accumulated development cost depending on the field size found. This again reflects historic experience. These costs are relatively lower on large fields, reflecting the economy of scale.

Using the above assumptions on exploration effort, exploration success rates, and the distributions of field sizes and development costs, the Monte Carlo technique was employed to produce a database of discovered fields found through time for the medium, low and high cases. Simulations were conducted separately for each of the five regions.

It was assumed that there would be a two-year time lag between discovery and the start of development in the Southern North Sea. For the rest of the UKCS the time lag was assumed to be four years.

From the sanctioned, 'probable', and the 56 'possible' fields, and the new discoveries from exploration, a profile of potential field developments over time was produced. The 'technical reserves' were then added, with constraints to the 'possible' fields. The constraints took the form of a ceiling on the total number of potential developments in each year. These were based on experience in the 1990s. For the medium case the ceiling was 15 new field developments per year, for the low case 12, and for the high case 20 new developments per year. If the number of new developments from the 'probable', 'possible' and new discovery categories was less than the ceiling, the Monte Carlo technique was used to sample from the bank of 'technical reserves', and the chosen fields were added to the 'possible' category. The development costs for these additional 'possible' fields were drawn from distributions with mean values $2/boe higher than those assumed for new discoveries. The standard deviations were again set at 20 per cent of the mean values.

All new fields and the incremental projects were subjected to economic testing. Using real discount rates of 10 per cent and 15 per cent, post-tax net present values were calculated. If the results were positive, the field development was triggered. The 10 per cent rate is generally employed in the results presented below. Where the 15 per cent rate makes a significant difference, attention is drawn to the effects. In the results the medium case reflects the effects of the combinations of medium price, exploration effort, and success rates. The high and low cases reflect corresponding combinations. The three elements of each case are not presumed to be causally linked.

3.2 Results

3.2.1 By field category

The results of the modelling can be shown to emphasize different features. One way is by category of field. This enables deductions to be made regarding the probabilities of different outcomes.

Figure 3.1 shows potential gas production under the medium case. In 2001 the total is 11 465 mmcf/d (million cubic feet per day), in 2005 12 942 mmcf/d, in 2010 7112 mmcf/d and in 2015 4299 mmcf/d. Production from the sanctioned fields peaks at 11 784 mmcf/d in 2002, then declines quite rapidly to 3622 mmcf/d by 2010. In 2004 the incremental projects contribute more than 1123 mmcf/d to the production of this category of field. By 2010 they contribute only 372 mmcf/d.

Poduction from the 'probable' fields rises quickly to peak in 2005 at 2739 mmcf/d, and declines to 1173 mmcf/d by 2010. Output from the 'possible'

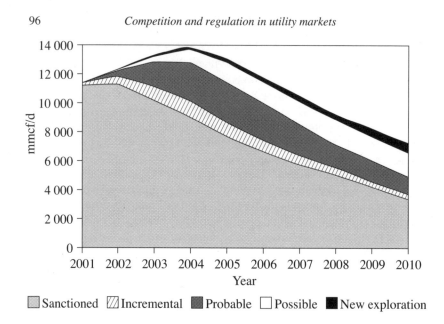

*Figure 3.1   Potential gas production by field category, medium case,
2001–10, (cost of capital 10 per cent)*

fields grows more slowly to peak in 2008 at 1653 mmcf/d and is 1600 mmcf/d
in 2010. With a 15 per cent cost of capital production from this category is
lower throughout, with a peak in 2006 at 1560 mmcf/d. Output from new discoveries grows much more slowly, to reach 695 mmcf/d by 2010 and 796
mmcf/d by 2015.

Production from the sanctioned fields clearly has the highest probability of
being achieved. There may be more incremental projects in the medium term,
which could further enhance production from this category of field. Significantly greater uncertainty is attached to output from the 'possible' fields and new
discoveries. It is noteworthy that in 2010 production from the sanctioned fields
still accounts for 51 per cent of total output. By 2015 the share is as high as
34 per cent.

Under the low case, production is not markedly different in the short term
because sanctioned fields dominate the total, but in the longer term the
difference becomes more marked as fewer new fields are developed and fewer
discoveries made. In 2005 total output is around 96 per cent of that under the
medium case. By 2010 it is 83 per cent, and by 2015 58 per cent. Production
from the sanctioned fields is even more important under this scenario. By 2010
output from this category still accounts for 62 per cent of the total, and by 2015
56 per cent.

There is not a major difference in output from the sanctioned fields under the two scenarios. A main reason for this is the importance in the total output of relatively 'old' gas contracts, where the influence of spot prices and/or those for new contracts is less. In the longer term the main sources of the substantially lower output under the low case emanate principally from fewer new discoveries and a lower number of field developments in the 'possible' category. Production from new discoveries under this scenario is small, being 11 per cent of that under the medium case in 2010, and 23 per cent in 2015.

Under the high case, production in the short term is also not markedly different from the medium case because of the predominance of the sanctioned fields in the total. In the longer term the differences become greater. In relation to the medium case, total output becomes 103 per cent in 2005, 111 per cent in 2010, and 119 per cent in 2015. These findings indicate that from the base of the medium case, the long-term responsiveness of output is considerably greater to the parameter values in the low case compared to those of the high case.

Consistent with the above, under the high case production from new discoveries in 2010 is double that in the medium case. In 2015 it is 163 per cent higher. Output from the 'possible' fields is 110 per cent of that under the medium case in 2010.

The results for the three scenarios indicate the sensitivities of long-term gas production to plausible variations in the factors determining activity levels. Some increase can confidently be predicted over the next few years, after which the rate of production decrease depends on a variety of factors. One implication of the findings is the importance of the maintenance of a substantial exploration effort. Exploration has fallen markedly in recent years, and has only slowly recovered despite the large increase in oil and gas prices.

3.2.2 By producing area

It is also useful to examine gas production by geographic area, as this has significant implications for infrastructure provision. Figure 3.2 shows potential production from each of the UKCS areas under the medium case. Production from the Southern North Sea peaks in 2004 at 4706 mmcf/d, then declines to 2321 mmcf/d by 2010, (2108 mmcf/d with 15 per cent cost of capital). By 2015 it becomes 1680 mmcf/d (1562 mmcf/d with 15 per cent cost of capital). It is noteworthy that the share of the Southern North Sea in total production holds up very well to 2015, despite the greater maturity of this basin and the fact that its share has decreased over the last decade. In 2004 it accounts for 34 per cent of the total, in 2010 33 per cent, and in 2015 39 per cent.

The Central North Sea has seen a large growth in output over the last decade. The results indicate that production (excluding the Moray Firth) will increase in the next few years, peaking in 2004 at 3725 mmcf/d (27 per cent of the total), and then decline to 1805 mmcf/d in 2010 (25 per cent of the total), and

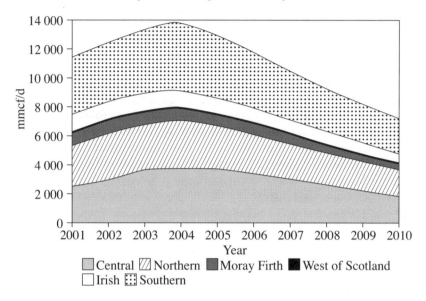

Figure 3.2   Potential gas production by producing area, medium case, 2001–10, (cost of capital 10 per cent)

909 mmcf/d in 2015 (21 per cent of the total). Output from the Moray Firth area peaks in 2002 and by 2010 becomes quite small. Production from the Northern North Sea will follow a path similar to that for the Central area. The volumes to 2010 are very similar. Production from the three areas is most likely to land at St Fergus, with implications for the provision of infrastructure. The findings in this study are that the combined production could peak in 2004 at 7903 mmcf/d. By 2010 they could be 4025 mmcf/d.

The results of the modelling indicate that production from West of Scotland is quite small throughout the period. This reflects the generally low levels of exploration success historically. Because large areas are as yet unexplored it is possible that substantial discoveries will be made, but the risks involved are high.

Production from the Irish Sea is estimated at 1271 mmcf/d for 2001. It falls gently to 689 mmcf/d by 2010.

Under the low case production is less in each area compared to the medium case, but there are significant variations across regions. These become noticeable in the longer term, when the effects of reduced exploration and new field developments become more noticeable. Thus in the Southern North Sea output in 2010 at 1660 mmcf/d is 655 mmcf/d less than in the medium case. The result is that this area accounts for 28 per cent of total production in that year compared to 33 per cent in the medium case.

In relative terms production is not reduced so much in the other areas under the low case. In the Central North Sea (excluding Moray Firth) it becomes 1511 mmcf/d in 2010, accounting for 26 per cent of the total. The share of the Northern North Sea increases over the period to account for 28 per cent of the total in 2010. In that year the aggregate output from Central North Sea, Moray Firth and Northern North Sea is 3214 mmcf/d, or nearly 55 per cent of the total.

There are several noteworthy implications of the results. The Southern North Sea fields contain dry gas, and so contracts with substantial swing factors can be made. In Central and Northern waters the gas is usually associated with oil or condensate, and large swing factors cannot readily be accommodated in contracts consistent with profit maximization from the production of liquids. (This point can, however, be overemphasized because maintenance work involving the shutdown of production facilities is generally concentrated in the summer months when gas demand is seasonally low.) The substantial sensitivity of the relative contribution of the Southern North Sea to the parameter values is of some importance given the high seasonal variation in UK gas demand.

Under the high case, while production in each of the areas is greater than under the medium case, the differences vary in the longer term. Output from the Southern North Sea is particularly responsive. By 2010 it is 461 mmcf/d higher than under the medium case and accounts for 35 per cent of total production. In 2015 the share from this region increases to over 40 per cent.

Production from the Central North Sea increases to a modest extent while that from the Northern North Sea increases by only a minor amount. The result is that in 2010 combined production for Central North Sea, Moray Firth and Northern North Sea is 4123 mmcf/d, or 52 per cent of the total.

4. SIZE AND LOCATION OF UK PRODUCTION AND RELATED NTS CAPACITY

The geographic location of future production is of interest because the infrastructure of the necessary size has to be available to receive the gas. Such infrastructure relates to terminal facilities and the National Transmission System (NTS). In recent years there has been some debate about the adequacy of the NTS capacity at certain points, notably St Fergus. The projections obtained in this study have been used to assess the extent of this problem. The destination by terminal of production from sanctioned fields (including incremental projects) is already known. The likely destinations by terminal of production from the 'probable' and 'possible' fields (including 'technical reserves') can be estimated with a reasonable degree of assurance, given the knowledge regarding the location of the fields and the offshore infrastructure. Production from new discoveries has *not* been included in this part of the study because of inadequate knowledge of their precise location. This probably does not affect the validity of any findings regarding the adequacy of the system because significant production from new discoveries will not occur until after total UK output has passed its peak. It is emphasized that the production figures are on an average annual basis.

Transco has made several estimates of NTS capacity at the different terminals. In Transco (2000) estimates are provided of the system entry point maximum unconstrained physical capacities for 2000/2001. In Transco (2001a and 2001b) various estimates are provided of the peak-day planned entry capacity based on the 1 in 20 winters licence obligation. Two cases are given. One is termed the 'St Fergus base' case. The second is the 'St Fergus expansion' case.

The projections of potential production arriving at the various terminals are now examined against the possible NTS capacities. Figure 3.3 shows the position at St Fergus. The production projections reflect the medium case. The unconstrained capacity as indicated in Transco (2000) is only slightly above the expected average production figure for 2001 and equal to it for 2002. There is no difference between the two cases until the later years of the forecast period. Up to and including 2004, capacity just exceeds production. When the recent BP contract involving imports from Norway of 163 million cubic feet per day for 15 years starting in late 2001 is added, there is very little spare capacity. When the peak winter situation is considered, the position is still tighter. In

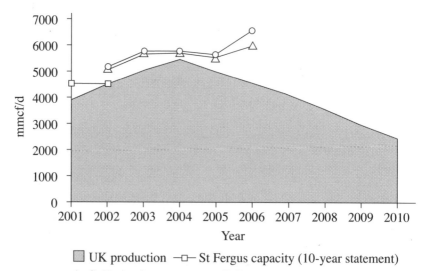

Figure 3.3   UK production and capacity at St Fergus, medium case, 2001–10

January 2001, 4342 mmcf/d landed at the terminal. Further imports may be expected. There will almost certainly be further significant UK production from new discoveries hoping to land at St Fergus. On the other hand some production landed at St Fergus is diverted away from the NTS to Peterhead power station. This has a capacity of around 1500 MW. It should be noted that no steps have yet been made to install capacity above the base case.

Figure 3.4 shows the position at Teesside. In this case the maximum unconstrained capacity as reported in Transco (2000) just exceeds the average production in 2002. Throughout the period the capacity indicated in Transco (2001b) is below the anticipated production. It should be noted that at Teesside there are substantial gas deliveries outside the NTS, mostly for power generation. These have recently been in the range 400–800 mmcf/d. This removes the apparent deficit. On the other hand there will probably be further production destined for Teesside from new discoveries in the Central North Sea and possibly imports from Norway in the longer term.

Figure 3.5 shows the position at Barrow. It is seen that under all cases there is generally a surplus of capacity at the NTS above prospective average annual production landing at Barrow. In this case the difference between average annual and peak winter production is very large because the Morecambe field has a large swing factor to meet winter demand. Thus in January 2001, production of 1768 mmcf/d landed at Barrow.

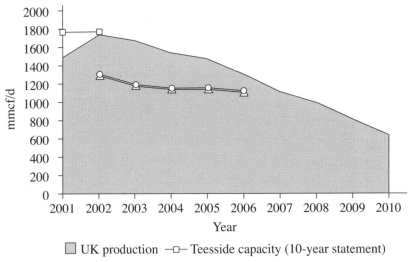

Figure 3.4   UK production and capacity at Teesside, medium case, 2001–10

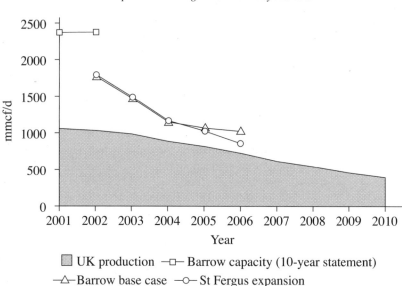

Figure 3.5   UK production and capacity at Barrow, medium case, 2001–10

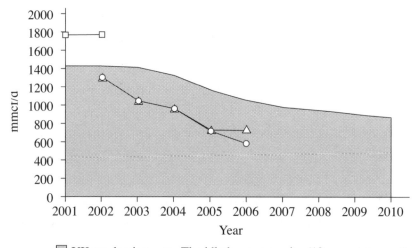

Figure 3.6   UK production and capacity at Theddlethorpe, medium case,
*   2001–10*

Figure 3.6 shows the position at Theddlethorpe. From Transco (2000) it is seen that the maximum unconstrained physical capacity exceeds the likely production arriving at Theddlethorpe. The Transco (2001b) scenarios indicate a deficit of capacity, particularly in the later years, with the St Fergus expansion case. It should be noted, however, that some gas which is landed at Theddlethorpe bypasses the NTS including, in recent years, around 350 mmcf/d destined for power generation. When this is taken into account the problem is not so noticeable.

Figure 3.7 shows the position at Easington/Dimlington. Capacity is far above prospective production levels. It is important to note that the capacity has to handle gas from the Rough field, which is employed for storage to meet peak demand. The gas deliverability from this field is as much as 1543 mmcf/d. When this is added to production, the total capacity requirement in 2004 exceeds 2500 mmcf/d.

Figure 3.8 shows the position at Bacton. This reveals that under both scenarios there is likely to be adequate capacity in the NTS. If the import capacity of the interconnector is eventually expanded to match its current export capability of around 2 billion cubic feet per day, there should still be enough overall capacity.

5. BALANCE OF UK PRODUCTION AND DEMAND

In this section estimates of UK demand are set alongside prospective UK production. Several recently published projections are used, namely DTI (2001b), Transco (2000, 2001a), and the Energy Contract Company (ECC) (2001).

The DTI projections are based on a large econometric energy demand model involving the disaggregation of final user demand into several sectors. Allowance is made for changes in energy efficiency. The effect of the climate change levy on demand in the business sector is incorporated. Six core scenarios are developed incorporating various combinations of GDP growth rates and energy prices. The high gas price scenario has delivered prices (expressed in 1999 values) rising to reach in 2010: (a) 24.3 pence per therm in the industrial sector; (b) 28.5 pence to the services sector; and (c) 62 pence in the domestic sector. Under the low price case the corresponding values are: (a) 12.3 pence; (b) 17.6 pence; and (c) 40.4 pence.

Transco's base case assumes a period of recession in the short term which causes a decrease in the rate of growth in demand for gas. Increased efficiency in the use of gas is assumed. The introduction of the climate change levy also impacts negatively on demand growth in the non-domestic sectors. Another assumption involves a further shift from manufacturing to services, which has a negative effect on demand growth. Further assumptions include the greater use of renewables in the combined heat and power (CHP) market and the absence of a further 'dash for gas' in power generation.

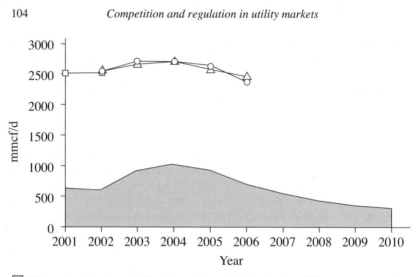

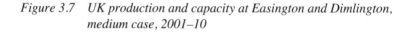

☐ UK production (excluding Rough) –□– E+D capacity (10-year statement)
–△–E+D base case (including rough) –○– Strong demand, St Fergus expansion

Figure 3.7   UK production and capacity at Easington and Dimlington,
            medium case, 2001–10

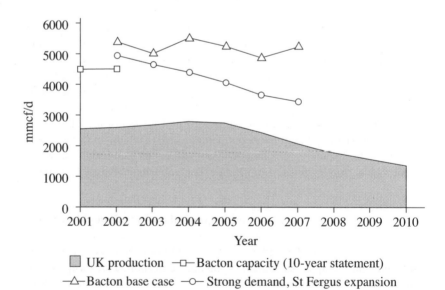

☐ UK production   –□–Bacton capacity (10-year statement)
–△–Bacton base case   –○– Strong demand, St Fergus expansion

Figure 3.8   UK production and capacity at Bacton, medium case, 2001–10

Transco's strong demand scenario incorporates relatively fast economic growth in all sectors of the UK economy while gas remains competitive in price terms. Power generation continues to grow, and the share of gas in power generation increases to 50 per cent.

In Figure 3.9 the scenario involving the medium case for UK production is shown, along with two DTI demand scenarios, namely central GDP growth and low and high gas prices (CL and CH). The results indicate that the UK remains self-sufficient on a net basis until 2006, after which the need for imports rises at an increasing rate. By 2010 they are in the range 3.8–4.4 bncf/d. These correspond to 35–43 per cent of primary gas demand under the CH and CL scenarios. By 2015 they could be as much as 7.5–8.8 bncf/d, which corresponds to 64–68 per cent of primary gas demand. It should be noted that the date of net imports commencing and the scale of the imports depend upon the export of the net surplus of UK production over the next few years. To the extent that the surplus is not exported, the date at which net imports begin is extended beyond 2006.

The balance of UK production in the low case was next compared with the various UK demand estimates. In this case the DTI projections relate to (a) high economic growth and low gas price (HL), (b) low economic growth and low gas price (LL), and (c) central economic growth and low gas price (CL). The result was that in most projections net imports are required in 2005. The surplus

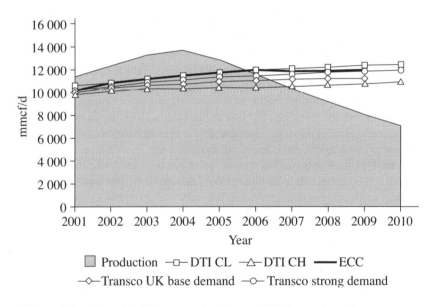

Figure 3.9   Potential UK gas production and UK demand, medium case, 2001–10, (cost of capital 10 per cent)

of production over UK demand over the next few years is also smaller. By 2010 the required net imports are in the range 3.8–5.3 bncf/d. Under the CL scenario these imports would account for 53 per cent of primary gas demand. In 2015 they would account for 81 per cent of primary demand. In that year they could be a massive 10.5–11 bncf/d.

In the high case the DTI demand scenarios employed are (a) high economic growth and high gas prices (HH), (b) low economic growth and high gas prices (LH), and (c) central economic growth and high gas prices (CH). Under most of the demand scenarios UK net self-sufficiency extends to 2007. The size of the surplus of production in the intervening years is greater than in the other cases. By 2010 the net import requirements are in the range 2.6–3.3 bncf/d. These correspond to 28–37 per cent of primary gas demand. By 2015 they are in the range 6.3–7 bncf/d. These correspond to 57–62 per cent of primary gas demand.

There are now substantial exports of gas from the UK. The Energy Contract Company (2001) estimates current long-term export contracts through the Bacton–Zeebrugge interconnector at around 1080 mmcf/d and exports to Southern Ireland at around 600 mmcf/d. To complete the picture of the balance between UK production and demand, estimates of committed exports were added to UK internal demand. A further case, where full use was made of the interconnector's export capacity, was also examined.

In Figure 3.10 the results are shown for the medium case regarding production, along with the Transco and Energy Contract Company's estimates of UK demand plus exports. Given the current export commitments in 2001, the balance between UK production and demand is fairly tight.

If full use were to be made of the interconnector for exports, there is no excess producing capacity above the sum of internal demand plus exports. Imports are required in 2001 and in 2002.

Under the low case the scale of the growth in gross imports from 2004 onwards becomes substantially greater, and the size of the surplus of UK producing capacity above UK demand and committed exports over the next few years considerably less than in the medium case.

In the high case with some of the internal demand scenarios the timing of the need for substantial gross imports is extended to 2006. The market remains relatively tight in 2001 and 2002. With full use of the interconnector for exports, significant gross imports would be required in 2001 and 2002.

6.   EUROPEAN GAS IMPORT DEPENDENCE

The results in Sections 4 and 5 have highlighted the possible extent of the UK's gas import dependence over the next 15 years and the consequent effect on the need for appropriate infrastructure for Europe. The Commission of the European

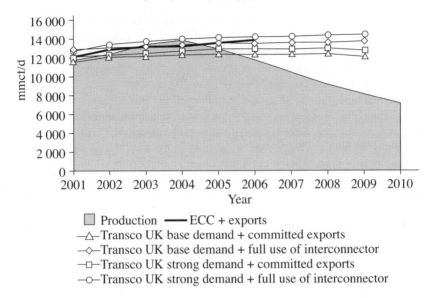

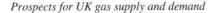

Figure 3.10 Potential UK gas production and UK demand including exports, medium case, 2001–10, (cost of capital 10 per cent)

Communities (2000) calculates that in 2000 for member countries 40 per cent of gas requirements were imported. Of these 41 per cent came from Russia, 25 per cent from Norway and 29 per cent from Algeria. The Commission estimates that by 2010 imports could account for 52 per cent of demand and by 2020 66 per cent. In the latter year as much as 38 per cent of *total* gas requirements could come from Russia, 34 per cent from Norway, and 23 per cent from Algeria. The IEA (2000) estimates that, for OECD Europe, imports could grow from 31 per cent of total gas requirements to 64 per cent in 2020.

These are high percentages of large absolute gas requirements (see Section 1). They clearly indicate the need for further infrastructure provision. They also raise questions regarding security of supply and the nature of the contracts between gas producers and buyers, which inevitably involve arrangements for access to the infrastructure.

7. INFRASTRUCTURE PROVISION

In the UK Transco has a responsibility to provide infrastructure, particularly in the form of a National Transmission System (NTS) and local distribution network. The regulatory system has been changed frequently over the years.

As far as provision of transmission capacity is concerned, recently there has been a debate about the appropriate long-term investment signals and incentives. The existing mechanism for determining the amount of long-term capacity in the NTS is the obligation placed on Transco to meet the peak aggregate demand which is likely to be exceeded only once in 20 years, taking into account the experience of the last 50 years. Ofgem believes that this scheme is not appropriate for a liberalized gas market. In particular, under the present system, if a shipper desired some (extra) capacity at a specified terminal, Transco has no obligation to invest in extra capacity so long as the 1 in 20 national peak day requirement is being met.

Ofgem is also concerned that the present system does not help to promote desired competition among shippers and suppliers. The regulator also believes that the determination of economic and efficient capital expenditure (which has been the subject of disagreement between Ofgem and Transco) can be better determined by other mechanisms.

Ofgem favours the employment of both short-term and long-term auctions of capacity for entry to and exit from the NTS. Short-term auctions are already employed. Ofgem (2000a) argues that in the short term price auctions provide the most efficient means of allocating the finite capacity. The system is based on willingness to pay and will reveal the true valuations placed on capacity by bidders. It is also argued that the mechanism permits buyers to place different values on capacity through time and at different entry points to the system. This system has been in operation since September 1999, when auctions began for six-month periods. With respect to the longer term, when the amount of capacity can be varied, Ofgem argues that the prices in long-term auctions provide signals to Transco regarding the need to enhance capacity at the different entry points. In Ofgem (2000b) it was emphasized that the auction system would also ensure that there was non-discrimination in the sale of capacity, which would help to ensure that competition in the supply of gas was not distorted. For the longer term auctions for five-year periods have been suggested. As with short-term auctions, shippers who require the capacity would make the bids. Trading in a secondary market would be permitted.

The proposals have aroused considerable controversy. Transco, shippers and producers have all expressed reservations. One area of controversy concerns the accuracy of investment signals provided by the system. It has been suggested by critics (Ofgem, 2000b and 2001) that shippers may well make bids based on short-term and diverse objectives rather than on the need for long-term capacity. Further, they may be unwilling to make long-term commitments to entry capacity faced with (a) one major competitor and (b) uncertainty regarding future market prospects. Sceptics have also pointed out that the experience to date with short-term contracts has not resulted in a stable, transparent or simple arrangement. Because there is a revenue cap under Transco's price control formula, a rebate to shippers is required if the auctions result in over-recovery of revenues by Transco. It has been argued that this could result in distorting bidding behaviour, with resulting distortions in the allocation of capacity. Transco supported this view (Ofgem, 2001), and concluded that it was unconvinced that long-term auctions would result in the provision of capacity at lowest cost. Transco also argued there was only limited competition among shippers, and this could result in bids not revealing the true valuations that shippers placed on capacity.

Ofgem generally has not accepted these arguments. With respect to the rebate mechanism whereby some of the revenues obtained in the auctions may be rebated to organizations which are themselves bidding, Ofgem acknowledges that a distortion in bidding behaviour might arise. Ofgem also argues, however, that, for a major player, the effect could operate in either direction. Thus while a bidder may overbid because he anticipates that a refund will reduce the net cost of the bid to him, a bidder that has a large market share may also attempt to exert its power by attempting to drive down capacity prices.

Ofgem also argues that it is only when large variations from Transco's target revenues can be predicted with reasonable accuracy that distortions to bidding behaviour can emerge. Given that bidders are uncertain about the extent of any over-recovery in revenues by Transco from the auction, then the higher the bid which any one shipper makes, the greater the overall cost which that shipper bears in relation to others. If his bid is relatively high, the rebate he receives may not compensate him.

Because of these uncertainties and their effects, Ofgem believes that shippers will have an incentive to ensure that bids closely reflect the value of the capacity to them. In support of this view Ofgem produced evidence from the experience of the short-term auctions that there was no clear relationship between a shipper's market share and the bids made.

Gas producers are keenly interested in the terms of access to the NTS. (Some, but not all, producers are also shippers.) From their viewpoint it is important not only that the costs of access are as low as possible but that capacity is available on stable, transparent and predictable terms. Increasingly the new gas fields in the UKCS are quite small. Problems of obtaining access to the infrastructure and the terms of such access can have a major effect on the economic viability of such fields.

Experience to date with short-term capacity entry auctions has hardly been reassuring. The prices can be claimed to be volatile and relatively high. Extraordinarily high prices have been paid at St Fergus (up to 12 pence per therm). The shortage of capacity at that terminal has been known for several years, but producers and shippers could legitimately claim that the response to date in terms of new investment has been very slow. Producers desire guaranteed capacity availability to reduce the risks relating to their investments. They would be able to purchase NTS capacity rights only in the secondary market. With respect to over-recovery of revenues from auctions by Transco, the rebate system currently employed distributes the excess in relation to the commodity (not capacity) charges under Transco's price formula. This favours shippers who move gas from the National Balancing Point. Arguably, this discriminates against those who directly incurred the original capacity charges.

There are, of course, other methods of allocating capacity. One is based on historic throughput using regulated prices. A provision of this scheme would withhold some capacity for new entrants. Ofgem does not support this mechanism on the grounds that it would favour existing major players and confer windfall gains on them when trading took place on the secondary market. Reserving some capacity for new entrants would run contrary to Transco's obligation to offer capacity in a non-discriminatory fashion.

The suggestion that capacity be allocated on a volume auction basis was also not favoured by Ofgem. Its concern was that this could lead to distortions. Shippers would have an incentive to bid for large volumes. Bids would have to be scaled down to ration the available capacity in the likely situation where the full market price exceeded the administered price. Some shippers who received allocations in excess of their own needs could then sell the rights on the secondary market at a profit. Ofgem also expresses concern that the use of volume auctions would mean that the true value of capacity to the users was not revealed.

Another possible allocation mechanism is through bilateral contracts, whereby capacity prices would be agreed between Transco and shippers. Ofgem is concerned that such a scheme would lack transparency, and might be discriminatory and not encourage competition. Ofgem fears that this type of scheme with tailored terms for each contract would inhibit secondary trading and lock-in capacity to an undesirable degree. The extent of these possible problems is open to debate. In some markets individual contracts are certainly compatible with effective competition.

Ofgem (2001) expressed surprise at the suggestion that shippers might be unwilling to commit to long-term purchases of capacity. The regulator feels that under a well-designed auction system shippers would be able to purchase capacity for a range of contract periods either in the primary auction markets or in the secondary markets. Ofgem believes that shippers affiliated to producers can obtain long-term contracts which should ensure that gas can be produced and landed without undue risks relating to the field investment. It is also argued that shippers who have long-term contracts with large customers such as power generators can effectively hedge their risks.

There are differing views on this issue. For effective hedging well-functioning futures markets are required. Gas futures markets have developed over the past decade. To date, however, there is a lack of liquidity in the long-term market, which is the relevant one in the present context. Whether effective hedging can be obtained on the necessary scale is thus debatable.

What difference does this make to the ability of shippers to sign long-term contracts? It is arguable that fully functioning futures markets are clearly desirable but perhaps not essential. In some cases, for example, the recent agreement between BP and Statoil, the parties in question can bear the risks because of the size of their equity in relation to the size of the contract. Where this circumstance does not prevail, shippers will be more exposed. The position in the gas market itself is clearly of major importance. To limit the shipper's risk exposure it is essential that the gas price indexation in the sales contract reflect the market risks in question.

In general it can be argued that, in the UK, where Transco is quite indepen-dent from the gas market itself and has an obligation to provide infrastructure on a common carriage basis, the risks on gas market participants are thereby reduced compared to the typical situation on the Continent, where the infra-structure provider is also a major participant in the gas market itself. Further, on the Continent the infrastructure provision is typically on an open-access basis rather than common carriage. This also means that the risks facing gas market participants are greater because access may not be guaranteed. In some countries the tariffs are also negotiable rather than determined by regulation.

A concern in the UK clearly relates to the volatility of capacity entry auction prices, which has been a feature of at least some elements of the short-term market to date. Both producers and shippers desire a more stable market situation. To what extent this can be expected when experience with long-term auctions has been obtained remains an open question.

A further concern in the UK is whether in practice Transco will respond in an expeditious manner to meet the needs of the growing and changing gas market. A related issue is the interpretation of the requirement to develop and maintain an economical and efficient infrastructure. It is certainly arguable that the definition expressed in terms of 1 in 20 peak days is now outmoded. The whole gas market has changed dramatically since this requirement was estab-lished. Not only has there been market liberalization, but the importance of the seasonality in demand has been considerably reduced. The increased use of gas in industry and for power generation, plus, in more recent times, exports through the interconnector, are responsible for this development. The overall growth in demand and the distribution of requirements at the different terminals has clearly not been fully anticipated. It is also generally agreed that future market uncertainties remain high. (It should be noted here that Transco's allowed capital expenditure has to be approved by Ofgem and generally Transco has wished to spend more than Ofgem desires. Thus for the next review (2002/3 – 2006/7) Transco wishes to invest £2.4 billion while Ofgem currently feels £1.9 billion is appropriate.)

In these circumstances it is arguable that a prudent interpretation of the obligation to provide an economical and efficient infrastructure should incorporate a safety margin to reflect these uncertainties. A modest element of excess capacity is likely to be very inexpensive from a national viewpoint compared to the costs caused by shortages of capacity. For example, for a typical annual domestic gas bill of £300 the NTS component is less than 4 per cent. The cost of every extra £100 million investment expressed in terms of the additional cost per domestic consumer is below 50 pence per year. This puts into perspective the costly effects of the shortage of capacity such as has occurred at St Fergus in recent years.

Use of long-term capacity auctions to provide investment signals to Transco needs to be supplemented by other incentives, including penalties for failing to provide the capacity. Recent experience indicates legitimate concern about whether the capacity will be provided at the required time. Looking ahead, with the prospective increase in demand, and given that long-term capacity auctions have not yet started nor the detailed rules been finalized, doubts remain about whether all the required capacity will be available at the right time and place.

On the Continent, where liberalization and competition have not proceeded as far as in the UK, the problems of provision of infrastructure will also have to be faced given the expected growth in demand and the concern about security of supply. Surprisingly, the Commission of the European Communities (2000), while acknowledging the need for infrastructure expansion, does not discuss in detail the issues noted above. As noted above, the current institutional structures and regulatory arrangements are generally different from the UK, with open access, often on a negotiated rather than regulated basis, being prevalent rather than common carriage. More fundamentally, transportation and trading functions are often still combined. It can be argued that these features will not be permanent because of their inherent problems. It is quite possible that major changes will be made to the regulatory framework incorporating many of the lessons from the UK experience. In the meantime the uncertainties leave an unsatisfactory investment environment.

Many of the issues which have been the subject of debate in the UK are likely to become live issues on the Continent over the next few years. For example, in the Netherlands there are disputes between Gasunie and the regulator on the question of whether tariffs should be cost-based or not, and whether tariffs charged should be published. Gasunie has also recently announced that it will separate its trading and transportation activities, though it has no legal obligation to do so, because it believes this is in line with evolving trends. In general, continued integration of the two functions is not only likely to inhibit the evolution of competition, but, where it is combined with a system of open access (rather than common carriage), it can inhibit the optimal growth of infrastructure capacity. The infrastructure owner may be reluctant to build more capacity when the prime beneficiary is a competitor to his own trading business.

8.   GAS CONTRACTS

Gas contracts may be made more efficient by the presence of an adequate infrastructure. The changing market structure in Europe, along with rising demand and the need for increased imports, also have major implications for the sources of supply and the associated contracts.

In the UK major changes occurred to gas contracts between producers and purchasers some years ago. The traditional field depletion-based contracts with a very high take-or-pay element have been modified. Typically there are volume contracts with somewhat reduced take-or-pay elements. Indexation is likely to be related to an inflation factor and the prices of competing fuels. The spot gas price may also be one of the elements in the indexation reflecting the opportunities of buyers to purchase in the spot markets.

On the Continent the typical long-term contracts for supplies from Norway, Russia and Algeria tend to be specified in terms of volumes with a very large take-or-pay element. The indexation is primarily to oil product prices. In recent years the weighting in favour of gas oil has increased compared to fuel oil, reflecting the reduced consumption of the latter. In some countries indexation is also linked to a main competing fuel.

How efficiently gas will be supplied to Europe in the future depends in part on the design of the appropriate contracts between producers and buyers. These have also to be seen in the context not only of the evolving liberalization and competition requirements but also of the conditions prevalent in the centres of production.

On the basis of the known reserves and likely future discoveries, it is clear that Norway and Russia will be major sources for many years. In Norway proven reserves are officially stated at 44 trillion cubic feet. Wood MacKenzie (2001) estimates that between now and 2012 new 'probable' fields containing recoverable reserves of 31 trillion cubic feet could be developed. A very high proportion of this gas is located in mid-Norway and the Barents Sea, where investment costs, including the provision of new offshore infrastructure, will be required. In the Barents Sea liquefied natural gas (LNG) is currently viewed as the most likely development concept.

Recently there has been a major change in the contractual situation regarding Norwegian gas exports. Under pressure from the EU, the arrangement whereby all export contracts were negotiated by one single group, led by Statoil and Norsk Hydro, and commonly known as the GFU, has been abolished. The EU has also instigated legal proceedings against Statoil and Norsk Hydro with the objective of requiring them to renegotiate the existing contracts. Whether this will happen and whether a more competitive export market will develop is still unclear. Statoil and Norsk Hydro are expected to challenge the EU Commission and to argue that the GFU scheme was imposed upon them by the Norwegian government. It is noteworthy that Statoil will also market the state's direct share of gas (now called Petoro). According to Schroder, Saloman, Smith, Barney (2001), this combination amounts to nearly 60 per cent of Norway's proven gas reserves.

It is also noteworthy that the combined shares of Statoil and Petoro in the giant Troll field amount to 55 per cent of the total. There is much uncontracted gas in this field, and to what extent other partners will enter into independent export contracts is unclear. A further relevant feature is the interventionist practice of the Norwegian government with respect to field development, depletion and exports. The ability to approve developments and contracts could also inhibit the emergence of competition among producers.

In Russia proven reserves are estimated at over 48 trillion cubic feet. While well over 80 per cent of Russia's current gas production comes from Western Siberia, incremental supplies will increasingly have to come from higher-cost and remote areas such as Yamal. The Russian gas industry is also faced with the prospect of major structural change, which adds a complicating factor from the viewpoint of contracts with Western Europe. Gazprom, a vertically integrated company, currently has a near monopoly of the industry, especially in transportation, and supply (including exports). In 2001 the government announced a proposal to deregulate the industry. The proposals involve the separation of Gazprom's transportation assets from those of production and supply, followed by separate accounting and the spinning off of Gazprom's pipeline business. Transparent tariffs would be established involving non-discriminatory access by third parties. At the production stage several subsidiaries of Gazprom would be established, with separate accounting. Subsequently they would compete with each other and with independent producers. As far as exports to non-FSU countries are concerned, for the foreseeable future Gazprom would probably retain a monopoly, though there is a possibility of other companies becoming exporters in the longer term.

These are far-reaching proposals, which would have major implications for all connected with the industry, including customers in Western Europe. Currently Gazprom not only has a near monopoly of the industry, but the pricing structure in the gas chain is far removed from structure of the related costs. United Financial Group (2001) estimates that under the transfer pricing system employed by Gazprom the transfer price between the production and transmission parts of the business is set artificially low. Thus 90 per cent of the company's total costs are allocated to transmission and only 10 per cent to the rest of the business. With a more accurate cost allocation the split would be around 75/25 per cent.

Whether these recent proposals will be implemented is a moot point. The very fact that the proposals have been made introduces some uncertainty. They come on top of a situation where Gazprom's total production has been falling (although its exports to non-FSU countries have continued to grow), and where concern has been expressed about the condition of the transportation infrastructure.

From the viewpoint of European countries importing increasingly large quantities of gas, the developments in both Norway and Russia noted above are of much interest. To what extent there will be competition among important producers can clearly affect the market price.

Other contractual issues are important in the supply of gas from producing to consuming countries. In the medium-term future the economic environment within which agreements are required will be significantly different from that typical in the past. The new fields in both countries will be more remote and generally costlier to develop, and there may be more competition at both the production stage and in the end markets for the gas. Producers like long-term take-or-pay contracts to reduce their investment risks. Purchasers have been willing to sign these because their market risks have been limited by entrenched near-monopoly rights. These are now clearly being eroded, though the pace of change still remains uncertain.

The future market situation clearly involves more risks. Producers will be keen to preserve substantial take-or-pay elements in their contracts. Purchasers may be more reluctant. The experience of British Gas in the 1990s, when it found itself with substantial 'excess' gas in its contracts with producers, will be remembered. The main established wholesalers, such as Gasunie, have already experienced large falls in their market shares.

As was noted above, there is currently still insufficient liquidity to enable effective hedging for large long-term contracts to take place on the necessary scale. Futures markets are, of course, likely to grow as the demand for the facility increases. It is likely, however, that contracts will have to become more flexible in their structure to deal with the changing market situation. From the producer's viewpoint it is essential that a market price be clearly obtainable. In a liberalized market there should be more gas-to-gas competition. In the European context it is the likely extent of this which is currently unclear. Long-term contracts can accommodate this uncertainty by the inclusion of price reopener/review clauses. These are already common to a limited extent in existing contracts, with three-year intervals between reviews being the norm. It is also understood that at least some recent contracts acknowledge the development of gas-to-gas competition by the inclusion of the spot gas price as one (small) element in the indexation formula. From this basis it is possible to see a basis for long-term agreements which could accommodate major changes in the gas market structure. This has, of course, already happened in the UK, but, arguably, the risks and likely field investment costs in the countries which are likely to be supplying large volumes of gas to Western Europe will be considerably greater.

Over the longer term there are many other possible sources of incremental gas for Western Europe apart from Norway and Russia. The Commission of the European Communities (2000) identified Algeria, Iran, Qatar, Nigeria and Turkmenistan. These countries all have very large reserves by world standards. Given the distances, the delivered costs are likely to be significantly higher than current levels. It is noteworthy, however, that there have been substantial reductions in the costs of developing and transporting gas in the form of LNG in recent years. Further progress is confidently expected over the next decade. Historically LNG contracts have had very substantial take-or-pay elements, and those to Europe have had indexation clauses heavily related to oil prices. Some adaptation to the likely new market situation will probably be needed.

9. CONCLUSIONS

Gas demand throughout Western Europe is very likely to grow substantially over the next two decades. This will have several consequences, particularly (a) a growing need for imports, which will become very substantial even by 2010, and (b) a need to expand the infrastructure network. The need for substantial imports in the medium term applies to the UK, where production is likely to peak within a few years and then decline at quite a fast pace.

The required expansion in the infrastructure will take place in the context of increasing liberalization in the gas market. The main infrastructure providers are all faced with heavy and changing regulation. The challenge for them and the regulators is to ensure that adequate capacity is provided at the right time and in the right place. Across Europe there is a variety of regulatory and incentive arrangements. In the UK, where there is a full common carriage obligation, the new system of providing incentives to the infrastructure provider is through the auction of capacity rights to shippers. How efficiently this system will function compared to other schemes, such as bilateral contracts between user and provider, or the judgement of the provider and regulator, is still unclear.

In the UK there is at least a settled basic industry structure of complete separation of infrastructure provider on a common carriage basis from the activities of gas production and supply. The problem for the provider is to deal with a liberalized market subject to considerable uncertainties at both the gas production and final market stages. A further complication concerns the uncertainties relating to the gas import landing points.

On the Continent the basic industry structures have generally not yet been settled. Infrastructure provision and gas supply are still widely undertaken by the same organization. Open access is common, but transparency and certainty for third-party users is often arguably inadequate. The structures as well as the regulatory arrangements are both subject to further change, but the pace and extent are still uncertain. The infrastructure providers thus have neither a settled industry structure nor a settled investment incentive scheme facing them. There is a clear benefit to all parties in the expeditious development of a settled industry structure and regulatory framework. The experience of the UK indicates that continuous regulatory uncertainty and changes increase the cost of capital to the infrastructure provider to the disadvantage of all parties. Shortage of capacity will impose large costs on the overall economy and a margin of excess capacity may be regarded as a relatively cheap insurance policy.

An efficiently provided infrastructure can help to facilitate long-term contracts between producers and gas purchasers. This market is also changing significantly. There are regulatory changes affecting Norway and Russia which may increase the level of competition among producers. The uncertainties regarding the pace and extent of (downstream) market liberalization may make the conclusion of long-term contracts more difficult, especially when high cost and very distant gas sources will be involved. The extent to which recent contracts have already incorporated some market liberalization in key clauses gives some confidence that future ones can accommodate a much more liberal market structure.

NOTE

1. This chapter appeared in the *Oxford Review of Economic Policy*, Issue on European Network Infrastructures, Vol. 17, No. 3, Autumn 2001 and is reproduced here with the kind permission of Oxford University Press.

REFERENCES

Commission of the European Communities (2000), *Towards a European Strategy for the Security of Energy Supply*, COM (2000) 769, Brussels, Annex Technical Document, p. 49.
DTI (2001a), *Development of UK Oil and Gas Resources*, London.
DTI (2001b), *Energy Projections for the UK*, Energy Paper No. 68, London.
Energy Contract Company (2001), *UK Gas Market Review, 2001*, Twickenham.
International Energy Agency (2000), *World Energy Outlook 2000*, Paris, p. 366.
Ofgem (2000a), *Long Term Signals and Incentives for Investment in Transmission Capacity on Transco's National Transmission System: a Consultation Document*, London, May.

Ofgem (2000b), *Long Term Signals and Incentives for Investment in Transmission Capacity on Transco's National Transmission System: Conclusions on the Framework*, London, December.

Ofgem (2001), *Long Term Signals and Incentives for Investment in Transmission Capacity on Transco's National Transmission System: The New Regime*, London, March.

Schroder, Salomon, Smith, Barney (2001), *Equity Research: Norway*, London, August.

Transco (2000), *Transportation Ten-Year Statement 2000*, Solihull.

Transco (2001a), *Transporting Britain's Energy: Consulting on Customer Requirements from Transco's Network*, Solihull, May.

Transco (2001b), *Transporting Britain's Energy: Conclusions of Transco's Consultation for Future Network Requirements*, Solihull, August.

United Financial Group (2001), *Gazprom: Brave New World*, Moscow, August.

Wood MacKenzie (2001), *North West Europe Upstream Report*, No. 180, Edinburgh, July.

CHAIRMAN'S COMMENTS

Callum McCarthy

Alexander Kemp and Linda Stephen's chapter has raised many issues. The fact that UKCS gas will not last indefinitely and hence, at some time, the UK will become a net importer is commonly known. However, it seems to have come as a surprise to some people and has raised all sorts of issues connected with security of supply and whether importing gas causes problems.

I should like to discuss the question raised of how to size the British gas network. As the chapter acknowledges, the debate surrounding this issue is often contentious but clearly of some importance for Ofgem. First I'd like to observe that taking, as a starting-point, this sort of econometric analysis of likely demand may take us further down a path of certainty about the future than is reasonable. I'm not arguing against an attempt to establish, by the best possible analysis available, a probable pattern of demand. But I think we shoild recognize the wide margin of error associated with any such attempt.

It's illuminating to look back at some of the past attempts at such analyses and see the margins of error associated with them; for example the 1982 Sizewell inquiry made a very determined effort to set out a range of scenarios which would encompass all possible outcomes. The inquiry set out five scenarios for the year 2000 and in none of the five was coal predicted to be below 50 mtoe; the actual outcome was, as we know, less than 20. In none of the five scenarios was gas predicted to be as high as 100; the outcome was over 140. So even at the most general level, forecasting is liable to produce very significant errors. At the detailed level, as I think the analysis showed, once we start looking at particular fields and particular entry points, the problem is even greater. In the present circumstances, for example, there's doubt as to whether new gas production will rise in the Norwegian sector or west of Shetland; whether producers will choose to land gas on the Continent, in the Netherlands, or in the UK; and if in the UK, at which entry point.

It's important to recognize that the investment and operational decisions to be made by Transco may be much more complex than some suggest. The demands on capacity at a particular entry point are not constant over the year; nor are they free from interdependence. Thus capacity constraints at St Fergus can be overcome, *inter alia*, by actions taken elsewhere; nor do they correspond to the administrative arrangements based on peak demand encapsulated in the 1 in 20 rule. So there is a whole series of problems that anybody trying to make decisions on investment has to recognize. The conclusion that Ofgem draws from this is that a mechanism is needed to identify changes in demand and translate this into an effective mechanism to incentivize Transco to invest, or not to invest, in response to changes in demand. As is well known, the approach that Ofgem has taken towards changes in demand, and Transco's responses to those changes, is set out in the proposals for the Transco system operator incentives. There are a number of important advances here over anything that has been done in the past under RPI–X regulation, and it's worth setting thoem out.

First of all, there are real incentives for Transco to respond to changes in demand, up or down. Transco, if it invests in additional NTS capacity and responds to demand, will be able to earn a return of three times its weighted average cost of capital during the price control period, and it is certain that the investment will count in its Regulatory Asset Value (RAV) thereafter. Unlike the present position, in which Transco has an incentive to delay investment until late in the five years of the price control, in future Transco will have an incentive to invest in a timely way. That is a very significant change.

My second point is that producers will for the first time have firm contractual rights to deliver gas to the NTS and will be able to exercise their rights. This will give them exactly the certainty that they are after, referred to in the chapter as one of the necessary features of a gas network. This is a welcome development, subject to some reservations about the form of the auctions, both by the UK Offshore Operators' Association (UKOOA) and by individual producers like BP, that long-term auctions do deliver what they want.

My last point is that incentives to Transco and auctions are integrally linked for the first time, so that there is a way of identifying demand and changes in demand, a way of giving certainty to both Transco and to producers and of establishing the necessary links. Although I have great respect for the scholarship demonstrated in identifying and predicting changes, the approach that we believe is necessary is not just based on as good an initial point as you can get, but a recognition that, however good that initial point is, there will be a need to deviate from it, and hence a need for mechanisms to do this.

4. The ingredients of effective competition policy

Irwin M. Stelzer

I begin with the usual declaration of interest: I serve as a consultant to News International, BSkyB, and a few of the energy companies that operate in the UK.

America has for over a century had as a cornerstone of public policy the belief that a vigorous competition policy is a good thing.[1] When Congress passed the Sherman Act in 1890, in part enshrining in statute law several long-standing common law proscriptions of a variety of trade restraints, it was reacting to growing public nervousness about the power of various 'trusts' that had acquired monopoly power in the oil, whisky, sugar and other industries. One hundred and eleven years later, the two basic provisions of the Sherman Act remain the core of American policy.

The first prohibits conspiracies in restraint of trade, the second bans abusive practices aimed at acquiring or maintaining a monopoly position. These provisions were later supplemented by separate statutes barring mergers that might substantially lessen competition, and incorporating certain consumer protections. Neither the original act nor its later supplements contain any provision attacking size as such.

The goals of this legislation are not immediately obvious to those who have not read the legislative history of these various acts. True, it is fair to say that the main goal is the preservation of a competitive economy. But that avoids the important question of just why the framers of the legislation and later generations of legislators and enforcement officials, as well as the American public, deemed this policy so important.

One reason is obvious: competition produces certain desirable *economic* results, to wit:

1. A policy that makes it difficult for businessmen to collude to fix prices guarantees consumers that the prices they pay for goods and services will reflect only the costs of producing the goods and services they buy, including a reasonable return on the capital committed to the production of those goods and services. As Alfred Marshall long ago stated, in the days when

the economic literature consisted of clear, equation-free prose, 'If the producers of a commodity are many in number and act without any concert, it is to the interest of each of them to increase his supply of it whenever he expects to obtain a price greater than its Expenses of production. So that the price of a commodity cannot long exceed its Expenses of production, if there is free competition among its producers.'[2]

2. A concomitant result of an effective competition policy is that competing businesses will be under pressure to produce in the most efficient manner – minimizing costs so that they are in a position to meet or beat the prices of their competitors.[3]

3. A vigorous competition policy should maximize the rate of innovation and the rate of introduction of new technologies, in the process denying what Hicks identified as the greatest monopoly profit – a quiet life.[4] I recognize that the economic literature on this point is ambiguous, since it recognizes the possibility that competition in product markets might deny innovators the ability to appropriate to themselves the fruits of their inventions, thereby discouraging expenditure on research and development.[5] But here I would like to draw on John Vickers's formulation, offered in a paper considering the relation between competition and productive efficiency: 'Competition seems very well in practice, but it is not so clear how it works in theory.'[6] But we can rely on a common-sense appraisal of real-life experience, which suggests that competition means a fiercer gale of creative destruction than does the cozier world of cartels and monopoly. Compare the level of efficiency in countries with and without competitive market systems; ask why Microsoft made such efforts and took such risks to deny innovators access to markets and to venture capital; recall the rapid introduction of new electric generating technologies when competition was opened up in the electricity market; and consider the innovative price/service combinations offered by the airline industry when competition replaced regulation. The list could be extended, but it suggests – more than suggests – that competition matters.

4. A vigorous competition policy also provides a tool with which to judge which mergers are in the public interest, and which are not. The dividing line is simple to describe, if not always easy to discern: any merger that has the probability of unduly reducing competition should be halted. Note: it is not necessary for any government agency to decide whether the merger is a good idea, and is likely to produce the anticipated savings (most do not), although officials often find that chore extraordinarily tempting; witness their inclusion of such considerations in the merger guidelines published in most countries. Fortunately, in most instances they resist the temptation to substitute their judgments for the market's.

5. Effective competition makes regulation unnecessary, and is far more efficient than regulation in allocating scarce resources.[7] It is important to distinguish competition policy from regulatory policy. Some industries contain large natural monopoly elements, and therefore must have their prices, performance and profits regulated lest they exploit their customers. In other industries, competition is possible but can be snuffed out or seriously diluted by the exercise of market power that in no sense flows 'naturally' from the economic structure of the industry. By preventing the untoward exercise of market power, the competition authorities preserve the market's ability to determine prices and allocate resources, making regulation unnecessary. In short, *ad hoc* interventions to preserve competition make ongoing regulation unnecessary, for where the invisible hand operates, the heavy hand of government is not necessary to assure consumers against exploitation.

But it would be incorrect to assume that these substantial *economic* advantages of a vigorous competition policy were and are the only, or even the main, goal of that policy. In addition to these economic advantages, a proper competition policy produces desirable *social* effects – the diffusion of economic power and the maximization of economic and social mobility. In an economy in which incumbent firms cannot create artificial barriers to entry, either by deploying their own market power in an anticompetitive manner, or by colluding with others, fledgling entrepreneurs are likely to flourish.

Such competitive entry prevents existing firms from resting on their laurels, and induces them to innovate in response to the innovations of new entrants. It also contributes to the maintenance of a society that is deemed to be fair and open by its citizens.[8] In America, the relative ease of entry into most industries has contributed to the mobility among income groups that has prevented the class warfare so common in other countries. Note, however, that it is precisely this result of competition policy, this social fluidity, that generates opposition to it by those in government who prefer to manage the rate of change in society, by those classes that prefer the status quo to a society in which *arrivistes* can eventually despoil the neighborhoods of those with 'old money' by moving there, and by businessmen with undepreciated sunk investment that will never be recovered if barriers to entry are eliminated.[9]

These, then, are the economic and social policy goals of competition policy. The economic goals are generally accepted by all proponents of vigorous enforcement; that social goals also play a role is disputed by adherents of the Chicago School who argue that the sole goal of antitrust policy is and should be the enhancement of consumer welfare. As you can discern without much difficulty, I am of a different view: the social dimension matters.

Of late, another reason has been advanced in support of a tough-minded competition enforcement policy: the relation that exists between the above-cited goals of what is essentially a microeconomic policy and the macroeconomic policy objective of maximizing productivity growth so that pro-growth monetary and fiscal policies do not trigger inflation. And governments around the world are certainly eager to see their economies grow.

This emphasis by governments on stimulating productivity and economic growth is not without an element of self-interest: long-term growth in productivity is a necessity if the economy is to grow, and living standards are to rise, and the Treasury's coffers to bulge. The programs of governments both of the right and the left require money to pay for them. And it is increasingly clear to most governments – Britain's may be an exception – that they are reaching the outer limits of their ability to extract from their citizens a larger portion of their hard-earned money. To the *political* difficulties of raising taxes add the *economic* fact that capital and labor are increasingly mobile and willing to migrate from jurisdictions in which taxes have become vexatious to more hospitable climes.

So any government, whether it is interested in a more fully funded defense establishment or an expanded welfare state, must rely largely on economic growth to throw off the huge sums of taxes that might at least partially satisfy its appetite – one is reminded of Queen Gertrude, whose appetite for the charms of King Hamlet increased 'by what it fed on'! So, too, do the appetites of governments increase even as the money flowing into their treasuries increases, for every increment in funds seems to stimulate the imaginations of those for whom no new government program is a program too far.

One source of the economic growth that governments crave is increased productivity. And one key to increased productivity is certainly a vigorous competition policy,[10] which requires emphasis now that 'new economy' advocates are pressing to confine our antitrust laws to the dustbin of history.

Indeed, in Britain, interest in a vigorous antitrust policy was generated not by microeconomic policymakers, but by the keeper of macroeconomic policy, the Chancellor. He divined that Britain's economic future depends on its ability to increase its productivity, and that the pace of productivity increase could only be accelerated if the cozy, cartel-like behaviour of British managers were replaced by an enterprise culture.

In emphasizing productivity growth the Chancellor has it right. Recent studies by economists at the Federal Reserve Bank of New York confirm earlier studies: 'The rate of productivity growth can have an enormous effect on real output and living standards ... Productivity growth is clearly a fundamental measure of economic health ...'.[11] Consider this example: if labor productivity grows at 1.5 percent per year (the US average from 1973 to 1995), output per hour would rise by 35 percent over 20 years. But growth of 2.7 percent (the American average from 1995 to 1999) raises hourly output by twice as much – 70 percent.

This is not the place to examine the myriad causes of Britain's historic record of poor productivity performance. Some lay the blame at the feet of Luddite trade unions; others blame the regulations that stifle new business formation and small-business growth;[12] others blame governments for siphoning off too large a portion of the nation's resources and imposing incentive-stifling tax rates; others blame managements that are loath to invest in new plant and equipment and resist compensation schemes that are genuinely related to performance in enhancing shareholder value; still others blame a civil service that for many years saw it as its role to manage economic decline in a way that minimized social unrest.

There is enough blame to go around, I suppose. But surely one contributor to suboptimal performance has been a culture that discourages confrontation and competition, a culture that when played out on the economic scene results in a comradely attitude not only on the shop floor but in the board room, and in an aversion to the risk associated with starting a new business.[13]

The replacement of such a culture, of the concept that 'it doesn't matter whether you win or lose, it's how you play the game', with one that says that winning is better than losing, cannot be accomplished quickly. Indeed, given the ancillary effects of such a cultural shift, Britain should think very hard before embarking on a path that, if trod, will surely make it more like America, a destination that many people in Britain do not feel is one at which they want to arrive.

But assuming that it is settled policy that Britain is to have an enterprise culture, one in which class mobility is increased, productivity rises, and economic well-being increases for all (even though income inequality may also increase), an effective competition policy is essential – not the only ingredient of such a shift in attitudes,[14] but one of the ingredients.

Such a policy starts with good legislation – laws that combine sufficient specificity with a good dose of flexibility. It is impossible to legislate a complete list of 'don'ts', practices that at all times and in all circumstances should be treated as *per se* illegal. Price fixing is one such, but it is difficult to think of others.

So sensible laws are proscriptive, not prescriptive. That is, they tell businessmen what they cannot do, not what a government regulator thinks they should do. Thus businesses are barred from colluding to fix prices, but not ordered to adopt a specific pricing policy; they are barred from merging with a competitor where the effect may be substantially to lessen competition, actual or potential, but they are not ordered to merge with some firm because a government regulator thinks that consolidation would be a good idea. In short, competition policy is about preserving the competitive *process*, and letting the *results* of that process fall where they may. I would hope that the new legislation, which will impose on the Office of Fair Trading (OFT) 'clear duties to promote competition',[15] will not cross the line and give the agency the authority to mandate forms of behavior or market structure outcomes that it feels are in the public interest.

For we must not confuse the competition policy appropriate to regulators of utility industries with that appropriate to enforcers of antitrust policy. Faced with industries that historically had monopoly power, and monopoly power that was granted to them by the state rather than won by their own superior performance in the market, regulators were given the affirmative responsibility of introducing competition. To say that the companies they regulate were unenthusiastic about allowing new entrants, and devised schemes for avoiding the erosion of their monopoly positions, is to put the case mildly. So regulators, with no *process* to rely on, were forced to get *results* by ordering the companies they regulated to take specific steps – orders to 'do this' rather than the orders of 'don't do this' that are appropriate to competition authorities whose job it is to preserve rather than establish competition.

I would also hope that the new competition policy includes enforcement mechanisms that make the law worthy of the attention of the business community. I have elsewhere made the case for criminal penalties for price fixers,[16] and will not repeat it here. I would like to add that allowing private plaintiffs to sue to recover some multiple of the damages inflicted upon them by dominant firms engaged in anticompetitive acts is another powerful deterrent, and one that adds resources from the private sector to those devoted by the public sector to enforcing the competition statutes. This sort of provision, combined with permitting lawyers to represent plaintiffs on a contingency fee basis, might produce some frivolous law suits, but my guess is that the 'loser pays' provision will keep these to a minimum, and the preponderance of those filed would be well-grounded actions that would otherwise never have been brought.

There are many other weapons in the enforcement kit, and an increasing number are being used in Britain to bolster the power of its competition law enforcers. Perhaps the best way to judge the efficacy of any proposed bit of competition legislation is to assume that its effectiveness is directly related to the decibel count of the complaints emerging from the CBI![17]

But no legislation, no matter how well drawn, is any better than the men and women charged with its enforcement. I won't repeat here the points I have made elsewhere about the need to recruit high-quality and well-trained men and women to the agencies charged with enforcement, a process well under way in Britain. For those who demand a fuller exposition of this point I commend to you my recent book of essays.[18]

But I should like to add to my list of the virtues of a good enforcement regime two other items. The first is that it be above political influence. On that score, we seem to be well served. The Director General of the Office of Fair Trading has announced that he will neither seek nor accept reappointment, making him immune to the blandishments of Number 10, assuming that he cares little about the honors list! The European Commission's competition enforcer has shown that political pressure generated by General Electric cannot deter him from refusing to sanction that company's acquisition of Honeywell. And in America, 'studies show that politics, as measured by the party of the President, and [by] the Republican versus Democratic composition of the House and Senate, does not have a clear impact on case activity'.[19] Indeed, in America it is more changes in economic fashion – reappraisal by academics of the nature and impact of vertical restraints, new definitions of predation, introduction and refinement of the contestable market thesis – than changes in politics that affect antitrust enforcement activity.

The second item I would add to any list of qualities one hopes to find in enforcement authorities is civility. The continued acceptability of antitrust enforcement depends in part on the ability of its defenders to demonstrate that they are not anti-business zealots. This is why I must confess that I am repeatedly astonished in dealing with the authorities in Britain and in Brussels at the number of ways in which they behave so as to lend credence to business complaints about the entire process of enforcement. Data requests are sent with no attention to the relevance of the information being commandeered, the cost of complying, or the time needed to do so. A favorite tactic is to drag a case out for months, and then send a massive request late in December, with a return date the first business day of January. A variation is to send a request on the last day of July, answers due on 1 September. And just last week I saw a request from Brussels that was received on Friday, answer due on Monday. It is as if the enforcement agencies are attempting to show the staffs of the companies under investigation that they have real power – the power to disrupt their holidays and family lives.

I am happy to say that the American authorities have no use for such silliness, which both degrades the quality of the information submitted and needlessly creates an opportunity for opponents of vigorous competition policy to argue that such a policy is aimed, not at preserving competition, but at harassing businessmen.

Lest I leave the impression that my only criticism of the enforcement agencies is their occasional burst of bad manners, I would like to focus on one important substantive economic issue that I believe has not been well handled by enforcement agencies in Britain – the question of market definition.

The beginning of any analysis of competition or its absence is the definition of the relevant product and geographic market, which is jargon for delineating the arena in which competition is occurring. 'A relevant market consists of all buyers and sellers of all products that are actual or potential competitors with one another.'[20]

In my experience, enforcement authorities are prone to make three conceptual errors. The first is to equate bigness with evil, to assume that large firms, especially those with large market shares, must have engaged in anticompetitive tactics. Now, I would be the first to argue that many have, and that it is entirely appropriate to have a double standard in enforcement that effectively denies to dominant firms some of the tactics in which smaller firms may be permitted to engage. But I would also point out that a large market share, even one that confers monopoly power, taken alone, is not objectionable. As American courts have put it, monopoly power that results from growth 'as a consequence of superior product, business acumen, or historic accident' is not illegal.[21] Or, to put it slightly differently, 'The successful competitor, having been urged to compete, must not be turned upon when he wins.'[22]

The second conceptual error is to equate market share with market power. I am aware that the European authorities say that they temper their judgment about the relation of market share to market power with a consideration of other factors.[23] But I would like to suggest that a review of enforcement decisions in the UK and in Europe, both in competition and in merger cases, might reveal a tendency to slight determinants of market power other than mere market share.

This brings me to the third conceptual error – a failure to accord appropriate weight to the restraint placed on the market power of an incumbent by the threat of potential entry of newcomers. It has been my experience that competition authorities tend to dismiss the possibility of new entry if they find that such entry requires substantial amounts of capital – as if capital markets do not exist.

I would hope that in the future authorities will take a harder look at, and give more weight to, 'contestability', or potential entry, as a constraint on the market power of incumbents,[24] perhaps as part of an overall abandonment of the tendency of some enforcement authorities to search for the narrowest (vaguely) plausible market definition so as to magnify the share of the company under investigation. This does not mean than I am an unreserved fan of 'contestability' theory, especially since Donald Hay and Derek Morris have pointed out in their textbook that the 'comforting conclusions' that free entry makes market dominance a non-issue depend on at least one 'implausible assumption',[25] that there are no sunk costs, or as Baumol and Blinder, devotees of contestability theory, put it, that new entrants can 'exit … without losing money'.[26] Costless exit is the exception rather than the rule.

Space does not allow me to attempt to review the enormous literature on the usability of the contestability doctrine in the appraisal of market power. It suffices for our purposes to make the common-sense observation that a credible threat of entry can operate as a constraint on the power of incumbent firms with large market shares. Just as we do not need 'perfect competition' to obtain benefits for consumers and gains in efficiency, so we do not need 'perfect contestability' to constrain market power. As Baumol and Blinder put it, 'The constant threat of entry forces oligopolists to perform well. Even monopolists must perform well if they do business in a highly contestable market.'[27]

Enough has been said to demonstrate that this is an extraordinarily complex issue, as is the question of market definition itself.

None of this implies that enforcement authorities err in wanting to know just how large a presence a firm is in a market. But the authorities must find out, in addition, whether a firm has a large market share, whether that share conveys real market power, or dominance, and whether that share was won and is being maintained by the use of anticompetitive tactics rather than merely by the exercise of business acumen. In short, defining the relevant market, to use the jargon of the trade, is only a first step, but an important one, in examining the state of competition in an industry.[28]

To measure a firm's market share it is first necessary to define the market in which it operates, and the sources of its competition. If a domestic manufacturer of, say automobiles, faces stiff competition from imports, foreign manufacturers must be counted among its competitors in computing its share. If newspapers compete with television for advertisers, the market share of any paper must be computed in light of that fact.

From this brief recitation it should be obvious that it is no easy matter even to take this first step in a competition inquiry: there are few hard-and-fast rules in the market definition game,[29] just as there are few bright lines to distinguish vigorously competitive behavior from anticompetitive acts – when is a price cut competitive, and when is it predatory? When does the legitimate protection of intellectual property become an anticompetitive attempt to stifle alternative technologies? That is why it is so important that the procedure used to reach a conclusion be designed to put as many facts and as many expert interpretations of those facts directly to the decision maker, consistent with the constraints I will mention in a moment, and why it is so important to have qualified people in charge of the enforcement process.

This is why I have always felt it so important for the Director General, particularly the skilled incumbent, to be exposed to as many points of view and hard information as possible. So I have been proposing that the Director General at some point summon before him the interested parties, and hear them out. Although I still worry that the staff controls the flow of information to the Director General, including summaries of its opponents' positions, I am no longer certain that my proposed remedy is optimal. For one thing, if the Director General actively shapes a case from the beginning by encouraging open discussion among the staff and with him, it is likely that more than one staff point of view gets considered and is questioned. For another, the pressures on the Director General's time make it infeasible for him to hear the views of the parties personally in more than a few cases; some of the data on which he is relying have been provided on a confidential basis, and therefore cannot be exposed to other parties for comment; the Director General can read submissions to him by all parties, which in some instances is more efficient than a face-to-face meeting. These are important points to which I had not previously given sufficient attention and thought, which I now must do. So let me leave it this way: existing procedure should be studied to see how it can be made fairer to the parties, and the information flow to the decision-maker improved.

I would not want to ask the Treasury to summarize the case for a reduction in petrol taxes, although I believe the staff would do its best to do an honest job. So I remain nervous about assigning a similar chore to the OFT staff. I am simply less certain that I once was both as to the magnitude of the problem and how to solve it, consistent with an optimal use of the Director General's time.

The procedure at the Competition Commission allows each interested party to have his or her say before the Commission. But even that procedure suffers from the inability or unwillingness of the Commission to summon the parties to a session at which it can hear the various answers to its questions, and the comments of each party on the presentation of the others, with cross-examination by each party of the others' experts allowed. There is also no satisfactory mechanism by which the staff can be queried by any of the parties, giving it a sheltered position from which it is free to reach conclusions without the disciplining effect of the knowledge that the affected parties will have an opportunity to confront it directly with evidence to the contrary.

Still, we cannot let these problems obscure the fundamental fact that the effectiveness of competition policy in moving Britain towards a more competitive economy has increased and is set to increase still further. This is why it would be a pity if the post-GE pressure to harmonize competition policy bears fruit.

The internationalization of many business enterprises certainly makes matters such as their business practices and any mergers in which they become involved of interest to authorities in more than one jurisdiction.[30] And no one can argue with the proposition that a greater exchange of ideas among authorities in Europe, the United States, the UK and other countries would be desirable, or that a coordination of data requests would reduce the costs and increase the speed of enforcement.

But in the end, competition policy is a reflection of national attitudes towards such things as the acceptable degree of income inequality;[31] the extent to which existing, small firms should be protected from the full force of competition; and the trade-offs between such things as environmental preservation and new entry that might require construction on greenfield sites.

If one believes in vigorous competition, and if one concedes that there is a range of support for such policies, extending from the most robust in the Anglo-Saxon countries to the least enthusiastic support in France, where highly competitive markets are viewed with alarm and policy positions do not easily bend to accommodate the views of other countries, then harmonization might quite possibly create pressure towards more lenient policies than some in the USA and the UK find acceptable and desirable.

In addition to this political problem there is a doctrinal issue, or issues. Reasonable men can differ on economic questions. The European authorities are convinced that mergers such as that proposed by GE and Honeywell can create an anticompetitive 'portfolio effect', or the possibility of 'bundling'. This theory holds that a merged conglomerate can 'leverage' its market power in one industry to gain advantages unrelated to its efficiency in another, or offer a 'bundle' of products that less diversified firms cannot offer. In its decision, yet to be published but shown to the press, the European Commission argues, 'The combined entity will be able to offer a package of products that has never been put together on the market prior to the takeover and that cannot be challenged by any other competitor on its own.'[32]

The American authorities rather hotly disagree with this analysis – they say that preventing mergers on this ground denies consumers efficiencies and other advantages that such mergers create. William Kolasky, the new head of the Department of Justice's international enforcement division, has unleashed an attack on Mr Monti and his decision that is unprecedented in its ferocity, demonstrating how strong his feelings on the subject are.

All of this speaks volumes about the possibility of harmonizing EU and US competition policy enforcement: it is simply not in the cards. Not a bad thing, in my view, since harmonization in any event is undesirable.

I do not want to leave you with the impression that I am unaware of the vast literature that contends, for one reason or another, that development and enforcement of vigorous competition policy is misguided. Some opponents argue that competition has unpleasant cultural side effects, producing a 'law of the jungle' attitude in commercial life that infects social, personal and political life; these folks reside primarily in France, but have allies in many countries. Some contend that competition may have been a good idea in the atomistic economy that Adam Smith studied, but that

> Competition among a small number of units each involving an organization so complex that costs have become indeterminate does not satisfy the conditions assumed by earlier economists, nor does it appear likely to be as effective a regulator of industry and of profits as they had assumed.[33]

Still others see enforcement of rules against price fixing and other anticompetitive practices as somewhere between unnecessary and inefficient. Finally, there are those who argue that 'new economy' enterprises, with their short-lived products and faced with the continuing threat of new entry, are discouraged from competing vigorously by the threat of prosecution by antitrust authorities who have no understanding of the economics of network industries and other modern enterprises.

You may have gathered that I do not agree with these critics of antitrust policy – some of whom would repeal the antitrust laws completely. In my view, competition contributes to economic growth, and to consumer welfare. On that ground I commend it to you. But competition creates an atmosphere that favors change, business rivalry, long days and sleepless nights, insecurity and class mobility – all of which I and most of my American friends take to be good things. You can have the economic advantages and these social consequences if you opt for a vigorous competition policy. But you cannot opt for the economic advantages only; they come in the same package as the social consequences.

NOTES

1. This brief historical summary is derived from John H. Shenefield and Irwin M. Stelzer, *The Antitrust Laws: A Primer*, Washington, DC: AEI Press, 2001 (4th edn).
2. Alfred and Mary Paley Marshall, *The Economics of Industry*, Bristol: Thoemmes Press, 1994, reprinting the original 1879 edition, p. 180.
3. 'In long-run competitive equilibrium, every firm produces at the minimum point on its average cost curve. Thus, the outputs of competitive industries are produced at the lowest possible cost to society.' William J. Baumol and Alan S. Blinder, *Economics: Principles and Policy*, New York: Harcourt College Publishers, 1999 (8th edn), p. 205.
4. J.R. Hicks, *Value and Capital*, Oxford: Clarendon Press, 1939.
5. In this connection see Donald Hay and John Vickers (eds), *The Economics of Market Dominance*, Oxford: Basil Blackwell, 1986, pp. 8–9.
6. John Vickers, 'Concepts of Competition', *Oxford Economic Papers*, **47** (1995), p. 1.
7. See, among many others, Alfred E. Kahn, *Letting Go: Deregulating The Process of Deregulation*, East Lansing, MI: Michigan State University, 1998. 'Competition is a better safeguard and promoter of the interest of both consumers and the public at large than regulated monopoly, wherever it is feasible – that is, except in cases where monopoly is natural, because competitive duplication of facilities would be grossly inefficient' (p. 2). And, of course, we have in recent years narrowed substantially the number of industries deemed to be natural monopolies.
8. In this connection see Hans B. Thorelli, *The Federal Antitrust Policy: Origination of an American Tradition*, now available from University Microfilms International, Ann Arbor, MI: Out-of-Print Books, 1992; Shenefield and Stelzer, *The Antitrust Laws*, pp. 11–15; and Stephen Martin, *Industrial Economics: Economic Analysis and Public Policy*, Englewood Cliffs, NJ: Prentice Hall, 1994, pp. 45–50.
9. See my 'Fostering High-Tech Competition', one of a series of *Essays in Regulatory Policy* published by the Hudson Institute, September 2001.
10. This is not the place to discuss the very difficult question of the determinants of the rate of productivity growth. A useful and readable summary can be found in Charles L. Schultze, 'The Sources of Economic Growth and How Important Each One Is', in his *Memos to the President: A Guide through Macroeconomics for the Busy Policymaker*, Washington, DC: The Brookings Institution, 1992, pp. 227–35.
11. Charles Steindel and Kevin J. Stiroh, 'Productivity: What Is It, and Why Do We Care About It?', 12 April 2001, pp. 1 and 25 (mimeo).
12. See *Economic Affairs*, Journal of The Institute of Economic Affairs, **21** (2), 2001. This issue is devoted to essays on the subject of 'Regulation and the Small Firm'.

13. There is at least some light at the end of this particular tunnel: the rate of new business formation in Britain has increased noticeably in recent years.
14. Others include a tax structure that does not penalize hard work and risk-taking, bankruptcy laws that allow failed entrepreneurs a second and even a third chance, and a system of planning permission that is not weighted in favor of incumbent firms.
15. Department of Trade and Industry, 'A World Class Competition Regime', July 2001, p. 16.
16. See my 'Competition Policy and Superior Economic Performance', in *Lectures on Regulatory and Competition Policy*, London: The Institute of Economic Affairs, 2001, pp. 94–5.
17. For a summary of the CBI's misgivings about recent and prospective changes in competition law see 'CBI Brands Competition Law Changes "Draconian"', *Financial Times*, 18 October 2001.
18. Irwin M. Stelzer (2001), *Lectures on Regulatory and Competition Policy*, Occasional Paper 120, London: The Institute of Economic Affairs.
19. Vivek Ghosal and Joseph Gallo, 'The Cyclical Behavior of the Department of Justice's Antitrust Enforcement Activity', *International Journal of Industrial Organization*, **19** (2001), p. 27.
20. Shenefield and Stelzer, *The Antitrust Laws*, p. 30.
21. *United States v. Grinnell Corp.*, 384 U.S. 563 (1966).
22. *United States v. Aluminum Co. of America*, 148 F.2d 416 (2d Cir. 1945).
23. The European Commission states that a dominant position 'would usually arise when a firm or group of firms accounted for a large share of the supply in any given market, provided that other factors analysed in the assessment (such as entry barriers, customers' capacity, etc) point in the same direction.' Commission Notice 97/C 372/03, reported in Garth Lindrup (ed.), *Butterworths Competition Law Handbook*, London: Butterworths, 2000 (6th edn), p. 2558. Hereafter *Butterworths*.
24. Baumol and Blinder, *Economics*, pp. 264–6.
25. Donald A. Hay and Derek J. Morris, *Industrial Economics and Organization*, Oxford: Oxford University Press, 1991, p. 608.
26. Baumol and Blinder, *Economics*, p. 264.
27. Ibid., p. 265.
28. 'Market definition is not an end in itself, but rather a step which helps in the process of determining whether undertakings possess, or will possess, market power.' OFT Guideline 403 (March 1999), reported in *Butterworths*, p. 2027.
29. For a concise review of the weaknesses of various methods see Richard Stead, Peter Curwen and Kevin Lawler, *Industrial Economics: Theory, Applications and Policy*, London: McGraw-Hill, 1996, pp. 25–6.
30. Simon J. Evenett, Alexander Lehmann and Benn Steil, 'Antitrust in a Global Marketplace', in *Antitrust Goes Global*, London: Royal Institute of Economic Affairs and Washington, DC.: Brookings Institution Press, 2000, pp. 1–3.
31. America is willing to tolerate a greater degree of income inequality than other countries. See Alberto Alesina, Rafael Di Tella and Robert MacCulloch, 'Inequality and Happiness: Are Europeans and Americans Different?', Working paper 8198, National Bureau of Economic Research, April 2001 (mimeo) p. 2. The reason for this difference seems to be that 'opportunities for mobility are (or are perceived to be) higher in the US than in Europe' (p. 20).
32. Reported in *Financial Times*, 4 October 2001.
33. Adolf A. Berle and Gardiner C. Means, *The Modern Corporation & Private Property*, New Brunswick, NJ and London: Transaction Publishers, 1991 (originally published in 1932), p. 308. But see the brief response to this line of thought in David Willetts, *Modern Conservatism*, London: Penguin Books, 1992, pp. 83–5.

CHAIRMAN'S COMMENTS

Derek Morris

In a brief chapter, Irwin Stelzer has swept through a wide range of economic, social and political issues surrounding competition policy, raising a whole host of interesting and challenging issues. Here I would like to raise a few questions and make one or two observations.

The first question is this. Stelzer referred on several occasions to opponents of competition policy – those who don't favour social fluidity; who prefer to manage the rate of change in an economy; anti-*arrivistes*; those opposed to class mobility. This is quite a strong statement, and I am curious to know who is meant. It cannot be consumers, small businesses or potential entrants; it certainly isn't, in my view, the competition authorities; nor, I would have thought, is it any part of the government's policy which has generated recent and prospective changes in competition policy. By elimination this appears to leave only big business, which I infer is where Stelzer feels the problem lies.

The second question is one to which we all want to know the answer: how much cartel-like activity is likely to be going on in the UK. Some say they would be surprised if this was an extensive problem, particularly among larger firms, given the 1998 Act and the role of internal compliance programmes. Others point to the USA, where experience indicates that, notwithstanding the risk of prison sentences and triple damages, hard-core cartels continue to come to light. This suggests that there continue to be powerful economic incentives for at least some US managers to operate cartels, and there is no obvious reason to think that UK managers are in a different position. In a sense this is an impossible question – no observer can really know – but the observations in the chapter are of special interest because of Stelzer's particularly advantageous position: someone from a US background and experience through and through but, spending six months a year in the UK, so that he can bring an external but none the less informed view to such issues.

I now turn to three observations arising from the chapter. First, Stelzer was critical of an approach which equated, or tended to equate, large size or large market share with 'evil' action, that is, anti-competitive behaviour or some other type of exploitation of consumers through the abuse of market power. In similar vein he expressed concern that competition authorities may equate high market share with market power. I cannot speak for other competition authorities around the world, and it may be that he had others in mind; but I do not believe that the authorities in the UK make the presumptions – which I agree would be unjustified – to which he has referred. In support of this view, the guidelines for assessing competition issues published by the OFT indicate that market shares, though clearly an aspect to be considered, are only a starting-point. As an example, the Competition Commission's investigation of super-markets found the largest four to have very sizeable market shares, particularly in some areas; nor did the Commission regard entry as anything less than very difficult. As always, however, it went on to look at the actual dynamics of price and non-price competition, the specific pattern of prices as well as the general level of prices and profits, quality, choice and so on, concluding that competition for consumer spending was intense. This reflects a well-known theoretical point: while there are determinate theories of oligopoly there is no unique such model. The same oligopolistic market structure can, dependent on history and circumstance, give quite different outcomes.

The second observation follows on directly. Stelzer suggested that perhaps not enough weight is given to the scope for entry as a threat which can directly constrain anti-competitive behaviour in a market. In particular he referred to the role of contestability in a market. Here I suspect we agree on two steps of the way but not necessarily a third and final stage. I certainly agree that consideration of entry conditions is not just important but essential. Any analysis which fails to address this issue is flawed. I also agree that the key concept here is the one that underlies contestability theory, namely whether there are sunk costs of entry, already incurred by incumbent firms but not potential entrants, which create an asymmetry between them to the former's competitive advantage. But I have concerns, originally raised in my book with Donald Hay to which he referred, that contestability, to use the jargon, is not 'robust'.

What does that mean? The traditional textbook model of perfect competition generated a fully competitive outcome. No one sees the model as being realistic. It is useful because it provides a conceptual benchmark. Real-world markets which have similarities to the benchmark are likely to be reasonably competitive in practice. Those which are a long way from the stylized conditions of perfect competition are the ones most likely to throw up competition problems.

A fully contestable market – one in which there are no sunk costs, and incumbents are vulnerable to hit-and-run entrants – is likewise not put forward as a realistic set of circumstances but as a benchmark against which to compare or rank real-world markets. The problem, as I see it, is that not only will markets which are a long way from being fully contestable be quite difficult to enter but, critically, also ones that are not so very far from being fully contestable. Why is this? If entering a market involves some, albeit limited, sunk costs, and if those entering cannot contemplate escaping, should the need arise, fast enough to avoid adverse consequences from the actions of incumbents, then the one-way option that exists under full contestability – the entrant may gain and cannot lose – which makes such a market so competitive, is lost; indeed it is reversed. Incumbents, if they do have market power, can threaten entrants with a rapid price-cutting response, or some other retaliatory measure which will eliminate potential gains and guarantee losses. There are three immediate caveats:

1. Incumbents need not actually threaten retaliation; the scope and rationale for it may well be enough.
2. Some potential entrants may, of course, still take the risk; this is not an argument that entry can't occur, only that even apparently quite low hurdles may be a barrier.
3. None of this will necessarily stop innovative or more efficient entrants with new products, new processes, lower costs and so on, but it still means that even limited sunk costs and time lags can sometimes prove a problem.

None of this undermines the basic point that entry conditions are critical. Indeed, conceptually entry conditions take precedence over market structure. This is because, on the one hand, no matter how concentrated a market, if there genuinely is so-called super-free entry, the market will perform competitively – that is the contestability insight; while on the other even perfect competition will not systematically generate a fully competitive outcome if the assumption of no barriers to entry is removed. There is, however, no reason to assume – outside the context of full contestability – that the threat of entry will necessarily constrain incumbent firms from behaving anti-competitively.

My final observation relates to procedures. Stelzer has commented favourably that, in a Competition Commission inquiry, parties have direct access to the Commissioners. Not only are all the parties' submissions – every single one of them – read, in their entirety, by the group of four or five members responsible for the outcome of the particular inquiry, and discussed by them, but there is also a series of face-to-face hearings in private in which, however confidential the material, parties can put their case orally, be questioned on it and engage in debate, it is hoped in a structured but none the less open and, to some extent, open-ended manner. Whatever procedural changes may occur in future, I am anxious to hold to this. But Stelzer was concerned at what clearly some have felt is inadequate access to Commission staff, to discuss the many aspects that typically arise in an inquiry. This I will certainly reflect on. There may be a misunderstanding in that, although Commission staff bring absolutely invaluable expertise to bear upon the investigatory and analytical process, decision-taking is for the members alone. There is therefore no reason in principle why substantial contact should not occur between the parties and the staff – indeed this has been a growing aspect of our work – provided our resources are sufficient; but parties cannot expect to get views, still less likely conclusions, from such meetings. Moreover, while the Commission puts much effort into alerting parties to the issues raised or concerns felt in an inquiry, members are actively exhorted not to move towards determining their findings until all the evidence, submissions and arguments are in.

None the less, significant changes in the regime are on their way; this will require re-examination of all aspects of the Commission's work – we currently envisage 12 major programmes for strategic change and development; and this will of course include procedure. It is therefore timely to have touched upon this here.

As I said at the beginning, Stelzer's chapter has raised a plethora of significant issues, broad and narrow. I have touched on only a few.

5. Regulatory incentives and deregulation in telecommunications

Leonard Waverman

INTRODUCTION

Economics is about incentives. Market economies provide certain incentives based on the information available to market participants. These incentives are somewhat different in competition or monopoly, hence the oft-quoted phrase about the monopolist preferring a quiet life. The constraints on firms also differ depending on the degree of competition they face. It is these incentives and constraints that regulation attempts to impose on utilities with market power.

The social policy behind promoting competition is that, given certain conditions, allocative efficiency is met – that is, there is no better allocation of resources so as to increase production. Competition is not an end in itself but a means for atomistic decision-making that maximizes output, given the incentives. Market participants are buyers and sellers of inputs and outputs. Their incentives are to maximize personal gain. The competitive market takes all these personal ideals and objectives, and with an 'invisible hand' provides incentives to maximize society's output. Think of the idealized competitive market. This used to be hard to do even in introductory economics, but now with Internet auction sites such as Free Markets, truly competitive markets are much easier to see. In the limit, the willingness to pay by the marginal consumer, the last one tempted to buy, is equated to the true resource cost of the marginal supplier, the last one tempted to produce. All producers in the market either make no economic profits or they earn some quasi-rent pertaining to some specialized asset, not perfectly reproducible. Most consumers in the market earn quasi-rents, increments to consumers' surplus above their willingness to pay.

Think of the incentives in this market. At the simplest level, producers are incentivized to minimize cost and consumers are incentivized to maximize satisfaction. But at deeper levels, the incentives are for producers to provide innovations, products, services which better those of their competitors. That is, the incentives are to compete to win customers. This is a difficult, expensive task and other incentives exist to pervert this basic process; hence we have laws on collusion, predation and bribery. It is important to emphasize here that dynamic views of competition focus on long-term incentives for investment and innovation. Temporary quasi-rents are the vehicle and reward for such socially beneficial innovations. Competition law is increasingly considering how innovation markets are structured and how they perform.[1]

There are numerous circumstances in which such dynamic competition, these incentives, do not work properly. The too-often used words of 'externalities' and 'market failure' come to mind. I do not wish to discuss these. What I do wish to discuss are three other key issues: *incomplete information, uncertainty* and *(un)contractability*. Incomplete information refers to differences in knowledge of key facts among producers or buyers. Uncertainty is not risk. Risk can be insured against and hence market participants can act correctly even with risk. Uncertainty is risk which cannot be insured against – the effects of a new innovation or unexpected entry, for example. Uncontractability refers to the inability of parties to a contract to write down all possible contingencies that may arise. Hence, there are incentives to renegotiate or abrogate contracts and as a result the parties may initially take actions which they would not take if there were full contractability. Note that incomplete information, uncertainty and uncontractability refer to dynamic markets.

What does all this have to do with regulation? Simply put, regulation is an attempt to mirror competitive actions. Crucially, it is an imperfect attempt because regulation invariably distorts incentives, and more so if regulated markets are dynamic. That is, since competitive outcomes are about getting incentives right, one has to consider how incentives operate under regulatory regimes, and with incomplete information, uncertainty and uncontractibility. My main message is fivefold, as follows:

1. Regulation can never truly replicate competitive conditions, especially in dynamic innovation markets; hence the need to move to competition law.
2. The incentive-distorting impacts of regulation – its presence and its process – are not fully reflected in regulatory design and in regulatory actions.
3. Uncontractibility is particularly important. In essence, regulation is an uneven game with the government/the regulator having the ability to rewrite the contract. This necessarily increases uncertainty and as a result distorts incentives.
4. Regulation tends to expand, not because of clear policy or intent but because the incentives of players in the regulatory area cause this expansion. Hence we all consider 'regulatory creep' as pervasive. Insufficient attention has been placed on how we curtail the incentives for this expansion. I will suggest a regulatory cap regime similar to price caps, which reduces the weighted average regulation over time.
5. While sector-specific regulation is necessary, and grouping complementary regulatory activities under one roof, that is, Ofcom, is sensible, the scope

and power of Ofcom appear to be too large. That is, I suggest Ofcom will be less easy to constrain in terms of the expansion of regulation.

Three specific issues are:

1. *Broadband*. Broadband is rolling out slowly, likely due to strategic misincentives among key providers. Providing new incentives, that is, subsidies, would be wrong. Continuing asymmetric regulation, that is, asymmetric incentives, is also wrong. Some current regulation, for example, examining wholesale prices to determine if they are too low, is constraining roll-out. The economics literature suggests ways to increase incentives: a prize to the winner, fast tax write-offs for ADSL and cable modems, or a tax on BT and cable companies relative to the gap between UK and average European performance – all these might change incentives. The best policy, however, is to minimize regulation.
2. *Mobile*. The mobile sector is over-regulated. Regulation under the guise of price caps is simply rent extraction. This extraction distorts incentives to invest. Regulation is a tax on shareholders and in addition holds back smaller firms.
3. *3G auctions*. Auctions generally are the most efficient, incentive-neutral, mechanism for transforming public assets to private uses. However, the UK auction appears to have been designed for maximum rent extraction, not just to transfer assets to private use.

THE SCENE

In 1991, only ten years ago, wireless was a figment of the imagination. While BT Cellnet and Vodafone had been licensed in 1983, total carphone customers numbered only 500 000 in 1991. Today, cell-phone customers number 45 million for four infrastructure operators. In 1991 the landline duopoly experiment in fixed-lines competition was viewed as a failure. The decision was taken to relicense and repackage the cable franchises and in addition to give incentives to the new cable providers to compete in telephony with BT. That is, the decision was made to engage in infrastructure competition. In 1991, the competitive telephony facilities providers in the UK were two, while today there are 1471 independent fixed-line telephony service providers and resellers. In 1992/93, BT's share of the telephony call minutes markets was 77 per cent of international, 89 per cent of national, and 96 per cent of local. Nine years later BT's shares are, for residential customers, 49 per cent of international call minutes, 66 per cent of national and 75 per cent of local. For business customers, BT's share has fallen to 18 per cent of international call minutes, 38 per cent of national and 60 per cent of local. Even on calls to mobiles, BT now has just over 50 per cent market share. Today, cable passes 50 per cent of UK homes and has taken over 15 per cent of the residential main lines market in ten years.

Remember that it was not until 1993 that the European Commission took the decision to liberalize telecoms in Europe generally and it was only on 1 January 1998 that liberalization began in much of Europe. Much has happened in a short period of time. But has the 'right' amount happened, that is, could we envision circumstances in which a different scenario would have occurred?

REGULATION AND INCENTIVES

Regulation is about incentives. In 1983, when Steve Littlechild wrote his famous report on how to regulate BT, the prevailing wisdom and methodology in North America for regulating privately owned utilities was rate-of-return regulation. The telecom provider – AT & T or Bell Canada, for example – had a monopoly franchise and the process of regulation was to limit the rate of return earned on capital. The reasoning was simple. Monopolies make excessive economic profit. Thus limiting economic profits to a slight premium over the cost of capital would prevent monopoly abuse. However, we learnt slowly that this system of controls had unforeseen negative impacts on incentives. Basically, rate-of-return (ROR) regulation was a contract between the state and the utility whereby the telco received back its costs of service plus a slight premium on the cost of capital. Such cost-plus contracts are called in economics 'low-powered incentive schemes', as the firm has little incentive to be efficient.[2] A number of other problems plague this regulatory scheme. First, each incremental 0.1 of a per cent on the allowed return on capital is millions of dollars. Numerous days of a regulator's time in Canada and the USA were spent assessing evidence for 8.25 per cent instead of 8.00 per cent for the allowed ROR – surely a social waste of resources. Second, economic analysis showed a second and much more important inefficiency – because capital earned a premium but other inputs only earned their costs, regulated firms had incentives to substitute capital for labour inefficiently – gold plating. Thus regulators had to determine if assets were 'used and useful' and if expenses were to be capitalized or written off. A screwdriver as an asset earned a rate of return but as a material expense it earned zero return!

But the incentive problems are even greater than these simple attributes. Laffont and Tirole[3] showed us that under asymmetric information – the firm knows its cost, the regulator does not – this regulatory game involves moral hazard. Simply put, under traditional ROR regulation, the firm is not itself largely responsible for excess costs, so that the moral hazard is that service tends to be high cost as there are few incentives to lower costs.

A regulatory contract is tantamount to a procurement contract where the government (society) wishes to purchase the goods (telecom services) at lowest possible cost. The firm's incentives are not necessarily aligned, as its incentives are, to maximize profits. Say profits are maximized at price 100. The competitive price is 75, costs are 70. If the regulator knew costs, it would not allow a profit of 25. The government/regulator, however, does not know the true costs. Therefore the firm's announced cost of 95, where the extra 20 is spent on items such as large offices, fancy boardroom walls, paintings and an excessive capital base, will work for the firm. A 'high-powered incentive' scheme instead of the 'low-powered' cost-plus scheme keeps costs down to 70 where the firm itself bears the extra costs.

The government in this procurement game could, as Laffont and Tirole argue, offer a fixed price, say 80. Then this high-powered scheme provides good incentives for the firm to lower costs: a pound saved is a pound earned. However, what if the firm offered the fixed-price contract convinces the regulator that its costs are 90, not 70? Then the fixed-price contract at 100 locks in high profits to the firm. There is then a regulatory dilemma. A cost-plus contract has few incentives for the firm to be totally efficient, but the process does minimize excess profits. A fixed-price contract maximizes allocative efficiency but allows excess profits. Hence the problem for governments in designing incentive-based regulation: is the true underlying social objective to be economic efficiency or low profits (rent extraction)? Each objective determines a regulatory scheme and each then has differing effects on firm behaviour.

If the true objective of society is efficiency, then use high-powered incentives. A long-term price cap scheme is used in most jurisdictions and this has, as its basis, an efficiency objective. If the true objective is rent extraction, then other regulatory schemes such as ROR, profit reviews, excess profit taxes will prevail, but these instruments engender inefficiency. The literature is clear. There is no ideal regulatory regime – there are trade-offs. When the price cap is squeezed after three or four years because the regulator or government considers that 'excess' profits are earned, the firm learns that a pound saved is not a pound earned but a pound lost forever when taken by the regulator. This does not provide correct incentives if the firm changes its actions and reduces long-run efficiency to escape the cap. Nor does the cap squeeze assist society in the long term if investment or innovations are frozen.

When incomplete information, uncertainty and the inability truly to commit to contracts (uncontractability) are added to the picture, the wedge increases between a regulatory structure that is efficiency-driven versus one that is rent extraction-driven. Today regulation in telecoms must recognize that the industry is not what it was in 1984.[4] There is no longer a simple and unique way of delivering voice signals to a black dial handset in a home. Communications is a converged dynamic sector which is a major contributor to economic growth.[5]

It appears to me that in the UK rent extraction is a major regulatory goal. Therefore, current telecoms regulation as perceived by firms may be low-powered; that is, the incentives for efficiency, dynamic efficiency, are not maximized.

We have now dealt with the basic intuition of one set of incentive issues in regulation. A second set has had far less attention in the literature – the incentives established by the very presence of regulation. There are three subsets of these incentives I wish to consider. The first is the incentive for firms to use regulation instead of the market to compete; the second is the incentive for regulatory creep, the third is the incentive structure for the regulator herself.

The Regulatory Game

Earlier I described the features of a competitive equilibrium. Consider how those features are altered under regulation. In a competitive market, firms strive to beat their rivals through strategic moves – price reductions, service innovations, advertising and so on. The presence of regulation, however, sets up a new avenue for 'competition', now with an added player – the regulator. Regulated firms will decide whether to devote one pound at the margin either to market competition or to regulatory competition. Hence incentives are altered. Depending on the scope of regulation and particularly the objectives of the regulator, firms are induced to compete for regulatory favours or 'wins'. There are good reasons for the proposition that incentives are shifted for firms quite critically to investing in the regulatory game and away from competing directly for customers. A pound spent on price reductions or advertising can be quickly met by rivals. However, a regulatory decision in your favour cannot be easily copied. We as a society do not want incentives for firms to over-invest in regulatory departments. Thus institutional design, due process and, as I will argue, an appeal mechanism, are critical to ensuring a 'correct' mix of firms' inputs directed towards the market versus directed towards the regulator.

The incentive for firms is to expand their use of regulation until they equate the marginal benefits of an extra pound spent on regulation with their marginal costs. And note that the marginal costs for the firms are simply their internal costs. The firm does not pay for the costs it imposes on others. Critically, the purpose of some regulatory intervention is simply to raise rivals' costs. It's all externalities! Therefore we must, as Gilbert and Sullivan suggest in the *Mikado*, raise the price for firms so that the price they see for using the regulatory scheme is the total social cost, not just their private cost. That is, we must put into place a system of appropriate penalties for all players – for the incumbents who use regulation to deter rivals and for entrants who abuse the process. That is, if firm Y requests that Oftel examine practice X of BT as it thinks it is anti-competitive or discriminatory and Y is wrong, firm Y gets the bill for Oftel's and BT's costs. If an incumbent lodges appeals against Oftel's decisions, and those appeals are dismissed, the incumbent pays the costs of the appeal for all parties.

My first suggestion, therefore, is that we investigate systems of penalties and appropriate fines for entrants and incumbents so as to ensure that regulation is not the strategic output that it is now.

Regulatory Creep

Misincentives for firms to expand their strategic use of regulation is one explanation for regulatory creep. However, regulatory creep is endemic to most current regulatory schemes in the UK or elsewhere, whether in telecoms or in energy. It is senseless to blame Oftel for this, as regulatory design almost guarantees that regulation expands. The reason is simple – the regulator's job is to regulate. Hence blaming them for regulating is like blaming fish for swimming. There are only ways to restrain regulatory creep: first, alter incentives for its misuse by firms (see previous section); and second, restrict the scope of regulation. The discretion given the regulator is large, its mandate vague and, as we saw above, there are incentives for players to overuse the regulatory regime.

I suggested above that there are ways of reducing excessive reliance by firms on the regulatory process – the demand for regulation. We also have to limit the regulator – the supplier of regulation. There are multiple avenues for increases in the supply of regulation. For example, under current telecoms regulation, firms with market influence, SMP, collective dominance or other usual terms have to act non-discriminatorily towards competitors. But the term non-discrimination is totally vague, and probably unworkable.[6] Think of BT: what conditions make its wholesale offers non-discriminatory relative to its retail offers? Competitors argue that all conditions are discriminatory – price, contractual terms, bundling of services, technical conditions, speed of access, delays in responding to competitors, charges for system changes ... the list is endless. The regulator is asked to deal with all of these. Hence we have regulatory creep. As long as the regulator considers most or all acts of discrimination by the firms with SMP bad, then regulatory creep will continue. In my view, regulators generally are the last remaining large group which indeed believes in perfect competition as an ideal. The EC in its 1999 Review wants to move telecoms regulation away from sector-specific rules to competition policy. This is indeed the only route – but how do we transit? Oftel sincerely believes that sector-specific regulation is needed in some issues, long term and in most areas, for another decade. Is this right?

I am concerned that there is no sensible path from sector-specific regulation to competition policy. That is, there is only a monopoly provider of UK telecoms regulation, no price for this supply and a basic economic law in operation –

supply creates its own demand. Let me suggest one idea to limit the supply of regulation, probably unworkable but at least a move in the right direction. Think of the idealized properties of a price cap mechanism. That mechanism operates by having a weighted average price of services constrained by some cap. It works because with incomplete information, allowing the firm to alter relative prices but constraining overall price, we control the firm with market power but allow it incentives to be efficient. The firm alters relative prices so as to increase profits – a socially efficient outcome. I've begun considering an analogue – a *regulatory cap for regulators*. This is my second suggestion. Let us assume we wish to have the aggregate level of regulation not rise but decrease at 10 per cent per year. We assign weights to each major regulatory activity of Oftel; these weights add up to one. We then have a weighted average measure of regulation. Call this WAR. Oftel is then permitted to change its policies but under a WAR –10 per cent policy.

The problems with WAR are obvious – how do we determine weights, what is the scope of regulation today, that is, what are the regulatory outputs that are akin to the firm's outputs in the price cap?

These are difficult questions, but posing them forces us to do the necessary – consider what is the scope and level of today's telecoms regulation. Is it socially optimal? Has it increased? I suggest we do not know the answers to these questions and, hence, it is crucial to begin framing them.

Incentives for the Regulator

What are incentives for the regulator? It is simpler to characterize objectives and ideal outcomes for market participants than for the regulator itself. What incentives does the regulatory system provide for the regulator to do the job properly? And what is the job – what objective should the regulator maximize? Again, institutional design is critical to ensure accountability. But similar design problems exist here as with the trade-off for the firm between efficiency and earning quasi-rents. That is, we could have a regulatory design that held the regulator totally accountable to parliament. Call this low-powered regulation, as it gives no discretion to the regulator. High-powered regulatory design gives the regulator a great deal of discretion. Consider two cases: first, a regulator who has a lifetime appointment and no appeals mechanism and no policy directives; and second, a regulator who has a six-month appointment. Consider the effects of these two differing design mechanisms – the regulator needing constant reappointment will do whatever politicians in power want. In contrast, regulators who are truly independent and long term may engage in 'rent appropriation' for themselves. I do not mean money transfers; I mean the ability to maximize some objective different from that of their political masters. Hence the trade-off, but in this case low-powered incentives lead to no 'appropriation' by regulators but require complete control by parliament.

Why not then provide very short terms of office for regulators, thus making them truly 'accountable and responsible'? The answer must be that the regulated firms would see no commitment value in regulation. If regulation is at the whim of short-run political expediency, then in an election campaign party Y can promise to reduce residential phone rates or increase X in RPI–X. In order to maintain credibility in a regulatory environment, it is necessary for politicians to cede such potential interference. This adding of legislative authority, however, makes the regulator's objective somewhat unclear – what is he to maximize: consumers' surplus, the well-being of small competitors, or what?

The problem of misalignment of the regulator's incentives with social objectives suggests to me some limits on the regulator's authority. Above I suggested a regulatory cap, a method to reduce the overall scope of regulation. Here I am discussing the relative weights that the regulator places on various policies. In my view, to make regulation effective, governments need to set the broad policies under which regulation operates. The UK has done this better than most. For example, it is not the regulator's role, I would argue, to determine whether competition in telecoms should exist or not. My example is the USA, where the courts had to overturn the FCC's refusal to allow MCl's Execunet service on grounds that Execunet was not simply private-line service. That is, regulators can become captured – in the literature by the firm being regulated – more generally by an idea, ideology or interest group. Policy questions such as should there be competition, and does the country need facilities based or service competition are questions for politicians, not regulators. The UK and Canada do it right; the USA can't seem to do it right. By right I don't mean that I agree with every policy, but at least most 'grand' policies come from the politicians.

Regulators everywhere do make policy, however, whether it is in the 'grand' (and I think they should not) or in the 'small'. The latter is the cumulative effect of day-to-day decisions. A theoretical view of best-practice regulation is to have technocrats who implement the details of the government's broad communications policy. This is far-fetched in reality. Many of the decisions of Oftel are policy. Let me define policy as compared to implementation. Policy is a decision or practice that affects firms' abilities to enter, exit or innovate. I thus see policy as determining the long-term structure of the industry. It is obvious that all regulatory agencies are engaged in policy-making in the 'small', and thus three consequences follow. First, these agencies must recognize that they are policy-makers and hence should introduce a long-term policy unit, as Ofcom does. Second, the government needs a mechanism to introduce policies into regulation, as the 1984 Telecom Act in the UK provides. Third, there must be mechanisms for the government and those regulated to appeal decisions of the regulator.

Canada handles this in two ways, one good, one bad. On the good side, the government can provide policy directives to the Canadian Radio, Television and Communications Commission (CRTC) for broad indicators such as competition. A poor policy in Canada is the government's ability to set aside CRTC decisions. This clearly undermines the regulatory process and has parties in a regulatory hearing, in effect lobbying politicians. Thus appeal procedures have to be carefully designed. In the UK they are far too limited. That is, the very limited appeal mechanisms in the UK cede too much authority to Oftel. By 'too much authority' I mean insufficient controls on the decisions of Oftel as the accountability process is by nature too vague and limited. Let me turn to specifics.

OFTEL

Oftel was established in 1984 and has had an impressive record of opening up the UK telecoms sector to competition. In late 2001, Oftel had 242 employees (full-time executives – FTEs) and an annual budget of £17.9 million, a growth of 86 per cent since 1996/97. But then enormous changes have arrived in the market. Table 5.1 provides some measures of the number of regulatory activities by Oftel in 2000–2001. These are categorized two ways: first into four areas of Oftel jurisdiction – (1) decisions/directions; (2) draft directions, statements, determinations, consultations; (3) research, and finally (4) investigations. Second, the activities are categorized by service area: mobile, Internet, broadcasting, customer access and so on. There were some 311 separate areas of Oftel interventions in 2000–2001 – 115 of these were investigations, 112 under Oftel's competition policy mandate. There were 140 draft directions, statements, determinations; 3 decisions, and 53 research studies. In contrast, the Competition Commission (CC) published 15 reports in the 1 April 2000 to 31 March 2001 period. There were 107 unpublished reports and inquiries in progress by the CC. The CC's total costs for 2000–2001 were £7.72 million. The OFT's 2000–2001 staff total was 443 FTEs, and its budget was £33 million, of which £13.7 million was for examining mergers and the general competition regime. Telecoms regulation uses nearly the same resources as that spent by the two competition authorities covering all the non-utility sectors. However, studying inputs does not tell much.

The UK government, not Oftel, has been the source of crucial policy such as the duopoly regime between BT and Mercury over 1984–91. The promotion of infrastructure competition is government-induced by providing new cable franchisees in 1991 and the ability to provide telephony while keeping BT out of video dial tone for ten years to 2001. Oftel's policies have matched these broad policy dictates, for example, in its reluctance to encourage service competition (no discount for resale, wholesale rates for systems providers only). However, as much as I prefer a clear division between policy and implementation, many of Oftel's regulatory stances and interventions add up to important policy dictates. I am not convinced that Oftel sees the policy forest in addition to the regulatory trees. I don't mean this as a criticism. I think it is evident in the incentive system that regulation has set up.

In effect, Oftel sees itself as the policeman of competition in telecoms, jealously managing its mandate of 'the best deal for consumers in terms of quality, choice and value for money'. Because of Oftel's keen desire to ensure that BT, Cable and Wireless, Kingston – all former 'monopoly' providers – do not abuse their position, complaints from deprived competitors flood in. The sheer growth in telecoms regulation as competition increases is a cause for alarm. Oftel has what I would call an 'elastic' supply function of regulation, through practising what I call 'narrow' regulation. An elastic supply function for the regulator combined with an elastic and outward-shifting demand function encourages excess use of regulatory services by entrants. By 'narrow' regulation I mean that Oftel takes a narrow view of competition. Competition to Oftel means that prices should reflect underlying costs and that the return on consumer equity by service and by decile of consumer group should be at or near the cost of capital.[7] 'The competitive process would tend to eliminate any excess profits over time.'[8] In its July 2001 review of competition in the fixed-lines market Oftel found that the profits on business and high-spend residential customers were 'significantly above the cost of capital' and that 'this is slightly paradoxical since these segments are the most competitive areas of the market'.[9]

I think it excessively narrow to examine profitability by service and by decile of consumer group. The purpose of regulation is not to ensure that prices equal some ill-measured accounting estimate of costs in such fine divisions of service segments. Neither Volkswagen nor NTL nor Sainsbury's nor Harvey Nichols price each item at some constant markup over Long Run Incremental Cost (LRIC). Markets do not function that way. Such oversupply of regulation provides perverse incentives and large regulatory costs. Competitors engage in micro-complaining and Oftel in micro-managing. Figure 5.1 provides a stylized graph of the supply of and demand for regulation. A 'narrow' view of competition leads, as I suggest, to an elastic supply curve of regulation, labelled S_1 in the diagram. A broader view of competition would lead to a less elastic supply curve S_2. For any demand for regulation, say D_2 note that the less elastic supply curve leads to less regulation (OB) than the more elastic curve S_1(OA). A regulatory cap would be S_3, and having it reduce by 10 per cent a year would see it moving leftwards.

As my second suggestion, therefore, I'd recommend that Oftel broaden its view of what competition is.

Table 5.1 Oftel activities summary, 2000–2001

Subject	Decisions/directions	Draft directions, statements, determinations, consultations, notices, guidance, etc.	Research, notes, reviews	Investigations
Broadcasting				
The bundling of telephony and television	–	–	–	1
Other (mainly Satellite/Digital TV)	1	5	1	–
Total	1	5	1	1
Carrier Pre-Selection				
Costs and charges for carrier pre-selection	–	4	–	–
Carrier pre-selection consumer guide	–	–	1	–
Other	–	7	1	–
Total	0	11	2	0
Customer Services (fixed/mobile telecom.)				
Telecom. metering systems & billing systems	–	1	1	–
Special tariffs for eligible public institutions	–	2	–	–
Telecom, universal service	–	2	–	–
Other	–	15	1	–
Total	0	20	2	0

149

Table 5.1   continued

Subject	Decisions/directions	Draft directions, statements, determinations, consultations, notices, guidance, etc.	Research, notes, reviews	Investigations
Internet Access (mainly dial-up Internet)				
Competition review of Internet connectivity	–	2	–	–
BT Surf Together pricing packages	–	–	–	1
Future interconnection arrangements in the UK	–	2	–	–
Dispute between BT and MCI Worldcom	–	3	–	–
Other	–	4	–	1
Total	0	11	0	2
Licensing & Enforcement Actions	1	24	0	0
Market Info				
Mobile market update	–	–	3	–
Fixed market update	–	–	4	–
Total	0	0	7	0
Mobile				
Orange/BT interconnection disputes	1	1	–	–
Determinations that Vodafone and BTCellnet have market influence under Condition 56 of their licences	–	6	–	–
Determinations of final/interim charges for the				

provision of indirect access services by BTCellnet to INMS (Intelligent Network Management Services)	—	—	5	—
Reviews on price control on calls to mobiles	—	2	—	—
Effective competition review: mobile	—	2	—	—
The profitability and efficiency of the UK network operators	—	1	—	—
3G mobile infrastructure sharing in the UK	—	—	1	—
Oftel's statement on BT's 100% ownership of BTCellnet	—	—	1	—
Other	1	—	7	—
Total	1	5	21	0
Pricing & Price Control				
Dispute between BT and other operators	2	—	2	—
A price index for mobile telephony	—	2	—	—
Other	—	—	17	1
Total	2	2	19	1
Local Loop Unbundling/High speed services				
International benchmarking of DSL&Cable modem	—	1	—	—
Co-location	—	—	4	—
Bow wave process	—	—	5	—
Charges for the provision of metallic path facilities	—	—	2	—
Access to bandwidth	—	—	6	—
Access to network facilities	—	—	2	—
Other	—	3	10	—
Total	0	4	29	0

Table 5.1 *continued*

Subject	Decisions/directions	Draft directions, statements, determinations, consultations, notices, guidance, etc.	Research, notes, reviews	Investigations
Numbering	0	16	0	0
Research & Initiatives				
Fixed	–	–	3	–
Mobile	–	–	6	–
Internet	–	–	2	–
Fixed & Mobile & Internet	–	–	6	–
Mobile & Internet	–	–	1	–
Digital TV	–	–	2	–
DSL Modems	–	–	1	–
Other	–	–	9	–
Total	0	0	30	0
Competition Bulletin (fixed/mobile)				
New cases	–	–	–	7
Completed cases	–	–	–	105
Total	0	0	0	112

Source: Oftel Annual Reports.

152

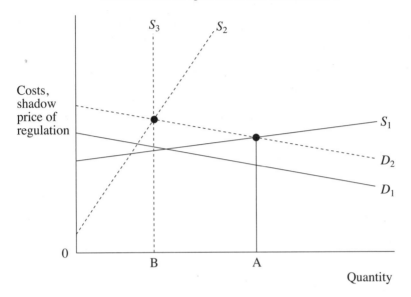

Figure 5.1   Supply of and demand for regulation

POLICY APPEALS AND OFCOM

Oftel is a model of openness. Formal accountability consists of the statutory requirements of an Annual Report, appearances before the Public Accounts Committee and Select Committees, public consultation procedures and six statutory Advisory Committees on Telecoms. Beyond these compulsory actions, Oftel has engaged the public through its website, surveys and research and through Advisory Bodies–Consumer Panel, Technical Expert Advisers' Panel, Panel of Economic and Financial Experts, Panels of Users. Oftel travels around the UK on important consultations and produces consumer guides.

In terms of outside controls, the Telecoms Act allows the Secretary of State to give the Director General general directions on the order of priorities.

A key constraint on a regulatory agency taking incorrect decisions is the appeal process. Appeals to Oftel decision are limited to two types. One is judicial review, which is limited to procedural unfairness. The second appeal is to the MMC, or now the Competition Commission, on the facts – the exercise of Oftel's statutory powers in a particular decision. These appeal procedures are far too limited; witness the lack of appeals.

Given the trends in regulation due to its misaligned incentives, that is, increased numbers of fish swimming, it is imperative to change incentives. It is necessary to add to my two suggestions so far – the proposed regulators' cap and broader views of competition, a third element – a process of limiting day-to-day authority. The only sustainable process of such limits on day-to-day activity is to provide a mechanism for those regulated to have reviews on the merits of a case. It is simply too easy for Oftel to convince itself that there is collective dominance in some sector, or that price needs to be controlled in another sector. The best constraint on such regulatory scope is to allow those regulated to appeal on the merits of the decision. This is the means of limiting as well as altering the incentives to impose regulation. Ofcom will be more powerful than Oftel. Its objectives are perhaps even vaguer, as it encompasses different sectors, broadcasting and communications. Hence there is a real potential for an even more elastic supply of regulation, and an even greater need for full appeals to Ofcom's decisions. A full appeal process will cause the regulator to reconsider the scope of its regulation.

Broadband

As of July 2001, broadband had rolled out to 232 000 subscribers in the UK, 170 000 using DSL (digital subscriber lines) and 52 000 using cable modems. I define broadband as infrastructure which allows 200 kilobits per second (kps) in at least one direction. Making the unrealistic assumption that these are all household users, then 0.9 per cent of UK households are on broadband. But only 38 per cent of UK households use the Internet, so a more valid figure is that 3 per cent of UK Internet households have broadband connections. Is this good or bad? And whatever the answer, is regulation to blame?

First, what is the experience in other countries? Sweden, Denmark, Singapore and the USA all have Internet penetration rates 50 per cent above that of the UK; that is, more than 50 per cent of households are on the Internet. Korea leads the world broadband race, with 58 per cent of households using it. Within Europe, Sweden at 13.8 per cent, Denmark at 13.2 per cent, Germany 7.8 per cent, even France at 6.4 per cent all exceed the UK's broadband household penetration. If we include ISDN lines (not broadband as it is 128 kps), then Norway has 60 per cent of the population using broadband (above 128 kps), Germany 45 per cent, Denmark 28 per cent, Italy 5 per cent, the UK 3.5 per cent. Clearly this is not a figure that meets the government's 'Broadband Britain' objective.

Why the UK's poor performance? There are several answers, but the full story is unclear. First, remember that broadband is new, ADSL (asynchronous digital subscriber line) modems only proved reliable and were standardized in 1996 and their price then was at least five times today's price. Second, in Sweden, Denmark and Norway, cable modems are important, at least as important in the market as ADSL. In the USA, which has 11 per cent of households on broadband, cable beats ADSL 2 to 1. Moreover, cable networks in the UK are new, post 1991, not needing system retrofitting to allow cable broadband modems. In the USA huge investments have been made in cable system upgrades not needed here. Why the cable delay? This delay is important in explaining the lag in ADSL, since telecom operators do not have great incentives to roll out ASL. Infrastructure competition between cable and telecom incumbents is key here and is surprisingly lacking in the UK.

A third culprit is the regulatory environment. Until the EU mandated local loop unbundling in 1999, the UK government and Oftel were opposed to service competition, that is, allowing entrants to roam on BT's infrastructure. One of Donald Cruikshank's last acts was to travel to Strasbourg to lobby the EU Parliament against mandated unbundling. Other pieces of regulation are important. First, Oftel alone among European regulators acted so as to prevent the UK incumbent telco – BT – from becoming the dominant Internet Service Provider (ISP). Only the UK mandated sharing local call charges with ISPs. Hence Virgilio (Italy), Terra (Spain), Wanadoo (France) are all large players in their country's ISP market. Name BT's ISP. Oftel also forced BT to offer a flat-rate Internet wholesale offering, not a regulatory policy in most other European countries. This may account for the UK's high share of Internet households. BT suggests these policies hampers broadband roll-out. The reverse may be true in the longer term: the greater the number of households already on the Internet, the faster should be broadband roll-out.

Certainly other regulatory policies, such as investigating whether ADSL wholesale prices are too low, are perverse. However, it's unclear whether forced unbundling is a major deterrent. It may be, or may not be; the evidence is unclear.[10]

I don't think service competition, that is, using incumbents' local loops to install ADSL modems – DLECs (data local exchange competitors) – is a viable business. Certainly, the collapse of the US DLECs, Covad, Rythms and others, is testimony to this proposition. Many US researchers believe, and I concur, that providing unbundled elements at forward-looking LRIC provides nothing but free options – subsidies to entrants.[11] In the USA, these entrants used these subsidies to fuel huge marketing spend in order to sign up customers. These customers proved elusive, and the customers who did sign up self-selected to be reluctant payers.

Germany is an interesting example of how regulation affects incentives. Germany has had local loop unbundling since 1997. Also ISDN is used by one third of residential Internet-using households. However, Deutsche Telekom AG (DTAG) upgraded its system so that almost all lines could use ISDN (integrated services digital network) well before regulation began. And DTAG has been very aggressive in marketing ISDN. The reason for this roll-out appears to be the inability of DTAG to raise analogue phone rates to costs and thus a strategic migration to ISDN is a revenue-enhancing strategy. Allowing rate rebalancing in Germany as in the UK might have deterred this ISDN roll-out in Germany! Regulation can indeed be perverse.

DTAG has rolled out 1.3 million ADSL lines some eight to ten times the UK experience. Only 30 000 unbundled lines are used by competitors to roll out competitive ADSL.[12] The ADSL prices in Germany are below those of the UK. Complaints were made to the Regulierungsbehörde für Telekommunikation und Post (RegTP) that wholesale and retail prices were predatory. (A good example of abuse of the regulatory process by competitors; they never argue retail prices are too high.) The RegTP decided that predation was not occurring and that low prices are part of a market penetration strategy. DTAG also uses (abuses) the regulatory process by appealing to stall the introduction of line sharing. Understanding broadband roll-out in any country needs detailed analysis.

Returning to the UK and to incentives, what are the strategic considerations guiding a duopoly (BT, cable companies) considering whether to invest in new technology? The economics literature shows that if costs are similar, we could have a stand-off – a kind of '*après-vous*' competition, with no one moving to invest. How does present regulation alter these incentives? I think it makes them worse.[13] Forcing unbundling on only one of the two potential players creates disincentives for both. Why should BT roll out its own package of ADSL, thus showing competitors that there is a market? How can cable compete when unbundled telecom network elements place a price ceiling on the price the cable companies can achieve? Hence asymmetric regulation is not an answer. Nor would regulating cable, say through open-access regimes, be of use.

Still, broadband roll-out is low, probably fuelled by incentives within BT not to cannibalize its more lucrative private circuit revenues. Since Deutsche Telecom had already eaten some of these profits with low ISDN prices, it has more incentive to roll out broadband.

What can the regulator/government do about 'slow' broadband roll-out? The economics literature on these duopoly investment games suggests some answers. One way of breaking the '*après-vous*' mentality is to announce a prize of say £50 000 000 for the first to wire up 5 per cent of households. A second answer is to provide tax incentives, say 100 per cent depreciation for ADSL modems to all competitors. A third strategy, if one concludes that indeed internal strategic considerations are holding back investment, is to tax the operators for any delay. For example, announcing a tax of £20 000 000 for every percentage point below the EU average roll-out, beginning in 2005, could provide incentives to firms to reconsider roll-out strategies.

These are three fanciful recommendations, all over-regulatory. The best strategy is to wait and see, since broadband is so new and since the economic/business case for large-scale take-up by users is still unclear.

Mobile

Many observers see continued regulation of mobile markets as unnecessary. How do incentives work in mobile markets and how does regulation interact with these incentives? Vodafone is the clear market leader, according to the recent NERA report,[14] the most efficient, and the most profitable. BT follows close behind, in terms of efficiency and profitability, while Orange and One2One are not yet cash flow positive.

Recently, Oftel referred the issue of continued regulation of mobile termination rates (the prices charged by a mobile operator to call this mobile customer) to the Competition Commission. Termination rates for BT and Vodafone had been in place since 1998 at RPI −9 per cent. Oftel had proposed continuing such regulation for four years past the due expiry date in 2002, extending capping termination rates to One2One (T-Mobile) and Orange and setting the cap at RPI −12 per cent.

The day this regulation was announced, Oftel was pleased that it could announce that it had saved consumers £800 million over the next four years. Well, has it done so? And is it the role of the regulator to extract rent? Labelling profits as 'excessive' in the aftermath of extracting £20 billion for 3G licences, and with the fallout of the entire sector, is odd public policy. Actually, Vodafone should be the least worried – after all, rent extraction negatively affects its competitors more since they have weaker financials. Society should trade off against the £800 million given to consumers the £800 million loss in producers' surplus (if we count only UK shareholders this figure falls appreciably). To the negative side of the ledger we have to add any increased power to Vodafone, decreased investments by all players and any loss in wages if these reduced 'rents' to the four lead to layoffs. Now it may be that total UK welfare does rise in the short run due to this action. However, much of the first-round impact is a transfer from shareholders to customers. If there are no dynamic or strategic consequences of the rent reduction, this is good for society. But this is a dynamic industry, and rent extraction will chill investment and innovation. The Haskins Task Force on Better Regulation agreed. Regulating termination rates is simply rent extraction. It is price controls, not a price cap.

3G Auctions

The messenger, the process – i.e. auctions of spectrum – is now being blamed for most of the ills of the telecom sector, if not the entire tech sector. It's not the messenger that is to blame. The companies would liked to have received again what they received with 2G licences – a free public resource (spectrum). Vodafone and BT are earning quasi-rents on resources on 2G spectrum they got for free. And they lobbied to get more free. Great incentives here. So the

UK and other smart European governments decided to charge for this valuable public resource.

Auctions in general, if well designed, have clear efficiency properties – they allocate scarce resources to those who value them the most. These are correct incentives. However, this does not mean that the actual auction design implemented produces correct incentives. The essential public question was – how many licences? Originally the rumour was that the Treasury wanted four licences so as to maximize revenue. Again the rumour was that Oftel intervened and forced a fifth licence for an entrant. If true, this was superb regulatory behaviour.

But why have the objective of maximizing revenue? The UK objective was clearly that – why else have asymmetric-sized licences for incumbents? It was immediately obvious that it was designed so that Vodafone and Cellnet would slug it out. But why? Designing an auction to place the spectrum in the best hands is different from maximizing revenue. In April 2000 the 3G technology was (and it still is) unproven and the exact spectrum required unknown.

Incentives are determined by institutional design. The UK 3G auction demonstrates this to a £20 billion T.

SUMMARY

Regulators can never mirror markets. It is a necessary transition from public/private monopoly to competition. No country has yet moved from entirely telecom-sector-specific regulation to competition policy. All analyses and reviews pay lip-service to the transition to competition policy. But we have implemented no procedures to take us on the road. In this chapter, I have recommended a set of actions to reduce both the demand for and supply of sector-specific telecoms regulation. There are ways to proceed, but what are the incentives to do so?

NOTES

1. Richard Gilbert and Carl Shapiro, 'Antitrust Issues in the Licensing of Intellectual Property', *Brookings Papers on Economic Activity, Microeconomics*, 1997.
2. Jean-Jacques Laffont and Jean Tirole, *A Theory of Incentives in Regulation and Procurement*, Cambridge MA: MIT Press, 1993.
3. See also Jean-Jacques Laffont and Jean Tirole, *Competition in* Telecommunications, Cambridge MA: MIT Press, 2000.
4. Laffont and Tirole, *A Theory of Incentives*.
5. See H. Roeller and L. Waverman, 'Telecommunications Infrastructure and Economic Growth', *AER*, September 2001.

6. Discrimination is one of those unfortunate economic terms like externalities. In economic theory, economic discrimination is in most cases socially desirable. In addition, dynamic markets are full of discrimination. We economists should have coined the phrase 'price distinction' instead of 'price discrimination', as distinction is good and discrimination bad.
7. See 'Competition in the provision of fixed telephony services', Oftel, 31 July 2001, pp. 16–20.
8. Ibid., p. 20.
9. Ibid., p. 21.
10. See B. Owen, 'Broadband Mysteries', AEI–Brookings Conference in Broadband, 4–5 October 2001.
11. See G. Hausman, 'Competition and Regulation for Internet-Related Services', AEI–Brookings Conference on Broadband, 4–5 October 2001.
12. Information from RegTP, 25 October 2001.
13. See M. Schankerman and L. Waverman, 'Asymmetric Regulation and Multimedia Markets', mimeo, LBS, 2001.
14. See OFTEL website: www.Oftel.gov.uk.

CHAIRMAN'S COMMENTS

David Edmonds

As expected, Leonard Waverman's chapter has covered a huge range of issues: it is provocative, challenging and I have considerable sympathy for much of what he says. I don't much like his new word: uncontractability. He applies it to the regulator and the fact that regulators change their minds. However, the best example I see of uncontractability is the total failure, particularly of the incumbent, ever to do what it says it will do over a reasonable period of time, making the job of the regulator even more difficult than it normally is.

I would like to make three or four points on the issues raised in the chapter, not necessarily in response to them but just by way of elucidation. The Treasury and Oftel worked closely together and in harmony on the 3G auction: the main role for Oftel was to persuade the government, and I was part of that, that having a fifth competitor in the auction wouldn't maximize proceeds but would actually produce benefits for the UK consumer, because we would have five competitors in the marketplace searching for custom rather than four. There was huge pressure on me from BT, Vodafone, Cellnet and Orange, amounting to: 'let's have four operators; leave it to us; we can do the job; you can trust us; we have done all right so far; let's not have a fifth player'. Fortunately, Peter Mandelson and then Stephen Byers accepted advice from Oftel which was strongly supported by the Treasury that there should be a fifth player.

A further point I would make is that anyone who quotes the Haskins Task Force Report in favour of his argument is on pretty weak ground. Those who have read the report will know that in relation to telecoms regulation, the analysis is often superficial, and the facts used to sustain its arguments are debatable. Some of the conclusions do not seem to have been logically thought out.

Waverman recognizes that the regulator's job is to regulate, but he stresses the dangers of regulatory creep. However, I see my job and the job of Oftel as, quite simply, to protect the interests of the consumer in the UK by promoting competition. He said that perhaps our analysis of competition was too narrow; if that is the case it is interesting that the whole of the European Union has endorsed a move towards a regulatory system based largely on the system we have here: that regulatory system is now being introduced across Europe, has gone through the European Parliament and has been endorsed by the democratic bodies in all EU countries. I suspect that the independence of the regulatory regime, which is at the heart of the new directives coming from Brussels, can only be sustained if parliaments continue, both at the European level and at the state level, to give regulators the kind of powers that Waverman is suggesting. This brings me to my next point. We do deal with a great many complaints by competitors to the incumbent about its behaviour, and these complaints have been increasing over the last few years, notwithstanding the use of competition law and sectoral powers. A particular example was the recent issue over partial private circuits (leased lines), where BT's competitors signed a contract with BT and the next day decided it wasn't a contract they liked in certain respects and so used the law, perfectly properly, to come back to Oftel and ask us to look at the bits they didn't like.

There are areas of increasing complexity flowing from sectoral regulation and competition law that have led to the series of directions, orders and instruments that Waverman quoted. I think it is misguided for anyone to believe that moving from sectoral regulation to regulation under the Competition Act will make either the life of the regulator or the life of the companies any easier. All my experience so far is that applying the Competition Act, albeit it according to the Competition Act guidelines which have been rigorously agreed between Oftel and OFT, makes for more complex inquiries; I am sure that moving towards greater use of the Competition Act is by no means the panacea for the problems set out in the chapter.

Finally a word or two in defence of what regulators do and then a word about Ofcom. I would agree that constraining the growth of regulatory departments in companies is one of the best things that could happen in terms of easing the load that regulation brings about. This is because, as is implied in the chapter, although to some extent I dissent from it, regulators do suffer from creep. But so too do regulatory departments in companies with their willingness to support their own existence by an ever-increasing series of complaints. This is to be abhorred, although what the solution is I am not sure.

In conclusion, I am a strong and committed proponent of Ofcom. If you look at the report that Towers Perrin, the consultants advising on the Ofcom structure, recently produced, you will see an Ofcom that is designed to carry out sectoral regulation for as long as sectoral regulation is in force and designed also to be a competition authority. It is not possible to decide in advance when to use competition legislation as opposed to sectoral powers. Deciding that out of context will subject the regulator to increasing pressure from challenges by the courts.

There is much food for thought in this chapter. I have a great deal of sympathy for many of the points made and I suspect that Ofcom will prove to be an organization that will adopt some of the principles put forward. However, it will have to embed itself firmly in the principles that we have developed in Oftel over the last 17 years. These principles I consider to have served the British consumer well over that period.

6. An end to economic regulation?

Robert W. Crandall

The end of the Cold War and the collapse of Communism in the 1990s have been attributed in part to the triumph of markets over government control of resources. Despite the Central Intelligence Agency's best efforts to overstate the national output of the Soviet Union, by the 1980s it had become evident to everyone – particularly to its own citizens – that the Soviet system could no longer continue to support an army and provide ordinary citizens a modern standard of living. This remarkable 'end of history'[1] came only about a decade after the beginning of the wave of deregulation that first gripped the USA, but then spread to the UK and – to a lesser extent – to the European continent. This suggests that, even in the West, the importance of markets was not fully appreciated until very recently.[2]

Despite its enormous success, the deregulatory movement may be stalled and even subject to reversal in the wake of the spectacular failure of California electricity 'deregulation', doubts about the UK's electricity and rail privatization/deregulation policies, and the spectacular collapse of the Enron Corporation.

In this chapter, I examine the case for eliminating the remaining pockets of regulation in the USA, but in doing so I look beyond the policies that we usually categorize as 'regulation'. There simply is not much left of traditional economic regulation except for telecommunications and electricity, and complete deregulation in either of these two sectors would be impossible in the current political environment. On the other hand, a wider assault against the myriad forms of inefficient government intervention in markets that continue in the USA, as in most developed economies, might prove more successful in mustering longer-term political support than would debates that focused solely on telecom or electricity. Trade protection, agricultural price supports, non-price allocation of water, regulation of airport landing rights, and government allocation of the electromagnetic spectrum could be targeted at the same time to build this broader reform coalition.[3]

1. WHERE HAS ALL THE REGULATION GONE?

Economists generally distinguish between 'economic' and 'social' regulation. The former is the control of prices, service quality and entry conditions in specific sectors, such as transportation, communications and energy. The latter is the regulation of risks to health, safety and the environment. This chapter deals primarily with economic regulation. I do not propose an end to health, safety and environmental regulation even though substantial rollbacks or reform would surely be justified even in these areas of public policy.

1.1   Traditional Economic Regulation

The deregulation movement of the 1980s and 1990s had a remarkable impact on the USA and many other countries. In the USA, which I know best, the entire national transportation sector was essentially deregulated,[4] the energy, financial and video distribution sectors were largely deregulated,[5] and even telecommunications saw a modicum of deregulation and substantial regulatory 'reform'. In some local jurisdictions, even taxi services were deregulated.

A list of the regulated and deregulated sectors of the US economy is shown in Table 6.1. I exclude some sectors that are regulated by local and state authorities, such as taxicab and limousine services. I also rather arbitrarily assume that

Table 6.1   The scope of economic regulation in the USA, 1975 and 2001

Sector or industry	Regulated in 1975	Regulated in 2001	Share of 1999 GDP regulated in 1975	Share of 1999 GDP regulated in 2001
Oil and gas extraction	Yes	No	0.0089	0
Railroads	Yes	No*	0.0025	0
Trucking	Yes	No	0.0125	0
Air transport	Yes	No	0.0102	0
Pipelines	Yes	Yes	0.0007	0.0007
Electricity	Yes	Yes	0.0119	0.0119
Telecommunications	Yes	Partially	0.0210	0.0105**
Radio and television	Yes	Partially	0.0070	0.0035**
Financial depository institutions	Yes	No***	0.0328	0
Insurance	Yes	Yes	0.0077	0.0077
Total			**0.1152**	**0.0343**

Notes:
*   Still some, largely irrelevant rate regulation.
**   Assumes half of industry output is deregulated.
***   Interest rates and entry are no longer regulated; solvency regulation remains.

Source: For share of GDP: US Department of Commerce, Bureau of Economic Analysis.

half of the communications sector's value added has been deregulated – long-distance services, telephone terminal equipment, and cable television – because local telecommunications and broadcasting are still heavily regulated. This tabulation suggests that the amount of regulation has fallen by roughly 70 percent.

1.2   Other Sectors

Before concluding from the above discussion that government intervention in the operation of markets has withered away in the USA, one should recognize that many other forms of economic 'regulation' of markets continue to survive despite the deregulatory political trend. I will exclude labor-market regulation though perhaps this reflects an American perspective. On the European continent, labor-market regulation may well be the most costly form of economic regulation.

The sectors of the US economy that are subject to some form of government control of prices and output are in fact quite numerous. Although we rarely consider such government intervention as economic 'regulation', these interventions generally involve direct or indirect control of prices or output. The obvious examples in the United States are:

- Housing – rent control
- Housing finance – government guarantees (subsidies) to home mortgage financing (FNMA, FHA, Freddie Mac)
- Agriculture – price supports; marketing agreements
- Trade protection – regulation of minimum import prices under 'constructed value' provision of 1974 Trade Act (applying mainly to metals and chemicals)
- Water supply – government prohibition on the use of market prices to ration water among competing uses
- Airport access – regulation of landing rights without regard to cost
- Health care – regulation of hospital rates and physician fees through public insurance programs that affect rates for services not insured by government
- Electromagnetic spectrum – government control of a large share of this valuable resource and non-price allocation of much of the rest of it.

This is a partial list – but a large and important one nonetheless – of government policies that we do not typically categorize as economic regulation even though the deregulatory movement has led to a modest amount of progress in reining in some of these programs in the USA. Unfortunately, much remains to be done in freeing water, spectrum and land from inefficient government controls. I return to the likely benefits from doing so later in the chapter.

2. WHY REGULATION? THE MODERN THEORY OF REGULATION

The University of Chicago is largely responsible for the modern theory of economic regulation. Stigler (1971), Posner (1971, 1974) and Peltzman (1976) provided a political-economy perspective on the demand for and supply of regulation. Politicians respond favorably to the demand for regulation by various interest groups – not only producers – as long as regulation's effect on the politicians' probability of being elected is not more than offset by the loss of votes from those who lose from the regulatory game.

Later, Becker (1983) provided a theoretical addendum that explained that there are stringent limits to the deadweight losses from regulation: such losses attenuate the political winners' gains or exacerbate the losers' losses or both. The winners and their agents, the regulators, do not wish to see their gains dissipated in foolishly inefficient regulatory policies. However, relatively efficient regulatory interventions can become exceedingly inefficient over time due to technological or other market changes, and such policies may be difficult to adjust because of political inertia. The allocation of valuable electromagnetic spectrum to broadcasting is an outstanding example. At first, too little spectrum was devoted to broadcasting. Today, very little should be allocated to this use.

In a later article Winston and Crandall (1994) provided an empirical analysis of the political response of voters to regulatory policies in the USA in the spirit of Peltzman (1992). Looking at presidential elections only, we found that an increase in *economic* regulation in 1952–92 generally inured to the disadvantage of the incumbent party or candidate, *ceteris paribus*, but that an increase in health, safety and environmental regulation had the opposite effect. This is consistent with the fact that the latter type of regulation increased during this period while the former became increasingly unpopular and declined.

The political sentiments were quite different in the 1900–48 US presidential elections. During this period, Winston and Crandall found that an increase in economic regulation had substantial and positive effects on the incumbent's probability of election, but an increase in health–safety–environmental regulation had negative effects. This was precisely the period in which economic regulation grew most rapidly in the United States. It was coincident with the movement to enact a highly progressive tax system, institute a large tax-supported retirement system, and institute massive agricultural and industrial price supports.[6] The driving force behind most of these policies was the redistribution of income, not economic efficiency.

The deregulatory movement in the United States began in the 1970s and continued through the 1990s, yielding partial electricity deregulation in many states, the opening of all telecommunications markets to competition,[7] and even proposals to privatize the nation's air-traffic control system. Whether this continues in the face of the prospective economic downturn, the California electricity fiasco, and the Enron débâcle remains to be seen.

3.   THE BENEFITS OF DEREGULATION – WHY MARKETS?

I turn now to the bright side – to the sectors of the US economy in which deregulation has occurred. How much do we know about the effects of this deregulation? My colleague, Clifford Winston, shows that our knowledge is far from perfect, but that deregulation generally improved economic welfare by much more than economists would have predicted *ex ante*.[8] The reason: economists had imperfect knowledge of how unregulated markets would operate, given decades of the distortions caused by government regulation. Furthermore, Winston argues that the movement to a new unregulated equilibrium can take years or even decades. For example, the US airline industry is still adjusting to an environment of unregulated competition 23 years after the passage of the Airline Deregulation Act.

The gains from deregulation have been impressive in the USA. In virtually every deregulated industry, there are substantial gains in both allocative and productive efficiency. The firms supplying the service – entrants and incumbents alike – produce this service at costs that are an average of 30 percent below the costs that would have been incurred under the previous regulatory regime.[9] But the relative prices also change because firms are no longer restrained by regulators from moving prices toward costs, and service quality improves. Finally, although earlier versions of the 'capture theory' of regulation might have predicted that deregulation would redistribute income from producers (and their employees and equity holders) to consumers, there is no general pattern of such redistribution. Some incumbents thrive, others fail, and new entrants emerge, but there is no *general* pattern of a decline in producer rents. A summary of the estimated effects of deregulation, drawn from Winston (1993, 1998) and Crandall and Ellig (1997) is shown in Table 6.2.

In his survey, Winston (1993) shows that economists generally were unable to predict the magnitude of the gains from deregulation. Morrison and Winston (1995) and Winston et al. (1990) find that deregulation led to savings in airline, trucking and railroad transportation costs to consumers of about $35 billion per year (1995$), and that these gains came almost entirely from improvements in efficiency rather than transfers from producers.[10] Similarly, the reductions in long-distance telephone rates derived from improvements in productive efficiency and from the Federal Communications Commission's (FCC) more efficient pricing of interstate carrier access, not simply from reduced producer profits in supplying the service.

Table 6.2   The effects of deregulation in the USA

Sector	Nature of deregulation	Consumer benefits
Airlines	Total	33% reduction in real fares
Trucking	Total	35 to 75% reduction in real rates
Railroads	Partial; rate ceilings and floors on 'monopoly' routes	More than 50% decline in real rates
Natural gas	Partial; distribution still regulated	30% decline in consumer prices
Telecommunications	Partial; local rates and interstate access still regulated	More than 50% decline in long-distance rates
Banking	Consumer rates deregulated; entry liberalized	Increase in rates on consumer deposits; improved productivity

Sources: Winston (1993, 1998); Crandall and Ellig (1997).

A recent study of natural-gas regulation by MacAvoy (2000) concludes that the USA's inadvertent foray into controlling the field price of natural gas in the 1960s resulted in huge losses in economic welfare. Between 1968 and 1977, regulators kept natural gas prices artificially low and thereby transferred $38.7 billion from producers to consumers. However, this regulation created shortages in natural gas that subsequently cost consumers and producers $58.7 billion (1982$). Subsequently, natural-gas deregulation was phased in over the 1978–84 period, and prices were kept artificially high during most of this time. As a result, ultimately there was a 'sell-off' of gas at artificially low prices that cost producers $45 billion (1982$) more than the gains to consumers. Thus, 17 years of regulating a competitive natural-gas extraction industry cost the USA more than $9.5 billion per year in 1995 dollars.

4.   WHAT WOULD COMPLETE DEREGULATION MEAN?

The successes of the deregulatory policies launched over the past quarter century should lead us to ask, 'Why not more deregulation?' Indeed, more than 30 years ago, Harold Demsetz (1968) asked an even more fundamental question, 'Why regulate utilities?' His question implicitly assumed that economic regulation was a response to the market failure of natural monopoly. His solution was to have the government auction off the right to dispense the natural monopoly service rather than to install government regulation. Competition for the monopoly privilege would replace ongoing government regulation.

At the time Demsetz wrote, however, the federal and state governments regulated financial services, trucking, airlines, radio and television broadcasting, consumer telephone equipment, air cargo, crude oil (through import quotas), natural-gas extraction, and long-distance telecommunications. All of these industries would have been highly competitive but for the heavy hand of government, as subsequent experience has shown. Demsetz's question is much more relevant today because the residue of formal economic regulation is largely in industries widely believed to be natural monopolies.

But how 'natural' are these monopolies? If we had no government control of entry and prices, would natural-gas and electricity distribution or local telecommunications be natural monopolies? And even if they were, would the loss in economic welfare be very great relative to the losses due to regulation? Sadly, we cannot answer such questions definitively because there have been no experiments in total deregulation of these sectors.[11] Nor are there even empirical 'guesstimates' from economic studies of such potential welfare losses.

There is reason to believe, however, that the 'natural' monopoly problem is neither severe nor extensive. Such economies derive either from economies of scale, large initial sunk costs, or economies of density. For the most part, these economies are in the distribution of energy, water, or communications services, not in production. Even in these distribution functions, it is not obvious that there are large *scale* economies. For instance, Shin and Ying (1992) find that scale economies are not important in the provision of local wireline telecommunications services. The natural monopoly problem in most such industries derives instead from economies of density or fill. It is widely believed that replication of the fixed assets required to compete with existing regulated distribution monopolies is simply too costly to assure that entry or the threat of entry can discipline incumbent behavior. But this belief has rarely been tested in many sectors, because of either government ownership or regulation. Given the rapid rate of technical change in many of these sectors, such as telecommunications, such a test may yield surprising results.

The natural monopoly problem, however small, is undoubtedly becoming even less severe due to improvements in information, increased consumer mobility and rapid technical change. Simply put, few of us are as hostage to any monopolist as we might have been a century ago. If local telephone rates rise, we can switch to a cellular service, a fixed wireless service, or – in some situations – cable telephony. If electricity rates rise or the utility service becomes unreliable, we can switch to our own generators or even begin to form a small collective to operate a small gas turbine. Certainly, large electricity customers have such self-generation opportunities. Were price discrimination impossible, these customers might be able to defeat a price increase, thereby eliminating the need for regulation. If my natural-gas utility exerts market power, I can switch to locally delivered propane or heating oil or even to electric heating. A water utility's market power is obviously constrained by its customers' ability to engage in self-supply, principally through drilling their own wells or purchasing water from other sources.

The degree of service substitution available to defeat attempted exertion of monopoly power by erstwhile regulated monopolists has clearly been increasing over time. For instance, US railroads may have had monopoly power on some routes 114 years ago when they were brought under regulation. However, they have been noticeably unable to exert it in the past 20 years under deregulation.[12] Trucks and airplanes have been added to waterways as significant competitors to the railroads. Regulation is therefore no longer necessary in transportation – if it ever was.[13]

4.1 Deregulation of the Cable Television Monopoly in the USA

It is instructive to begin with one example of recent deregulation in an ostensibly 'natural' monopoly industry – cable television in the USA. Because of a protectionist spectrum allocation policy, competition in the distribution of video programming was limited to three or four national broadcast services before the development of coaxial-cable distribution. Cable systems developed in the 1950s in local markets whose topography created reception problems. These cable systems quickly discovered that they could offer more than the local signals, but they were soon blocked in attempts to pull in distant signals by the FCC, which acted to protect the local broadcasting monopolies. Eventually, these restrictions were removed, and in the 1980s cable systems expanded their channel capacity and grew rapidly. By the early 1990s, cable provided dozens of channels to 60 percent of the country's households.

Having displaced one 'unnatural' monopoly – off-air broadcasting, cable soon came under attack as the newest communications monopoly. Most cable systems had been granted monopoly franchises by local governments, and their rates were at least informally regulated by these municipal or state authorities. Although such exclusive franchises were barred in 1984 by a federal law that also deregulated cable rates, very few markets experienced competitive entry – 'overbuilding' by new cable companies. In this deregulated environment, cable companies raised rates sharply after 1984, but they also greatly expanded service now that they were free from FCC restrictions on signal carriage.[14]

The sharp increase in rates led to a popular demand to regulate this apparent monopoly, and Congress obliged in 1992, voting to override the President's veto. Rate regulation was placed in the hands of the FCC, and the result was disastrous. With no cost basis for setting permissible rates, the Commission used regression analysis to measure the extent to which competition would have reduced rates – defining 'competition' as the existence of a second cable system in a market, the provision of the only service by a municipal authority, or the subscription to cable by fewer than 35 percent of households. Rates were rolled back to this estimated level for a few years, and cable companies responded by reducing the rate at which they expanded the quality of their service – that is, by reducing the expansion of channel capacity.

The overall loss of consumer surplus due to this reduction in service quality was about $5 billion per year.[15] Regulating a 'natural' monopoly succeeded in reducing output by suppressing overall rates because regulators could not mandate service levels in an industry that delivers highly differentiated entertainment products. Fortunately, the FCC began to reverse course by simply ignoring rate increases, and later Congress ratified this decision by deregulating virtually all cable television rates in the 1996 Telecommunications Act. The result has been an increase in rates, but there has also been a resumption in the growth of service quality, spurred by the entry of high-powered satellite service, rate deregulation and the need to upgrade system capacity to offer (unregulated) cable modem service.

There is more to this story. The political movement to regulate cable television in 1992 derived from the popular view that cable television is a monopoly – even perhaps a natural monopoly – that shifted wealth from consumers to cable system owners.[16] But this monopoly status derived in no small part from regulation itself, namely, the restrictions placed on telephone-company 'video platforms' and the slowness of the FCC to license spectrum for high-power satellite broadcasting. These limitations on the telephone companies, in turn, derived from regulators' fear that these companies might leverage their local telephone monopoly positions into other markets, but these monopoly positions reflect decades of entry barriers and cross-subsidies erected by the regulators themselves.[17] Regulators not only blocked entry into the telephone sector by new wireline carriers, but they limited wireless competition by initially allocating only two 25 MHz blocks of spectrum to commercial wireless (cellular) uses while allowing hundreds of MHz to remain unused as UHF television spectrum, a policy dutifully followed by other countries in the ensuing years.

The moral to the cable television story in the USA is clear. There is no reason to believe that multi-channel video distribution is a 'natural' monopoly, nor even to believe that it ever was. Even if it is, however, we now have convincing evidence that regulating cable rates is a grievous error. It costs consumers more than it benefits them. Unregulated monopoly is better than regulated monopoly in this market with its highly differentiated products.

4.2   The Likely Effects of Further Deregulation in 'Monopoly' Industries

The most important of the sectors that continue under formal government economic regulation are telecommunications and electricity. How might total deregulation of each affect economic welfare?

4.2.1   Telecommunications

Although one cannot foresee how the telecommunications sector will evolve under continued regulation or deregulation because of the incredible rate of technical change that affects it, it is difficult to see how total deregulation could possibly reduce economic welfare. The principal remaining potential locus of monopoly power is in the provision of local access to residential and small-business subscribers. Even this market might be competitive if rates were set at levels that are close to long-run average incremental cost and if all regulatory barriers were eliminated.

In the USA, there are approximately 195 million switched-access lines, of which 150 million are residential or small-business lines. Most of the large-business lines are likely to be in dense business districts in which competition now thrives. Thus full deregulation of local access/exchange service would affect 150 million lines, 20 million of which are small-business lines. Two important factors limit the economic welfare loss from any attempt by dereg-ulated incumbents to raise rates. First, the demand for access is extraordinarily price-insensitive, meaning that rate increases would transfer income from consumers to producers but would have little effect on output and the allocation of resources.

Second, any attempt to raise local rates very much would induce substantial substitution of cellular, fixed wireless, cable telephone, or competitive local exchange carrier services. As an extreme assumption, assume that subscribers would not switch in large numbers to these alternatives until incumbents *trebled* local rates – from approximately $20 per month today for residences and perhaps $40 for small businesses to $60 and $120 per month, respectively. At these rates, subscribers could switch to national wireless plans that offer 1500 or more minutes per month without any further increase in telephone expendi-tures. If the price elasticity of demand for local service is –0.05, surely the upper end of recent estimates, a trebling of residential rates would result in a loss of just 7 million lines and $1.68 billion in annual deadweight economic loss. A trebling of small business rates would result in the loss of 1.1 million lines and a deadweight loss of $530 million per year, again assuming a price elasticity of demand of –0.05. Thus, even under these extreme assumptions, local telephone regulation creates only $2.2 billion in net annual economic welfare gains in the local market, *ceteris paribus*. Of course, under these assumptions regulation transfers substantial rents from producers to consumers – about $77 billion per year.

It is likely, however, that consumers would begin shifting to other forms of network access long before local residential rates reached $60 per month. Subscribers who use their phones very little and younger users are already substituting cellular service for wireline access. At a monthly rate of $40 to $60 per month, cellular subscribers may now purchase 'national' plans that provide free national calling to all 50 US states. Moreover, if local rates were to rise to $30 or $40 per month, cable television systems would surely accelerate their deployment of cable telephony and Internet telephony. Thus the above estimate of the potential welfare cost of local telephone deregulation is surely much too high. Nevertheless, even this estimate pales in comparison to recent estimates of the cost that continued regulation imposes on us.

Full deregulation would convey enormous offsetting benefits in two ways. First, regulators' inefficient pricing of local and long-distance services, defended as 'universal service' policy, would end. Deregulated firms would not pursue these reverse 'Ramsey' prices. The gains to the economy from just this change would be as much as $7 billion per year (Crandall and Waverman, 2000). Second, regulation inhibits entry and investment in new services. Hausman (1997) has estimated that regulatory delays in licensing cellular systems and in approving Bell-company offerings of voice messaging in the USA cost consumers as much as $51 billion per year for each year of regulatory delay. These estimates, even if high by a factor of ten, surely swamp any potential gains from continuing telecommunications regulation.[18]

4.2.2 Electricity

I am on less firm ground in providing a rough estimate of the cost or benefit to economic welfare from full electricity deregulation. Full deregulation without any attention to the structure of electricity distribution would surely be unwise. There is no evidence of which I am aware of the potential for competitive transmission grids or competitive local distribution networks. However, as I write this chapter, I look out on utility poles that now carry three communications lines past my home – two fiber-coaxial cable lines and one copper telephone wire. I cannot see the fourth network, but my cellular phone can! For some reason, only one set of electrical lines passes my home. It is not obvious to me that a second electrical line could not be strung over this pole line or through underground conduits.

Unfortunately, we have no experience with full deregulation in electricity. Competition exists in some jurisdictions in the supply (generation) of electrical energy, but the transmission grid generally remains a public or private monopoly or a set of interconnected public/private monopolies.

The facile answer to the monopoly distribution problem in electricity is long-term contracting, as Demsetz suggested nearly fifty years ago. But as Newbery (1999) points out, it is likely that an *existing* grid operator would obtain large monopoly rents in such a contracting process. Without a competitive alternative, there is no reason to expect the monopolist not to exploit its market power in the contracting process, and it is unlikely that anyone would build a parallel grid to wrest the contract from him in ten, twenty, or thirty years when the contract expires.

One of the lessons from 25 years of deregulation in other sectors, however, is that we cannot predict how a deregulated market will evolve from observations drawn solely from a politically controlled marketplace. In the case of electricity, some contend that deregulation would lead to a much more decentralized system of electricity supply and distribution. It may be that no one would respond to deregulation by building a second regional distribution network in the eastern USA to connect large numbers of generators to me and my neighbors. But 50 or 100 of my neighbors and I might invest in a small combined-cycle gas-fired turbine to provide our own electricity through wires strung in parallel with our current distributor if we could get access to the poles. Alternatively, we might confront our distributor with the threat to build our own small network if he does not enter into a long-term contract with us at competitive rates. In turn, the bargaining power of large numbers of such potential sub-networks might cause the grid operator to grant relatively competitive rates for transmitting power from large, distant generators.

I do not mean to suggest that operating an electricity network and pricing access is simple, nor that we understand how a more fragmented electricity market could work without some regulation. Indeed, California's recent experience with limited deregulation and the substitution of spot market transactions between generators and utilities for the formerly integrated structure shows how a simple error can translate into enormous transfers of wealth in an industry in which the short-term price elasticity of demand and supply are very low.

One might argue that California provides a good basis for estimating the 'cost' of deregulation in the short term under the most pessimistic assumptions. Could complete deregulation possibly be worse? In 2000–2001, California's failed approach to deregulation allowed generators to exploit the short-term scarcity of power created by natural forces, such as a shortfall in precipitation and a rise in fossil-fuel prices, because California forbade utilities to enter into long-term contracts. The result was an increase in the state's electricity bill of approximately $12 billion per year.[19] Since the total bill in 1999 had been about

$22 billion, the increase due to the failures of deregulation was about 55 percent. Assume that this is a worst case for the effects of full deregulation, that is, that rates would increase by 55 percent in the short run if regulators were simply to walk away. Moreover, assume that this increase would decline steadily over subsequent years as technologies, distribution networks and energy substitution would mitigate but not eliminate the monopoly problem. For the USA as a whole, the transfer from consumers to producers would be about $142 billion per year in the short run.

The net cost to the economy would be much less. With a short-term demand elasticity of –0.15,[20] the annual deadweight loss (additional loss in consumer welfare) would be only $5.5 billion in the short run. The deadweight loss might well *increase* even as prices fell because consumers might substitute socially more expensive electricity for the electricity available from incumbent suppliers at prices above marginal cost. Ultimately, the cost to the economy would depend on how much efficiency was sacrificed by moving away from regulation to new institutional arrangements.

Even this rather superficial projection of the potential adverse effects of full electricity deregulation serves to emphasize an important point: regulation is generally more effective as a device to transfer rents than one to increase economic efficiency. The deadweight loss of allowing electricity monopoly pricing is swamped by the transfer from consumers to producers. But even this deadweight loss might be overestimated if our experience with deregulation in other sectors is any guide. Regulation stunts incentives to invest and innovate. An unregulated market might result in substantial pockets of market power, but the unregulated firms might have much lower costs than the regulated firms. Indeed, one of the underlying goals of the California 'deregulation' of electricity was to allow utilities to shed billions of dollars of wasteful expenditures and unproductive assets accumulated during decades of regulation.

4.3 Summing Up

Although it is highly unlikely that we shall experience total telecommunications and electricity deregulation anytime soon, even a worst-case scenario would suggest that total deregulation in these two sectors would be beneficial. The gains from telecom deregulation would likely offset any prospective short-term losses from electricity deregulation even if competitive electricity transmission and distribution networks did not materialize. The worst-case scenario in electricity would, however, result in politically unacceptable transfers of wealth from consumers to producers, as the Governor of California recently discovered.

5. THE COST OF GOVERNMENT CONTROLS IN OTHER SECTORS

It is certainly possible that complete economic deregulation might lead to short-term losses in economic welfare in certain sectors, particularly in electricity. If complete deregulation were to be part of a constitutional compact that forbade government intervention in controlling prices and output in other sectors, however, the net gains could be enormous. In this section, I try to summarize the prospective gains that can be identified from the existing literature.

5.1 The Electromagnetic Spectrum

Only recently have governments begun to privatize the electromagnetic spectrum by auctioning rights to it for various commercial purposes. Unfortunately, only a very small share of commercially usable spectrum has been auctioned; the remainder is still allocated by governments without regard to its economic value in alternative uses. The potential gains from freeing the remaining spectrum from government management, particularly that set aside for defense and public safety, are extremely large. The recent prices paid for the rights to use the spectrum in the USA provide at least a starting-point for estimating this value.

In the most recent US auction for cellular spectrum, bidders paid an average of $4.18 per MHz per person in the population.[21] Given a population of 275 million, this translates into $1.15 billion per MHz. A single cellular band generally has 30 MHz; therefore, bidders were willing to pay $34.5 billion for a cellular band in the USA. Since these bids are generally for spectrum that is currently occupied by various other users, the winning bidder incurs the liability for moving these incumbents to other parts of the spectrum or simply compensating them for abandoning the spectrum. Thus the $34.5 billion value is a measure of the *net* value of this resource from improved allocation of it.

The amount of usable spectrum is enormous, but it is not all of equal value for all uses. Nor would the above estimate of the marginal value of just 30 MHz be invariant against the amount of spectrum allocated by auctions. If the US government were to auction immediately all spectrum that has not yet been sold by auction, the marginal value would presumably decline substantially. No one has an estimate of the demand for all such spectrum. However, assume that all of the US *commercial television* spectrum were to be auctioned tomorrow. There is about 400 MHz of such spectrum in very desirable bands. It is not unreasonable to assume that the $1.15 billion per MHz value realized at the last auction is the value of this spectrum also. This translates into about $460 billion in total value.

The abandonment of television broadcasting would leave some households with dark television sets. However, given that only 15 percent of US households now watch television off the air, it would not cost much to shift them to cable television or direct broadcast satellites. Assuming that the marginal cost of shifting these households would be $20 per month, the annual cost would be $240 per household, and the present value of these costs in perpetuity, evaluated at a 5 percent discount rate, would be $4800. With just 15 million households to move, the total cost would be $72 billion. Therefore, the net gain from moving a small part of the spectrum to a higher-valued use would be nearly $400 billion. It is obvious that a total shift to a market allocation of spectrum would be enormous.

5.2 Water

Water might be even more important than the electromagnetic spectrum. Most of us recall the early economists' discussions of the difference between marginal and total value! Unfortunately, despite the volumes that have been written on cost–benefit analysis of water-resource projects, such as dams, and many individual studies of the inefficiency of government allocation of water, I am unable to find a comprehensive estimate of the social cost of failing to use the price mechanism for this scarce resource. I can only assume that it is quite large and move on to other government failures.

5.3 Airport Landing Rights

Air space is an abundant resource whose scarcity is largely contrived by those who regulate it. In many countries, the air traffic control system has been privatized. In the USA, the Federal Aviation Administration (FAA) controls air traffic and government-owned airports impose weight-based landing fees. The combination of FAA and airport regulation of the use of the air-traffic infrastructure has created much more congestion than is necessary or optimal. Morrison and Winston (1989) estimate that a shift to congestion fees for air traffic, better pricing of aircraft landings, and improved investment decisions in building runways could lead to an annual increase in economic welfare of $11 billion (1988$). In current dollars, even with only the 1988 traffic, this estimate rises to more than $16 billion per year.

5.4 Rent Control

There is some new theoretical literature that suggests that the cost of limiting rents on residential properties has been overstated. Neverthless, it is well known that such controls have a deleterious effect on the supply of new housing although the magnitude of this effect is subject to some debate. In addition, Glaeser and Luttmer (1997) find that the cost of misallocation of the existing housing stock across consumers due to rent control is likely to be more than $500 million per year in New York City alone. Fortunately, most US cities have avoided the folly of rent control, but the cost in those where it exists is likely to be substantial. Unfortunately, there is no comprehensive study of rent control for the entire country.

5.5   Trade Protection

Despite a general movement toward free trade since World War II, many countries still resort to trade protection in response to special pleas from various industries or labor groups. In the USA, a protectionist trend began with the passage of the Trade Act of 1974, which allowed the use of 'constructed value' as a benchmark for evaluating allegations of dumping charges. In addition, the maritime, apparel and textile industries enjoy direct protection from a variety of direct and indirect quotas. The President of the USA has now very unwisely added steel to this list, attempting to protect many of the declining US integrated companies from extinction for one more election cycle.[22] Hufbauer and Elliott (1994) estimate that the cost to consumers of trade protection in 21 large US industries was $10.4 billion in 1990. The President's recent steel decision will increase these costs. Were the costs to be estimated across all industries, they would surely be much larger.

5.6   Agricultural Price Supports

The USA, as many other countries, has had some form of intervention in agricultural markets to increase farmer incomes for decades. These programs transfer roughly $20 billion per year from consumers to producers. In the 1980s, these programs cost the American economy about $5 billion per year in lost output because they used acreage controls and reduced output to generate the income redistribution.[23] Since 1996, however, these payments have come directly from the US Treasury. The net cost of the various agricultural programs has fallen to $0.8 billion per year, but – ominously – there is now political pressure to return to the older system in order to reduce the overt cost to US taxpayers, but such a change will sharply increase the real economic cost of the program.[24]

5.7   Adding Up the Costs

Although I cannot neatly total the cost of the US government's mismanagement of resources through these various programs, it is clear that the annual costs run into scores of billions of dollars.[25] Simply using the price mechanism to allocate the broadcast spectrum would be worth at least $10 to $15 billion per year, depending on one's estimate of the social cost of capital. Eliminating trade protection, government control of airport landing rights and agricultural price supports would generate another $26 billion in net economic benefits. Extending market mechanisms to the allocation of water and the rest of the electromagnetic spectrum would surely add substantially to these estimates of the gains from an expansive program of 'deregulation'.

6.   AVOIDING COSTLY NEW REGULATION

A policy of complete economic deregulation would not only rid us of some very costly and unfortunate current government interventions in markets, but it would protect us from new ones. We hardly need a course in current events to remind us of the dangers of government intervention during periods of instability. Recent events in the USA surely portend substantial instability and the prospect of political lurches into renewed regulation. Even more troubling is the view spreading across OECD governments that regulators can accelerate competition in sectors where they had been responsible for blocking it for decades!

6.1   Regulation in Response to International Disruptions

The recent terrorist events in the USA have opened the door for a vast new set of regulatory and other interventionist proposals. The Federal Aviation Administration – after years of mismanaging air traffic – was close to political extinction before 11 September. Now, it is likely to get vast new powers in the name of controlling airport and in-flight safety. New programmes to subsidize airlines, steel companies and agriculture appear daily.

One only has to recall the US response to the OPEC oil shock in 1973–74 to see how governments resort to new exercises in regulation in the name of protecting the public. The USA enacted a vast new program of oil and refined-product price controls during 1973–75, and established an 'entitlements' program that allowed refiners with no domestic oil to share in the regulated low-priced oil developed by the more far-sighted integrated producers. Because the entitlement was tied to the amount of imported oil used, this program increased the demand for OPEC oil, increasing the cartel equilibrium price and transferring even more of US resources to the Arab oil producers. This surely was a curious form of income redistribution for the US Congress to support.

6.2   Regulation and Economic Recessions

In the USA, some of our worst regulatory interventions began during difficult and unstable economic periods. Railroads were first regulated in the late 1880s after they had woefully over-invested in infrastructure and during a period of an unstable macro-economy. The regulation of trucking began in the depths of the 1930s Great Depression, when the railroads and truckers were under enormous financial pressures. The regulation of communications also began in the Depression, fed by erroneous concerns of 'chaos' in using the electro-magnetic spectrum without government controls. Airline regulation began in 1938 after allegedly 'ruinous' competition for postal air mail contracts in the Depression. Oil price controls and 'entitlements' – a government policy of increasing the transfer of income from the USA to OPEC – were established in 1974–75 after oil prices soared, inflation accelerated and the economy became quite unstable.

6.3   The New Threat – Regulation to Promote Competition

Each of the above examples of new regulatory regimes began, in part, because firms and their employees sought government assistance to ease market pressures that were exacerbated by a weak economy or international disruptions. However, such pleas are not confined to periods of instability. The recent spectre of firms appearing before the European Union's competition authority or the US Justice Department to inflict damage upon their rivals, such as occurred in the Boeing–McDonnell/Douglas or General Electric–Honeywell mergers or in repeated sorties against Microsoft, are but selected cases in point. At one time, these self-interested protestations from rival firms, rather than customers, would have been treated very skeptically by US antitrust authorities. In the last eight years, however, the competition authorities have been much more receptive to complaints from competitors.

This type of behavior is repeated every day before the various OECD countries' telecommunications regulatory commissions. Given the likely importance of telecommunications in the continued growth of developed economies, we should be extremely concerned about preventing further regulatory incursions in this sector. For more than a decade, telecom regulators had been moving in the right directions – substituting price caps for 'cost-based' regulation and exercising regulatory forbearance. As markets became contestable, regulation was substantially lightened or eliminated altogether. Now, just as new technologies are wreaking havoc with incumbents, regulators are leaping into the fray with new vigor, imposing wholesale regulation on incumbents and looking earnestly for other ways to restrain these old-line firms from engaging in aggressive price competition. The result is already becoming apparent in the USA.

In the 1996 Telecommunications Act, the US Congress devised a very complicated scheme of wholesale regulation for incumbents, described as 'interconnection policy' by the *cognoscenti*. This approach has been copied to some extent by many other OECD countries as the result of multilateral trade negotiations. Indeed, the USA has spent most of the last five years trying to force this type of regime on Japan and other countries.

The new regulatory regime has two related problems: an extensive 'unbundling' regime and a new policy to set rates on the basis of detailed cost estimates. As entry into telecommunications has become much easier because of technical change in wireless systems, satellite systems and fiber optics, regulators now worry that the cost of the 'last mile' may prove to be an insuperable entry barrier. Their response might have been manageable if it had been limited to apparently essential facilities and if it had been limited to, say, five or ten years.[26] Unfortunately, despite some dissenting views from the US Supreme Court, the Federal Communications Commission was successful in requiring the unbundling of virtually everything in the incumbents' networks. And if this were not enough to satisfy the new entrants, the FCC even imposed conditions on incumbent mergers that required these unbundled elements to be rebundled into a single 'platform' at low, wholesale rates.

Requiring that incumbents provide entrants access to their networks is of little consequence unless the regulators specify a price for such access. In a surge of theoretical elegance, the US regulator, the FCC, decided that it should attempt to replicate the operation of a frictionless, competitive market. It decided that the wholesale rates for network elements should be based on the reproduction cost of those assets, and it therefore established Total Element Long Run Incremental Cost (TELRIC) as its standard. Of course, it could not know what such costs are since it could not find cost data for a network that was built just yesterday. The result was a four-year effort to develop an engineering cost model of a local exchange network designed to deliver yesterday's services with today's technology from switching centers that were sited decades ago – all of this guided by thousands of interventions by interested parties. But why would anyone build a network to deliver the old mix of voice and data services over copper wires?

Even if it had been possible to divine the costs of building this essentially obsolete network at today's cost, there remained a fundamental problem. No one would build an expensive network with enormous sunk costs to lease to its rivals on a month-to-month basis at rates that are calculated to return the investment and the opportunity cost of capital over the full anticipated useful life of the assets. Leasing network facilities at these rates allows the lessee to obtain a 'free option' on the investment, delaying indefinitely the need to build its own plant.[27] For instance, why would anyone build a new steel mill at a cost of perhaps $10 billion if they could persuade the government to force someone else to build it for them and lease it to them on a month-to-month basis at, say, $100 million per month? The lessee could force the builder to assume the risk that steel mills will be redundant in three or five years – many of the newest ones already are.

This approach to regulating 'interconnection' so as to encourage entry is too new in most countries for one to assess whether it has worked. However, in the USA we have had seven years of entry and continuous regulatory skirmishing. The result has been less than satisfactory. Most of the new entrants who rushed in to offer telecom services are either failing or have failed. Those that have relied heavily on the wholesale services or facilities of the incumbents have been most likely to fail. At one time, the new entrants had a market capitalization that totaled nearly $100 billion, as investors subscribed them capital to exploit the FCC's regulatory largesse. When it became apparent that most of these new companies had little to offer their customers in terms of new or lower-cost services, their share prices began to fall. When the stock market declined severely in 2000, in no small part because investors began to realize that telecom firms had been overcapitalized, the rush for the exit accelerated. Today, these entrants' market value is less than $5 billion.

Were the telecom industry not regulated, so many new entrants might never have appeared, and the failure of those that did would be treated much like the passing of Olivetti typewriters, Douglas DC-7s, or Betamax VCRs. But in a regulated industry, the losers have a forum in which to petition for more assistance – the regulatory commission. In the USA, AT & T tried to enter the local telecom market in various ways, including by paying $110 billion for cable systems that are today worth perhaps $60 billion and by trying to resell incumbent services. Now, it is fighting a rear-guard action at regulatory commissions, asking that the incumbent local companies be structurally separated into wholesale and retail operations so that wholesale rates can be pushed even lower.

There are enormous risks to this new, cost-based telecommunications regulation. First, evidence is already accumulating that low wholesale rates have depressed investment in fixed assets, allowing entrants to invest mostly in marketing instead.[28] Second, there is at least anecdotal evidence that this regulation has reduced the incumbents' investment in new facilities to deliver broadband. Third, to the extent that many entrants use incumbents' facilities, leased at artificially low rates, those entrants who build their own facilities are less likely to thrive.

None of these results should be surprising. Trying to regulate a changing, rivalrous market creates enormous pressures to shield firms from market forces. In the 1930s, the regulators' clients were the incumbent transportation firms –

the railroads and the airlines. Today, they are the new entrants in telecom and the incumbents in the television broadcasting sector.

7.   CONCLUSION

The USA has reaped substantial economic benefits from the deregulation of transportation, energy, communications and financial markets over the past 25 years. Further deregulation, particularly in telecommunications, would likely add billions of dollars in annual net economic benefits to producers and consumers. Mustering the political support for such deregulation, however, will be difficult. If the net is cast more widely to include a variety of other forms of government intervention in markets – from trade protection to managing the electromagnetic spectrum – the benefits can be increased immeasurably and the narrow interest-group politics that supports continued regulation might be overcome. The interesting target for deregulation at present is electricity, but no one can be sure how a fully deregulated electricity market would operate. Whatever the short-term economic losses from such deregulation, they are likely to be swamped by the short-term income redistribution it creates. Nevertheless, a decision to end government intervention in pricing and output decisions across the economy would surely yield large benefits to the economy – benefits that would undoubtedly swamp any short-term costs of electricity deregulation.

NOTES

1. Francis Fukuyama (1992).
2. As late as 1985, the most influential US basic economics textbook, Samuelson and Nordhaus (1985) offered the view that, 'The planned Soviet economy since 1928 has grown more rapidly than the economy of Czarist Russia and has outpaced the long-term growth of the major market economies. Only Japan and the United States in its rapid growth phase approach Soviet economic growth.' Six years later, the Soviet Union collapsed, and no one could find the accumulated benefits of this 55-year period of such astounding growth. Surely it was a chimera.
3. In the USA, a large number of deregulatory measures swept through the Congress in the era of 'stagflation' that began during the Vietnam War and continued through the two major oil shocks into the 1980s. These laws were part of a package (misleadingly) promoted to reduce inflation.
4. See Winston (1993), for a discussion of transport deregulation.
5. Some regulation remains in each of these sectors, but it does not generally involve the control of prices or entry conditions.
6. The attempt to legislate far-reaching industrial price and output controls through the National Industrial Recovery Act was overturned by the US Supreme Court.
7. Unfortunately, liberalization of local telecommunications was not accompanied by rate deregulation. See the discussion below.
8. Winston (1993, 1998).

9. Winston (1998).
10. The exception is less-than-truckload trucking in which producers lost a substantial amount of capitalized economic rents when entry was liberalized in 1980.
11. New Zealand attempted to deregulate telecommunications fully, but years of legal wrangling resulted. As this is being written, New Zealand is debating the restoration of telecommunications regulation.
12. See Winston (1993) and Crandall and Ellig (1997).
13. There is a considerable literature on railroad pricing and regulation, much of which suggests that US railroads had overbuilt their networks and were engaged in aggressive price competition before 1887 when federal regulation was first established. See MacAvoy (1965) and Kolko (1965).
14. US General Accounting Office (1989).
15. Crandall and Furchtgott-Roth (1996). See also Hazlett and Spitzer (1997).
16. There was no popular discussion of the effects of this monopoly on output and resource allocation. Government investigators counted the number of channels of service provided only to address the cable system owners' contentions that they had not raised the price per *channel* offered.
17. See the discussion in the next section.
18. Even under this extreme assumption of a trebling of local rates due to deregulation, the total transfer of income from consumers to producers is only about $77 billion per year. If the efficiency costs of regulation designed to prevent such a transfer are as much as $58 billion, this is an extremely inefficient mechanism for redistributing income.
19. The total increase appears to have been about $20 billion, but about $8 billion of this increase would have occurred due to drought and fossil-fuel price increases. See Joskow (2001) for a discussion of California's travails.
20. Taylor (1975).
21. These data may be found at http://www.fcc.gov/wtb/auctions/35/.
22. This decision was announced on 6 March 2002, at the end of a lengthy 'escape clause' (Section 201) process.
23. Gardner (2001).
24. Ibid.
25. The largest cost of government intervention may be in the healthcare sector, but there is simply no comprehensive estimate of these costs. Nor is there a consensus on the effects of implicit government guarantees of securities backed by home mortgages.
26. This is the approach taken by the Canadian regulator, the Canadian Radio-Television and Telecommunications Commission (CRTC), in 1997. Predictably, the new competitors are now petitioning the CRTC for an extension of time and lower rates for unbundled elements.
27. See Hausman (1999).
28. See Eisner and Lehman (2001).

REFERENCES

Becker, Gary (1983), 'A Theory of Competition Among Pressure Groups for Political Influence', *Quarterly Journal of Economics*, **98** (August), 371–400.
Crandall, Robert W. and Jerry Ellig (1997), *Economic Deregulation and Customer Choice: Lessons for the Electricity Industry*, The Center For Market Processes, George Mason University.
Crandall, Robert W. and Harold Furchtgott-Roth (1996), *Cable TV: Regulation or Competition?* Washington, DC: The Brookings Institution.
Crandall, Robert W. and Leonard Waverman (2000), *Who Pays for Universal Service? When Telephone Subsidies Become Transparent*, Washington, DC: The Brookings Institution.

Demsetz, Harold (1968), 'Why regulate utilities?' *Journal of Law and Economics*, **11**, April, 55–65.

Eisner, James and Dale E. Lehman (2001), 'Regulatory Behavior and Competitive Entry', paper presented at the 14th Annual Western Conference, Center for Research in Regulated Industries, 28 June.

Fukuyama, Francis (1992), *The End of History and the Last Man*, New York: The Free Press.

Gardner, Bruce L. (2001), 'Has the FAIR Act Failed?', paper prepared for the Luther Tweeten Symposium, Ohio State University, 10 September.

Glaeser, Edward L. and Ezro F.P. Luttmer (1997), 'The Misallocation of Housing Under Rent Control', National Bureau of Economic Research, Working Paper 6220, Cambridge, October.

Hausman, Jerry (1997), 'Valuing the effect of Regulation on New Services in Telecommunications', *Brookings Papers on Economic Activity: Microeconomics*, 1–38.

Hausman, Jerry (1999), 'The Effect of Sunk Costs in Telecommunications Regulation', in James Alleman and Eli Noam (eds), *The New Investment Theory of Real Options and Its Implications for Telecommunications*, Boston: Kluwer Academic Publishers, pp. 191–204.

Hazlett, Thomas and Matthew Spitzer (1997), *Public Policy Toward Cable Television: The Economics of Rate Controls*, Washington, DC: The American Enterprise Institute.

Hufbauer, Gary Clyde and Kimberly Ann Elliott (1994), *Measuring the Costs of Protection in the United States*, Washington, DC: Institute for International Economics.

Joskow, Paul L. (2001), 'California's Electricity Crisis', National Bureau of Economic Research, Working Paper 8442, August.

Kolko, Gabriel (1965), *Railroads and Regulation: 1877–1916*, Princeton, NJ: Princeton University Press.

MacAvoy, Paul W. (1965), *The Economic Effects of Regulation: Trunk-Line Railroad Cartels and the Interstate Commerce Commission*, Cambridge, MA: MIT Press.

MacAvoy, Paul W. (2000), *The Natural Gas Market: Sixty Years of Regulation and Deregulation*, New Haven, CT: Yale University Press.

Morrison, Steven A. and Clifford Winston (1986), *The Economic Effects of Airline Deregulation*, Washington, DC: The Brookings Institution.

Morrison, Steven A. and Clifford Winston (1989), 'Enhancing the Performance of the Deregulated Air Transportation System', *Brookings Papers on Economic Activity: Microeconomics*, pp. 61–112.

Morrison, Steven A. and Clifford Winston (1995), *The Evolution of the Airline Industry*, Washington, DC: The Brookings Institution.

Newbery, David M. (1999), *Privatization, Restructuring, and Regulation of Network Utilities*, Cambridge, MA: MIT Press.

Peltzman, Sam (1976), 'Toward a More General Theory of Regulation', *Journal of Law and Economics*, **19** (August), 211–40.

Peltzman, Sam (1989), 'The Economic Theory of Regulation after a Decade of Deregulation', *Brookings Papers on Economic Activity: Microeconomics*, pp. 1–41.

Peltzman, Sam (1992), 'Voters as Fiscal Conservatives', *Quarterly Journal of Economics*, **107** (May), 327–61.

Posner, Richard (1971), 'Taxation by Regulation', *Bell Journal of Economics and Management Science*, **2** (Spring), 22–50

Posner, Richard (1974), 'Theories of economic regulation', *Bell Journal of Economics and Management Science*, **5** (Autumn), 335–58.

Samuelson, Paul A. and William D. Nordhaus (1985), *Economics*, New York: McGraw-Hill.

Shin, Richard T. and J.S. Ying (1992), 'Unnatural Monopolies in Local Telephone', *Rand Journal of Economics*, **23** (2), 171–83.

Stigler, George J. (1971), 'The Theory of Economic Regulation', *Bell Journal of Economics and Management Science*, **2** (Spring), 3–21.

Taylor, Lester D. (1975), 'The Demand for Electricity: A Survey', *The Bell Journal of Economics*, **6** (Spring), 74–110.

US General Accounting Office (1989), *National Survey of Cable Television Rates and Services*, Washington.

Winston, Clifford (1993), 'Economic Deregulation: Days of Reckoning for Micro-economists,' *Journal of Economic Literature*, **31** (September), 1263–89.

Winston, Clifford (1998), 'U.S. Industry Adjustment to Economic Deregulation', *The Journal of Economic Perspectives*, **12** (Summer), 89–110.

Winston, Clifford, Thomas M. Corsi, Curtis M. Grimm, and Carol A. Evans (1990), *The Economic Effects of Surface Freight Deregulation*, Washington, DC: The Brookings Institution.

Winston, Clifford and Robert W. Crandall (1994), 'Explaining Regulatory Policy', *Brookings Papers on Economic Activity: Microeconomics*, pp. 1–31.

CHAIRMAN'S COMMENTS

Penelope Rowlatt

First, I would like to say that I particularly enjoyed Robert Crandall's short history of the benefits of deregulation in the USA. Most of it was new to me, and I found it quite fascinating.

Second, I think this is the first time I've encountered a really serious argument put forward for a total deregulation of the utilities. In the UK, when we deal with something that looks like a natural monopoly, people don't usually ask whether or not it needs to be regulated. Instead, they tend simply to seek the best way to regulate it. It has been taken for granted that we had to regulate. In that context, when, on the Better Regulation Task Force, we called in the stake-holders and asked them what they thought was good and what was bad about the regulation of utilities, none of them suggested that we should deregulate totally.

Third, I appreciate Crandall's emphasis on the importance of the distributional effects of regulation, as opposed to the efficiency effects. This is a point very well worth making. There is a great deal of stress on the fall in prices that has followed the restructuring of the industries and regulation of the markets, and we don't generally separate it into these two parts.

Finally, I know you find it troubling that people are signing up to the idea that regulators can facilitate or accelerate competition. It would be interesting to read about a development of those views.

7. Mutualization and debt-only vehicles: which way for RPI–X regulation?

David Currie[1]

INTRODUCTION

When I agreed the title of this chapter, it seemed a well-defined and narrow topic that merited attention but was not centre stage. I had counted without Railtrack and Stephen Byers. I had also not anticipated the growing swell of opinion that the RPI–X regulatory model needs reconsideration. I would therefore like to set this chapter in a somewhat broader context. I will first address what I think are the key issues around mutualization, debt-only companies and related issues. But then I will draw from that some implications for regulation more broadly, and some conclusions about the continued relevance of the RPI–X model.

I start by putting these issues in a broader political context. The RPI–X model proved robust in the early years of privatization in protecting customers from the possible abuse of monopoly power by the newly privatized utilities, and in passing considerable benefits to customers in the form of lower prices. However, the unexpectedly large efficiency gains made by many utilities meant that profits were typically high and shareholders did well. This fuelled the debate within the opposition Labour Party about alternative models of regulation, including profit-sharing and other modifications of RPI–X. It was also driven by the political wish to develop an alternative both to the then government's thinking and to the unpalatable Old Labour preferred solution of renationalization.

As I argued earlier, before Labour's election victory in May 1997, a number of these proposals for reform of RPI–X, notably profit-sharing, were ill conceived (see Currie, 1997), and were quietly dropped in the first year or two of the Labour government. Change took the form of the cleverly designed and implemented windfall levy, used to fund the government's welfare-to-work programme, and described by Christopher Chataway, perhaps over-optimistically, as 'the last gasp of Old Labour'. More positively, in respect of the gas and electricity sectors, it led to the Utilities Act of 2000, which left untouched the RPI–X model of regulation but provided a more coherent definition of regulatory objectives, provided a clearer framework for the balance between competition and regulation, established a broad framework for regulation in place of the individual regulator, and cleared the way for the introduction of genuine wholesale competition in electricity in the form of NETA.

What has led to the renewed questioning of the RPI–X model? I would identify three factors. First, there is the need in certain sectors for very major investments in renewal, environment, safety or capacity expansion. Thus, in water, we have major investment in EU-driven environmental standards; in rail the need for capacity expansion and increased safety; and in gas, major investment in network renewal driven by the Health and Safety Executive (HSE). Some praise the RPI–X model as being an effective way of incentiviz- ing the sweating of existing assets, but question its efficacy in incentivizing long-term investment. I return to this question later.

Second, there was the last RPI–X determination in water concluded by Ian Byatt. That left the shares of all water companies trading well below the price implied by their regulatory asset value, and led many to question the viability of financing major prospective investment programmes from equity and debt markets. We have yet to see any funding crises in the industry, but these concerns remain live, fuelling interest in alternative models, including mutuals and debt-only vehicles, the topic of this chapter. We have also seen the successful launch of Glas Cymru. If there is a problem in the sector, it remains an open question as to whether this is a failure of the RPI–X model itself, or is rather a more particular problem arising from the over-zealous pursuit of price cuts within that overall model. These are questions to which I will return.

Finally, there is Railtrack and the government's recent decision to pull the plug on the equity model in this part of the rail industry. This has catapulted a minority interest in debt-only vehicles to the centre of the political stage. I do not want to attempt to analyse the vexed issues that surround this development, especially the rights and wrongs of the dispute between shareholders and Stephen Byers. Instead I want to argue that this development is not of great relevance to the debates in other utilities sectors. Of all the privatizations, rail was the most problematic because of the continued reliance on state subsidy, whether paid through the train-operating companies or through assistance to Railtrack's investment programme.

On this, Michael Beesley demonstrated his usual percipience. In his lecture on rail privatization (Beesley, 1997), he made two key points. First, he argued that the form of privatization, with the separation of rail and wheel, was inap- propriate since effective competition over the rail was not realistic. Instead he argued for privatization of integrated businesses. This would have led to a much simpler industry structure to regulate, more akin to water. Instead we created a complex industry structure, and then responded to growing difficulties by adding corresponding regulatory complexity. This error has not been repeated in other sectors, which are generally divided into parts where competition can flourish or monopoly parts be subject to price-cap regulation.[2]

Beesley also argued that the assumed tapering of subsidy to the industry was unrealistic, and in that he has sadly been proved right. We seem to face an industry whose viability depends on continued and very major support from government. This raises profound questions over the viability of the equity model in such circumstances. Railtrack exemplified that problem: a FTSE100 company that relied for its major return on handouts from government. Stephen Byers was right to accuse Railtrack of becoming an effective machine for seeking those handouts, for that must surely have been the case if the directors of Railtrack were fulfilling their fiduciary obligations to maximize shareholder value. That just highlights the problem of the equity model in an industry dominated by subsidy. But it is a problem specific to rail, and not relevant to the other utility sectors.

DEBT-ONLY VEHICLES

I now turn to the core subject of my chapter. There has been an upsurge of interest in the possibility of non-equity models for utilities. This interest has been strongest in water, with the as yet unsuccessful Kelda proposal followed by Glas Cymru, and the recent refinancing of Southern Water to move to 90 per cent debt finance; but there has also been consideration of the relevance of such a model for monopoly utility companies such as NGC and Transco. I want to divide my discussion into two: first, I will consider the financial aspects of non-equity models; and then I will move on to consider the control aspects.

On the finance side, it seems to me that, leaving the implications of the control question to one side for the moment, the issues are relatively straightforward. Equity provides the front-line cushion against unforeseen adverse shocks that impact on the company's bottom line. Debt provides a second-line cushion, possibly tiered depending on the covenants attached to such lending. The mix of debt and equity in the company's balance sheet alters the company-specific risk characteristics of that company's equity: higher borrowing goes together with higher gearing of equity to performance and therefore implies both a greater company-specific equity risk and a higher β. If financial markets can diversify the company-specific risk, then only the higher β impacts through a higher equity cost of capital. But a shift to a higher gearing increases the importance of lower-cost debt in the overall cost of capital.

In some circumstances, when the assumptions of the Modigliani–Miller theorem do not apply, it is possible to show that increasing gearing lowers the overall cost of capital until gearing reaches its optimal level. Increased gearing beyond that point will increase the overall cost of capital once more. One factor that may influence this relationship is the fact that higher gearing may increase the pressures for managerial efficiency: the share price will be more sensitive to changes in performance, and this may sharpen incentives on management, either in itself or through incentive schemes linked to the share price.

Ofwat has regularly commended to the water companies a higher level of debt gearing, on the grounds just outlined that thereby they can reduce their cost of capital. One way of formulating the question about debt-only vehicles is to ask whether there are circumstances in which the optimal debt level is 100 per cent, so that equity is eliminated. I find it very hard to see how this could be the case if it is solely the level of gearing that is changing through a swap of equity for debt. For if a company has only debt, then that debt assumes the role of equity, being at risk in the event of an adverse unanticipated shock.

In the case of Glas Cymru, the exchange of debt for equity was such as to leave the company with a cash reserve against future contingencies, thereby reducing (or even eliminating if the reserve is judged large enough) the equity role of debt. But it is hard to see how that exchange alters anything material. It is possible, I suppose, that Glas was the beneficiary of a divergence of view between debt and equity investors on the prospects for the market, possibly arising from the fact that debt investors did not fully appreciate their equity role. That is a weak basis for the sustained viability of the debt-only model. More plausibly, something else may be seen as changing. What that might be I will return to, but first let me address the question of corporate control.

CORPORATE CONTROL AND MUTUALS

A key advantage of an equity-based company is that the structure of corporate control is familiar and clear. In the event of a company getting into trouble, whether for reasons within or outwith the control of management, the share-holders have the clear incentive and power to replace the incumbent management. This is true even if high gearing means that equity accounts for only a very small part of the company. And although shareholder passivity may well mean that *de facto* control is with management in normal times, share-holder power is usually exercised when the going gets rough.

If equity is totally withdrawn, then matters become less straightforward. Debt invested in a debt-only vehicle is very likely to be lent on terms that are covenanted in ways that give debt-holders considerable influence and control over what happens when things go wrong. It may be possible that the terms of such covenants reproduce *de facto* the ownership rights that lie with share-holders in the equity model.[3] In that case debt essentially serves in the same way as equity; and although it is unclear what the switch to a debt-only vehicle has accomplished, at least there is no weakening of corporate control. But if issues of control are left more ambiguous than in the equity model, then the risk is muddle and drift if the company gets into difficulty.

This risk is all the greater if ownership is vested in a mutual model, however hedged around by covenants. Mutuals are notorious for their weakness in decision-making, sometimes because of confused powers of control but also because of an absence of incentives for efficiency. We need only look at the shift from mutual to equity ownership for markets, the shift away from mutual structures in the building society movement and in other areas. Those not familiar with the history of the British Labour movement often assume that mutual structures will appeal to the present generation of Labour politicians. But this overlooks the fact that many of them are all too familiar with the weaknesses of mutual structures of decision-making, not only in the political process but also in the old Co-op movement.

A key difficulty with mutual structures is that, when the mutual structure gets into trouble, the resolution of the problem is muddled and confused, in contrast to the equity model. This weakness may also be shared with the debt-only model, unless structures of control are clearly laid down. A possible response to this is that the separation of asset ownership from asset operation can eliminate risk from the mutual or debt-only vehicle. It is to this point that we now turn.

SEPARATING ASSET OWNERSHIP AND OPERATION

The standard model for achieving competition in formerly monopolistic utility sectors has been to separate monopolistic distribution from supply, and to promote the conditions for effective competition in supply. However, there is a widespread, though not universal, view that establishing effective competition in the supply of water, along the lines of electricity and gas, is not realistic because of the high cost of transporting water and the consequent lack of a fully developed national network. An alternative model for the water industry is to separate asset ownership from asset operation, and to promote the conditions for effective competition in asset operations to develop, while asset ownership remains a local monopoly. The mutual or debt-only models have been advocated for the asset-owning company, though it is important to note that some advocates of the ownership/operation split remain firm advocates of the equity model.

Thus the proposal is for an asset-owning company to franchise out the operations of its assets on a competitive basis. If this structure is widespread, it is conceivable that a healthy market will develop in the provision of operation services, and the emergence of a competitive price for such services. This would have important implications for the operation of the regulatory regime: if the price of asset operations emerges from a competitive process, then the regulator has no need to take a view on the appropriate price cap for this part of the business. Controversies over Opex become less vexed, though there remains the difficult issue of the trade-off between Opex and Capex. We return to this key point. However, it is important to note that it is far from automatic that healthy competition will emerge in this way, particularly in view of the legacy of the old monopoly structure.

The separation of asset ownership from operation allows the asset-owning company to pass some classes of risk to the competitive provider of operation services. These include all the risks associated with the direct operation of the assets. This therefore alters the risk profile of the asset-owning company. A key question is whether there are any classes of risk that cannot be transferred in this way. Clearly there is the risk of catastrophe, now much more in our minds since 11 September 2001: the destruction, for example, of a reservoir, or the introduction of disease into our water systems. A well-run company may guard against such risks, but reasonably may be unable to eliminate them. Such risks may also be impossible for any company either to bear, however deep its equity, or to insure against. In that case, the regulator or government will have to help. This is largely irrespective of financing vehicle or regulatory regime, and therefore such risk, crucial though it is, does not bear on our argument.

A more relevant risk concerns the quality of decision-making in the asset-owning company. Clearly the asset-owning company cannot pass on the risks that arise from the failings of its own decision-making. Such risk is particularly relevant in view of my earlier comments about decision-making in mutual structures.

Some commentators play down the importance of such risk. I believe this to be a profound error. Subcontracting the operation of assets is an activity that requires skill on a number of dimensions, including knowledge of the sector and how it works as well as negotiation skills. This is no trivial task, and one in which different management teams will exhibit different levels of skill. It is made more difficult when the question of new investment is considered. Who will make the decision about what assets to acquire or replace? This must surely lie with the asset-owning company, yet will profoundly affect the asset operator. How will the asset owner decide between two rival bids for asset operation, one posited on one type of forward investment and the other on another? It may well require, for example, practical hands-on knowledge of operations to identify profitable Capex/Opex trade-offs, together with the appropriate incentives to look for them. Will the operation franchise be for a short period of time, introducing a number of agency incentive problems between the interests of the asset owner and the asset operator; or will it be on a longer-term basis (as for example in France), with the danger that the development of the competitive market in operation services will be held back?

It is important to note that these problems are likely to cumulate over time. With the initial split of asset ownership from operation, the asset-owning company is likely to retain knowledge and experience of the sector, so that its decision-making is likely to be informed and high quality. Thus we should not fear too greatly about Terry Burns and his colleagues at Glas making bad decisions. But what will be the position in five or ten years, when the management team has changed? How easy will it be to attract first-rate management to replace the current team, and to devise an executive package that incentivizes excellence within a non-equity context? Is not the danger that an informed and skilled management team will be replaced in time by one that is less informed and of lower quality, especially if expertise derives from experience of operations? The oft-cited example of the oil industry that relies heavily on outsourcing is not helpful in this: there is a great deal of excitement and reward (often through share-based options) in running a global oil business, even with outsourcing on a large scale. Indeed, without outsourcing, the management task would be impossible. But this is very different from running a small asset-owning utility in the UK, even with some sensible diversification. These difficulties are all the greater if contracting of operations is on a long-term basis so that the management of the asset-owning company has little to do between franchise bids.

THE REGULATORY CONTEXT

I now draw the threads of my argument together and examine the implications for the regulatory regime.

First, I summarize the case for debt-only or mutual-asset-owning companies, franchising the operation of assets to competitive suppliers of such services. The argument is that this enables a competitive market in asset-operating services to emerge, with two benefits. First, it will relieve the regulator of the key, but very difficult, task of forming a judgement on current and future Opex. And, second, it will introduce genuine and effective competition into a key part of the water industry, to the benefit of customers.

I should make it clear that I see the point of the second part of this argument, though I do have doubts about whether effective competition will arise. The level of competition will depend on the number of contracting companies, and this is a sector that in the past has had a poor record of competitive behaviour. I also have no difficulty in principle with the separation of asset ownership and operations, especially if this facilitates the emergence of vigorous competition in operation services, with real benefits to customers.

What I have much greater difficulty with is the notion that this will necessarily relieve the regulator of the need to make judgements about current and future Opex. For, as I have indicated, the task that falls to the asset-owning company, that of making decisions on the franchising of the operations of its assets, is a complex and difficult one. And I do not see how Philip Fletcher or his successor could simply take the actual level of Opex expenditure thrown up by this franchising process, without questioning whether the management of the asset-owning company had performed its task well. Although the market delivery of operation services will throw up important data to inform the regulator's decision, the regulator will need to continue to examine the comparative performance of companies to give a benchmark for the performance of the monopoly owners of the assets, and to ensure that the less effective catch up with best performance. That is not very different from now: franchising will help regulation, but not eliminate the need for it.

It follows, I believe, that we should be very wary of mutuals or other structures prone to confused or poor decision-making processes in the event of difficulty. Suppose several mutuals emerge in the water sector. Suppose, as I have suggested, they find it difficult in due course to attract dynamic and efficient management, and they make poor decisions. In time, the regulator will identify this, and set them a more ambitious target to catch up with best, or possibly even just average, performance in the sector. What happens if they do not succeed and they run into financial difficulty? Who will rescue them? How can they be rescued if it is the decision structure itself that is at the root of the problem? If the result is to undermine the financial viability of such companies, will this make it more difficult for the regulator to set them tough targets? Will this mean that customers end up paying more? Will this be the result whether or not the company is formally owned by customers, as in a mutual, or takes some other debt-only form?

The contrast with the equity model is marked: when an equity-based company gets into difficulty, there is an established route for changing the management. Thus, for example, when Swalec got into difficulty, there was a smooth transfer of ownership and management. The rescue routes for the mutual and debt-only models are much less clear.

I have deliberately posed my argument in the form of a set of questions, because my mind is not altogether made up. Convincing and robust answers to each of these questions could persuade me that debt-only vehicles with the right control structure should be allowed more generally than the exception allowed in the case of Glas. But I have not seen answers to these questions, perhaps because they cannot be given. And in their absence, I remain opposed to changing the nature of the British regulatory model by the back door, through a change in ownership and control which forces the hand of the regulator. It would be disastrous for the industry to presume an implicit financial guarantee from the regulator or government: part of the Railtrack fiasco derives from that assumption on the part of shareholders, and we do not want a repeat of that.

THE FUTURE OF THE REGULATORY SYSTEM

Instead of back-door change, I would prefer to see an open debate about the regulatory system and its future.

Part of that debate should concern the state of the water industry after the last periodic review. In my opinion that review went too far in the drive for immediate price reductions. I never understood the case for large P_0 (initial price) reductions followed by subsequent price increases. And I shared the concern that the water companies had been pushed, if not to and over, certainly close to, the financial edge (though it is significant that none of the companies appealed against Ofwat's price determination).

Against that, it is interesting to observe that the initial large discount to regulatory asset value has narrowed: how far that is a reassessment of the fundamentals of the review and how far a short-term response to the value of the utility sector as a recession hedge remains to be seen. It is also worth recalling that the so-called 'smash and grab' raid on British Gas by Ofgas led to a similar large discount to regulatory asset value, but that rapidly disappeared once the benefits of the restructuring of British Gas, separating supply and distribution, worked through. Time will tell whether restructuring in the water industry, if it comes, will have the same result.

This is not to say that we should be complacent about the current regulatory model. It has undergone significant evolution over the past five years or so. There has been the development of collective board responsibility for regulation in gas and electricity in place of the individual regulator (a development that will be extended to telecoms and broadcasting with the expected passage of the Ofcom bill through the next parliamentary session). This should also be extended to water when expected legislation is forthcoming. There has been growing convergence in regulatory practice as a result of better consultation between the regulators. There have been improvements in the processes of regulation, not least in greater openness, though more can be done in that direction. And there have been significant steps towards much greater competition in telecoms, gas and electricity.[4]

I also take seriously the question of whether the current way in which we apply RPI–X price controls is well suited to encouraging long-term investment in capacity expansion, rather than encouraging better sweating of the assets. I am not sure that the evidence supports the case for concern, for I see no evidence of deteriorating performance of the networks and very large levels of investment in both the gas and electricity networks. If there is a case for change, it is for modest reform to RPI–X rather than its abandonment. In particular, I would identify several directions for change.

First, I think it important that regulators are as clear as possible about the way in which they account for investment and carry it forward through time.

Consistency and clarity in that is essential to incentivizing long-term investment. That was a major reason why Ofgem decided in the course of the Transco price review not to reopen the vexed question of a focused versus unfocused approach to the definition of the regulatory asset value: to have changed that definition after so long and after so much previous review would have been to introduce major and quite generalized regulatory uncertainty, whatever the merits of the case for a focused approach in line with other sectors had it been initially adopted. The development of consistent regulatory accounting that carries forward the consistency of treatment from one periodic review to the next is helpful in this.[5]

I think it is also the case that the move from individual to collective regulators, in the form of a board, is helpful in this respect: the staged replacement of members that this makes possible greatly increases the prospect for continuity and consistency through time.

Second, it would also be helpful to see if there are ways in which our treatment of the cost of capital in RPI–X can be improved. It has always struck me as odd that regulators take the cost of capital at a point in time, determined by financial market conditions around the time of the periodic review, and apply that to the following four or five years. This is despite the fact that companies raise the finance for their investment throughout the period, in possibly quite divergent market conditions. It seems to me that there should be a way for regulators to allow for these divergencies, possibly through an adjustment at the subsequent periodic review.[6] However, care would be needed to ensure that the adjustment was sufficiently robust that it could not be readily gamed to advantage by the regulated companies.

Third, I think that it is well worth monitoring carefully and taking further the developments on capacity that Ofgem has introduced with respect to Transco. These include establishing auctions for capacity to guide forward investment decisions and rolling incentives for capacity expansion that recognize the greater element of risk associated with such investment.

Finally, and more radically, I wonder whether we cannot find ways to address one key, and somewhat odd, feature of RPI–X, namely the time profile of returns to investment. The standard treatment of Capex rolls it into the regulatory asset base, and remunerates it at a real rate of return. However, the financing of Capex is typically through debt finance yielding a nominal return. The consequence is that the financing costs of investment are front-loaded, while the returns are back-loaded. In old-fashioned business terms that my finance colleagues would thoroughly disapprove of, the pay-back period to investments is very long indeed. That would matter less if investment had a smooth profile over time. But if investment is gearing up for a major expansion of capacity, it can matter. It would also matter less if the return were certain, as it would be in the idealized RPI–X model. But the presence of any form of regulatory uncertainty, because of the factors cited above or other reasons, means that this delayed profile of return assumes much greater prominence.[7]

Of course, it would be perfectly possible to treat investment differently, by applying a nominal return to the regulatory asset base and modifying the formula for updating it. That could be made to ensure the same overall rate of return, but with a profile of return more skewed to the present, matching better the profile of debt servicing. This would make the regulated company much less exposed to regulatory, and possibly other, uncertainty, and might therefore encourage long-term investment.

The case for treating investment in the way we currently do is on grounds of intertemporal fairness: investment should be paid for by customers over the lifetime of the asset, not front-loaded on current customers. And, of course, capital markets are meant to be able to facilitate such intertemporal smoothing. I take those points fully. But it is worth reflecting whether the back-loaded profile does not lead both companies and capital markets to look more warily at major long-lived investment programmes (particularly when an element of regulatory uncertainty is present, as it must be), thereby inhibiting investment in new capacity to the common detriment of current and future customers. If that is so, then that risk factor might be reduced by some move in the direction that I am suggesting.

CONCLUSIONS

I have strayed some distance from my central topic, but not quite as far as it may appear. My central point is that we should not be driven by the circumstances around one key price review to throw out the RPI–X model, whether directly or by the back door, when it has served us well. And we should look very carefully at apparently plausible propositions to understand their consequences. I believe that regulators have been right to look warily, and indeed with scepticism, at proposals for equity withdrawal and shifts to old models, such as mutuals, that have failed in the past and will fail us again. Instead we should seek to build on the strengths of the current system and apply some careful and intelligent modifications where, after careful thought and analysis, they seem to make sense. The RPI–X model of British regulation has delivered enormous benefit to consumers, to business and the broader economy. We should build and develop it to deliver the utility services that we need for the twenty-first century.

NOTES

1. The views expressed in this chapter are personal and should not be interpreted to reflect the views of the organizations with which the author is associated. In particular, they do not reflect the position of Ofgem (the UK energy regulator), of which the author was a non-executive board member when this chapter was written, stepping down in April 2002, nor of Ofcom (the new UK communications regulator), of which he was apponted Chairman in July 2002.
2. The exception is telecoms, where the dominant player is vertically integrated, posing considerable problems for regulation. It seemed that BT was planning to separate its network activities from its supply activities, which could have facilitated regulatory withdrawal by Oftel, but with its new chairman current intentions are less clear.
3. Thus there is a continuum from senior secured debt to pure equity, with subordinated debt and convertible bonds in the middle. Some debt comes close to equity not only in its risk characteristics but also in its control rights.
4. I would cite the recent review of the state of competition in mobile telephony for telecoms, and the introduction of genuine wholesale competition in electricity through NETA and the opening up of metering to competition in gas and electricity.
5. I suspect that it is an intrinsic feature of British regulation that forward commitments of this kind cannot be made absolute, essentially for reasons that spring from the British constitution. In caricature, the divine right of kings passed to Parliament and in the area of regulation was passed to regulators. Since Parliament cannot bind its successors, regulators cannot. But they can probably do more to give assurance, even if not absolute.
6. This presupposes the first point, a reliable and open way of carrying forward commitments of this kind through a system of regulatory accounts.
7. The point made in note 6 above is germane here.

REFERENCES

Beesley, Michael (1997), 'Rail: The Role of Subsidy in Privatization', in (ed.) *Regulating Utilities: Broadening the Debate*, IEA.

Currie, David (1997), 'The Labour Party's Approach to Utility Regulation: An Appraisal', in Michael Beesley (ed.), *Regulating Utilities: Broadening the Debate*, IEA.

Stones, Clive (2001), *Changes in the Pipeline: Economic and Public Policy Implications of Water Industry Restructuring*, Social Market Foundation.

CHAIRMAN'S COMMENTS

Philip Fletcher

David Currie brings a high degree of penetrating analysis and very broad perspective to this whole series of issues. I shall confine my comments mostly to the water sector, but come back on a few of the issues raised, largely on matters of degree and emphasis rather than fundamental disagreement.

Many of the issues and questions Currie has raised will only be resolved over time. We shall have to see how the unfolding position develops and whether it does work as indicated. The issues include the quality of management of companies like Glas Cymru, the owner of Welsh Water/Dŵr Cymru.

I am convinced that the last water periodic review was tough but fair, and not over-severe. In relation to Railtrack, I should just mention that its exposure to the continuing need for heavy public subsidy does introduce an element that is not present in the other main utility sectors, and is clearly not present in relation to water. To have no reliance on public subsidy, is I think, a significant factor.

RPI–X is being questioned in relation to water, as in relation to other sectors. My view, similar to Currie's, is that, like democracy, it is not necessarily the best system but it is the best we have, and we should be very wary about trying to change it to any significant degree. There are some alternative systems that I am convinced we should not even consider, including rate-of-return regulation as practised in the USA.

One or two commentators have suggested that RPI–X is not capable of coping with very large investment programmes. I think the water sector gives the lie to that. RPI–X has coped with a very large investment programme ever since privatization in 1989; I can see no reason why it should not continue to do so. The Wild West period of regulation, if it ever existed, has passed into myth or history. The settled period does not make RPI–X any less valid. It can underpin a more stable system as regulation and as the privatized monopoly companies develop.

But the subject of the debate is debt-only vehicles, and in that context it is worth making the important distinction, as Currie did, between debt-only vehicles like Glas Cymru, the owner of Welsh Water, and the Kelda proposition for a community asset mutual, which raises a different series of issues, including rescue if something went disastrously wrong. Currie raised the question of what happens if the management is not up to it: does the regulator step in and 'rescue' the company by putting the bills up? My answer would be definitely 'no'. In relation to the equity model, there are well-tried forms of rescue, known as takeover, and they are not ruled out in relation to the sort of model Glas is developing for Welsh Water. Glas is the holding company, Welsh Water is the regulated company. In the last resort the latter company can be sold.

If my comments have a value, it is from the regulator's perspective. I fully believe that it is not for the regulator to dictate the structure of the industry. It is not for regulators to suggest a perfect model which everybody should seek to follow, and that is certainly not how I am interpreting my duty at the moment. It is for me to respond as regulator when a company presents a model. In the water sector, where customers have no options, the interests of those customers must be properly protected and regulatory effectiveness, both for the appointed company and for the industry at large, must be maintained. This includes in water the important business of comparing performance across the sector, and specifically that safety and quality are properly safeguarded and risks of failure minimized. Ian Byatt, looking at those criteria in relation to the Kelda mutual proposition, decided they were not met. I think he was right. I looked at the issues in relation to the different Glas model with just the questions that Currie has been raising: would its debt finance structure be sufficiently robust to withstand cost shocks? Would the incentives for continuing efficiency be adequate? would it maintain proper control over its outsourced functions? I concluded not that it was all for the best in the best of all possible worlds, but that it stood a reasonable chance of succeeding. On that basis, it is going forward: see the *Financial Times* (13 November 2001). I agree with David that the incentives are not as strong as under the shareholder model, but Glas put in place other possible mechanisms to try to compensate.

I also agree that the mere outsourcing of functions does nothing to make the regulator's job easier; it is an option for all companies, not just those who choose the debt-only approach. Mere exposure to competition at the contractual level does nothing to ensure that the most efficient answer will be produced; that will depend on all the expert business of setting up the contracts properly and then managing them properly. So, it will be a matter of testing over time how well Glas, or any other company that chooses to follow a significantly different model, actually does in practice.

There are, of course, potential and actual countervailing benefits; the significant initial reduction in the weighted average cost of capital which Glas achieved is obviously one of them. So is the prospect of extra benefits to customers, which, arguably, could be an offset for a degree of extra risk within a permissible minimum risk to which such companies are exposed.

I would like to finish by touching on the next set of developments in the industry, which, as Currie has said, have been developing since the Glas model last year. The trend now seems to be not towards fully debt-financed companies, but companies that adopt a tranche of thin equity balanced by high gearing. There is the Scottish Power proposal for Southern Water immediately in the news; there are proposals and, in some cases, completed execution of proposals by water-only companies: Mid Kent, Sutton & East Surrey, Brockhampton (Portsmouth), for example. Currie noted that Ofwat assumed higher gearing than the then company average at the last periodic review. We assumed 50/50; companies are now at 50/50. Incidentally, a very similar view was taken by Ofgem on the distribution price control for regional electricity companies.

Some commentators have wrongly implied that Ofwat seeks debt-only or very thin equity as the answer to keeping the cost of capital down. Not so; it is a deliberate choice by companies to beat the weighted average assumed at the last periodic review. This clearly has implications for risk – the risk borne by the financial stakeholders of all sorts in the companies who adopt this approach. It is for the stakeholders to assess that risk, not just to rely on a regulator who has decided that that model can be allowed to go forward. It is not my job to provide a complete safety net for financial stakeholders. Ofwat has seen no reason to oppose the models that have come forward so far, but it does not hold up the resulting structures as a model for companies in general to follow.

We think the equity model has worked well; there again I agree with Currie. It has produced strong efficiency gains, which have enabled very substantial environmental and water quality investment programmes to be undertaken while consumer prices have gone up by much less in proportion. That has been made possible by the efficiency gains of the companies. Our job is to ensure that the financial structures of the appointees are robust, and that they remain capable of financing their present and prospective capital investment programmes readily and at reasonable cost. We also want to continue to treat all companies, whatever their structure, on a fair basis. That will not be a straightforward process as we come to the periodic review in 2004, but it is certainly going to be my endeavour.

Future market developments will, of course, have a bearing on the assessment of the efficient level of gearing at the next periodic review, and I shall not speculate where we shall finish up in four years' time. If we were to see that higher levels of gearing than the current 50/50 do not result in increases in risk premiums equal to or greater than the incremental value of the tax-shield; that such gearing levels were consistent with credit ratings comfortably within the investment grade envelope; and that these may reasonably be expected to be sustainable in the long term, then we shall obviously look at all that evidence. But we have not yet seen anything to justify significantly higher gearing than we have got across the industry as a whole, so I do not see us as in the business of forcing companies to adopt a very highly geared structure.

Where will that take us? To a large extent the benefits that have been claimed in the case of all the refinancing so far result from the present availability of terms in the debt market that are more favourable than those that applied a couple of years ago. Such savings are really no different from those achieved by outperformance of other regulatory assumptions. They may, however, be transitory; they depend on future market conditions. So, I find myself in agreement with Currie that very highly geared capital structures may imply greater risks for holders of both debt and equity, as such structures reduce a company's financial flexibility. You can only go very highly geared once. Highly geared companies face potentially higher interest rates and, potentially, greater refinancing risks, and all those risks need to be assessed.

I therefore see the RPI–X model as still valid. In relation to Currie's point about the back-end loading, I think we must always weigh the 'rough-edges' argument, which pushes us constantly in the direction of more sophistication, against the danger on the other hand of becoming over-complex, of making regulation more opaque, of obscuring the fact that the price limit represents a package which a company takes or leaves – leaves in the form of appeal to the Competition Commission, or accepts rough with smooth.

My job remains to protect the customers from unacceptable increased risks but not to provide a general safety net for all investors in the company. It is not my job to identify a single best model, and so far I have not seen anything which undermines my belief that Ian Byatt took the right decision on Kelda's mutual proposition and that the view I took on Glas is equally so far, so good. But time will tell; I shall continue to take a very close interest in whatever other restructuring proposals may come forward.

The regulatory structure, as Currie rightly said, is not itself immune from change. I rather agree that depersonalization is highly desirable; that is one of the reasons that I am looking by administrative means to create a proper board within Ofwat, and why I shall be quite happy if the government eventually legislates to make arrangements for Ofwat similar to those made for gas and electricity.

8. International mergers: the view from a national authority[1]

John Vickers[2]

INTRODUCTION

Does the role of national authorities in international merger control need rethinking? I will look at this question from the pure and unbiased perspective of a national authority – the UK's Office of Fair Trading. My answer will be a qualified 'yes'.

In reaching towards that answer I shall put less weight than some on the proposition that the merger process would be less costly if more internationalized. That proposition is correct, but perhaps not quite to the extent sometimes argued. It is a proposition put forcefully by, among others, some business interests. But care is needed in making the point, lest it be heard by some as a plea that international mergers should simply be easier to bring about. Of course they should not encounter needless and wasteful hassle. But if there is a serious question that an international merger might substantially lessen competition – to the ultimate detriment of consumers – then it is important that it be scrutinized, and be seen to be scrutinized, by competition authorities, and moreover by competition authorities with public legitimacy. Such scrutiny is good, not bad, for the international business system in so far as it maintains the competitive market infrastructure that drives its effectiveness and sustains its public acceptability.

The argument for (somewhat) more internationalized merger control that I want to explore in this chapter is not lower costs but greater effectiveness, especially when it comes to remedies.

VIEWPOINT

In the global scheme of things the UK is at least a medium-sized economy. In terms of GDP at current prices it is about the fourth largest in the world – smaller than the USA, Japan and Germany and on a par with France and Italy. The UK long has been, and remains, a very open economy in terms of trade and international capital flows. Much multinational business is UK-based, and London has a leading position in terms of international capital markets.

The open nature of the UK economy means that a disproportionately large volume of cross-border mergers will involve UK businesses. If multilateral controls over mergers were having a seriously adverse effect on the situation, we ought to be some of the first to know. In practice it is difficult to detect such adverse effect. The OFT's mergers team is not aware of mergers that have been deterred simply by the volume of notification requirements, but who knows what might have been? My focus will be on the actual mergers with an international dimension that have been before us in the recent past.

In the following I shall consider:

- how the OFT appraises mergers in general terms;
- what different types of 'international' mergers there are and whether this has implications for the way they are handled;
- some practical examples of 'international' mergers recently examined by the OFT; and
- the implications of all this for international (especially European) merger control.

THE PRESENT SYSTEM IN THE UK

The UK has had law controlling mergers since 1965. In our system, the OFT is the first-phase investigator. The OFT decides whether a merger raises sufficient issues to justify a full three- or four-month consideration in depth by the second-phase investigator, the Competition Commission (formerly the Monopolies and Mergers Commission). The OFT is also responsible for negotiating remedies, whether that remedy is instead of an investigation by the Competition Commission or following one. At present there is a third element in the system – the Secretary of State for Trade and Industry, a government minister. She decides whether to endorse my recommendation on whether a merger should be referred for investigation by the Competition Commission and, following a report by the Commission, will decide on any necessary remedy.

UK MERGER REFORM

The government has decided to take ministers out of this process (save for exceptional cases that raise national security issues), leaving decisions entirely to the independent competition authorities – the OFT and the Competition

Commission. Legislation is shortly to be laid before Parliament to secure this. The change has been widely welcomed. The opportunity is also being taken to update and strengthen other aspects of the law. For example, the test for mergers in the law, which is now of the effect on the public interest, will be replaced by a competition test – whether a merger will lead to a substantial lessening of competition. This change is less radical than it sounds – in analysing mergers, prospective effects on competition are paramount already; other public interest issues generally play little part, if any.

Other changes to the law affecting mergers are essentially fine-tuning. Over the years the law has proved quite robust and, on the philosophy of 'if it ain't broke don't fix it', we are aiming to preserve the better features of the UK system, while changing those which don't work so well. Thus we will continue without any compulsory notification system. Although unfashionable among competition authorities, companies have made clear that they like this – it gives them flexibility on whether to notify and on the contents and the timing of any notification, and companies are not fined for a failure to notify. But our scrutiny is not restricted to notified mergers, and the absence of a notification system does not, we believe, result in a failure to examine important mergers.

We will also continue to have a 'share of supply' test as one jurisdictional measure. This test is emphatically not a market share test, which would imply a substantial amount of market definition analysis before jurisdiction was determined, but is a test of the share of supply (or demand) on any reasonable definition of goods and services. It has proved useful in giving jurisdiction over small but potentially problematic cases.

We will also continue to take jurisdiction at relatively low levels of corporate control – 'material' influence as against the European test of 'decisive' influence. In other ways we will approach the European norm more closely – as the other jurisdictional test we will move from gross worldwide assets to one assessing turnover – though turnover solely in the UK.

The Competition Commission will publish the equivalent of a statement of objections in second-phase cases. It will also have the ability to impose fines for failures to provide information.

UK PROCEDURES

We do not intend to make any substantial changes to the way the OFT conducts first-phase investigations. The resource input into these cases is compact and the timescale short. We aim, and generally manage, to give a decision within 45 working days of notification; with the new regime this will be reduced to 40 days. In some cases we are under a statutory obligation to reach a decision in 35 working days; that will be reduced to 30.

We will continue to put the more difficult cases to our Mergers Panel for their views on the grounds for a second-phase investigation. The Mergers Panel is a committee drawn from other government departments with relevant information, and is chaired by my officials (and occasionally by me). Some lawyers in commercial practice give the appearance of viewing the Panel with suspicion, as though it could allow political influence into decisions. That is not so, and if I felt vulnerable to such influence I would shut down the Panel. The Panel makes no decisions. It is a way of bringing the expertise lying in other departments to merger analysis so that the OFT makes better-informed decisions. Our decisions on whether to advise referral of the cases in question are taken at separate, subsequent and exclusively OFT meetings usually chaired by me. In future the decision whether a case goes to a second-phase investigation will lie solely with the OFT. For now we advise the minister, and our advice is independently given and invariably accepted.

For the past year or so that advice has been published for all (non-confidential) cases that have been to the Mergers Panel. There is a slight delay between a decision and such publication, to allow commercially confidential information to be excised. So far there have been 36 cases published (to 30 September 2001). These are listed in the Appendix.

Some of the cases in the Appendix involve international companies but not international markets; some others involve national or local businesses operating in international markets. Some were notifiable in a number of other countries, others not. As I will discuss below, four of those considered in the UK last year involved repatriation (or maybe I mean patriation) to the UK from Brussels and hence involved markets that are no more than national. And as I shall also illustrate later, others might have lent themselves to expatriation from the UK to Brussels.

As to the overall scale of activity, in the year 2000 the OFT considered 315 mergers. Of these around 45 (or 14 per cent) were considered by the Mergers Panel and 14 (or 4 per cent) were referred to the Competition Commission, on the OFT's advice, for a second-phase investigation. A further four cases (or a little over 1 per cent) involved the acceptance of undertakings instead of such a reference.

THE UK AND THE EUROPEAN COMMISSION

Of the 18 cases that were referred or made subject to undertakings, it is noteworthy that three involved the reference back to the UK, under Article 9.2(a) of the European Community Merger Regulation (ECMR), of mergers notified to the European Commission. A fourth reference back, C3D Rhone/Go Ahead, subsequently lapsed when the bid was not agreed. As with these four, cases may be referred back to a Member State when a merger threatens to create or strengthen a dominant position within a distinct market within that Member State as a result of which effective competition will be significantly impeded. The need to demonstrate that threat within three weeks of notification has proved a demanding requirement, which may have discouraged Article 9 requests. So might, perhaps, a past perception of reluctance on the part of the European Commission to agree. Things are, however, changing and the four cases referred back to the UK in 2000 are as many as were referred back to the UK in all the preceding lifetime of the ECMR.

Furthermore, in 2001 the Commission for the first time referred back to the UK another case under Article 9.2(b). This, less demanding, provision requires only an effect on competition in a distinct market that does not constitute a substantial part of the European Community. This case was *Govia/Connex*, which affected certain railway routes south of London.

Two of the four Article 9.2(a) cases – AngloAmerican/Tarmac and Hanson/Pioneer – involved ready-mixed concrete, for which the markets are highly localized. C3D Rhone/Go Ahead involved bus services in South London – again a very local market. It may be that in future it will be easier to seek such cases back under Article 9.2(b), though it is not obvious what the Commission would consider to be a non-substantial part of the Community. The fourth case involved the brewing and distribution of beer, where the British penchant for ale as well as lager helps make markets no more than national. This was the Interbrew/Bass merger, which has now achieved some celebrity.

If the European Commission is now more willing to consider references back to Member States, as seems to be the case, it may be primarily for two reasons. One is the vast increase in mergers notified in Brussels, which has put the Merger Task Force under considerable strain. The other is the welcome momentum created by the modernization proposals for handling agreements and abuse of dominance, which will transfer some of that responsibility to Member States on the principle of 'best-placed acts'.

HOW MANY MERGERS ARE INTERNATIONAL?

What counts as an 'international' merger? From a producerist perspective, the answer might be a merger that involves firms from two or more countries. For present purposes this is the wrong answer, which is fortunate in that it disposes of the need to get into increasingly meaningless questions about the nationality of firms – is it the location of the workers, the shareholders, the plant, the HQ or what that matters?

A better answer, having regard to the ultimate purpose of competition law, is more customer-focused: a merger is international if it potentially affects competition, and, ultimately, end-consumers in multiple countries. Among such mergers, it is important to distinguish between:

- those where the question is whether the merger substantially lessens competition in a market that is international; and
- those where the question is whether the merger substantially lessens competition in several national (or subnational) markets.

A closely related distinction is between:

- international mergers where if, upon investigation, there are competition problems, the appropriate remedies have international effects; and
- those where there are national (or indeed subnational) remedies.

International mergers of the first kind require at least international policy coordination, and may best be handled with a degree of international centralization of policy – such as exists with the ECMR. Measures of international coordination – where information disclosure provisions allow – are important in any event although I do not believe that, for the foreseeable future, it would be realistic (or even desirable) to propose a global authority to handle such cases.

With mergers of the second kind, the gathering of information at national level is obviously essential, and I would argue that it is important more generally. The whole is better understood if the parts are understood.

This has (negative) implications for the savings that would come from reducing multiple notifications: much of the information would have to be gathered in any event, whoever takes the decision. A one-stop (or few-stop) shop is likely to want a good deal of the same information, though it might achieve economies of scope in gathering it.

Distinctions like those above are easily made in theory. In practice one generally doesn't know, at least at the outset of the investigation, what sort of merger one is dealing with. In any case there are all sorts of possible hybrids.

PRACTICAL EXAMPLES

Several merger cases that were repatriated to the UK under Article 9 of the ECMR have already been mentioned. International issues have arisen in a number of other merger cases recently considered in the UK. Of the 36 cases listed in the Appendix, at least ten (more than a quarter) appear to involve international markets. These are:

1. Kodak/Bell & Howell – micrographics equipment
2. Tessenderlo/Atofina – the supply of benzyl chloride and related products

3. RCG Holding/Doncasters – superalloys
4. Transocean Sedco Forex/R&B Falcon – mobile offshore contract drilling
5. Reed Elsevier/Harcourt – scientific, technical and medical publishing
6. Schlumberger/Baker and Hughes – seismic data from the North Sea
7. City Technology/Marconi – gas sensors
8. BASF/Takeda – vitamins
9. Grundfos/Baxi – water pumps
10. Thomson/Primark – electronic supply of financial data.

What are the general lessons to be drawn from these cases for the conduct of international merger control?

I will refer shortly to a few of the mergers in this group. But first I want to mention the merger that was proposed in 2000 between the London and Frankfurt stock exchanges. It would have raised fascinating issues, which OFT officials were relishing. Sadly for them, however, the merger was halted even before it was formally notified. None the less, German and British officials had already begun intense cooperative discussions on such vexed questions as market definition. It was clear that only such close cooperation between the OFT and the Bundeskartellamt (BKA) was likely to resolve satisfactorily some of the issues which arose from that merger. I believe that, had it proceeded further, the deal would have been analysed efficiently and well on the basis of international cooperation.

Arguably, though, given the number of companies from other countries listed on these exchanges, this was a case that would have been more appropriately handled by the Mergers Task Force in Brussels, had there been satisfactory machinery for making this transfer. Article 22 of the ECMR is intended to provide this counterpart to Article 9, but unfortunately it is now less than adequate for these purposes.

An example of a cross-border merger, sensibly handled, was the recent Proctor and Gamble/Clairol case. This fell outside the thresholds for the ECMR and consequently had to be notified in nine different European jurisdictions as well as, presumably, a number of countries elsewhere. The parties' lawyers targeted first the countries in which the merger appeared to raise some concerns but notified all nine European jurisdictions within about a month, in similar terms. The countries involved were the UK, Austria, Germany, Greece, Ireland, Italy, Norway, Portugal and Spain. The parties received clearance from all nine within about two more months. The process began in June 2001 and was over by the beginning of September. Because the merger did not give rise to significant issues in any of the countries, there was no need for active coordination.

We took the view in the Proctor and Gamble/Clairol case that the shampoo and hair conditioner markets might well be no more than national. It probably makes sense – at least it seems not unreasonable – that when markets are national or subnational in scope, a merger should be looked at by the individual author-ities. Whoever looks at it, data at that level will need to be gathered and assessed.

Another example is ready-mixed concrete, which sets very quickly and cannot be transported far. Ready-mixed concrete markets may, therefore, have a very small geographical compass. We usually think of these as being no wider than 15 miles or so from a population centre. And in part because population centres are often more than 15 miles apart, we do not think there are usually chains of substitution to extend the geographic scope. Thus in the Lafarge/Redland case in 1997 both the UK and France successfully sought to have the same case repatriated from the European Commission. Obviously we looked at the UK overlaps and the French looked at the French overlaps. We decided that in the UK there was no competition problem requiring remedy; the French decided that in France a remedy was required. These decisions are not inconsistent; they simply reflect the different circumstances in the two countries. Given the scope of the markets, it made sense for the UK and French authorities each to look at this merger, rather than the European Commission.

From a competition authority's perspective, the cases that need or would merit some single, or at least coordinated, examination are those which have similar possible adverse effects on competition across the relevant countries. The case for coordination is even stronger when it comes to remedy. Obviously, the parties are likely to gain from consistent, coherent decisions from the author-ities. And the merger control process itself may benefit.

I do not intend to debate the pros and cons of GE/Honeywell, but suppose that the European Commission's analysis was right and the remedy appropri-ate. What would have happened if the case had fallen to individual national authorities in Europe? Assuming that those individual countries had shared the European Commission's analysis and its views on remedy, could they have imposed the same remedy? This seems to me highly questionable – they did not individually have the same supranational standing. For example, in terms of population, the EU is larger than the USA, while no individual country is more than a fraction of its size. It also seems to me questionable whether the remedy – an inherently international remedy – would have been proportionate for a single European country to impose. What is proportionate for all might not be proportionate for any.

At least two recent mergers considered by the UK authorities – BASF/Takeda, and Reed Elsevier/Harcourt – could have raised similar issues.

BASF/Takeda involved the supply of vitamins C and B2. The geographic market is global. The merger would have produced two-firm concentration rations of between 60 and 80 per cent and Herfindahl indices of between 2700 and 3000. In recent history both BASF and Takeda, with others, had been heavily fined by the US Department of Justice for their roles in the global cartel which had controlled the worldwide vitamins market. They were also fined in Canada.

The case did not cross the ECMR thresholds, and so for the UK it fell to the OFT for first-phase investigation. We took the view that there was a significant possibility, requiring further investigation, that the merger would substantially lessen competition in the relevant markets serving UK customers. The case was therefore referred to the UK's Competition Commission. It concluded that there was likely to be new entry, at least into the vitamin C market, and that substantial competitive pressures, particularly from the Chinese, would be likely to prevent tacit or explicit collusion. The merger was judged not to have adverse effects in the UK, and the issue of remedy therefore did not arise.

What concerns me, however, is the hypothetical question of what could have been done if the UK Competition Commission had concluded that there were adverse effects requiring remedy. Although BASF had UK subsidiaries, it is not a UK company. Takeda had business but no presence in the UK – its business is handled by an agent. Both companies' UK business represented a relatively small part of its overall turnover. It seems to me that the ability to impose a UK structural remedy would have been very limited. Behavioural remedies might have been possible, but behavioural remedies, where they address the symptoms rather than the cause of a problem, can be less than satisfactory.

I cannot help thinking – and I thought at the time – that the competition questions raised by this case would have been better addressed at European level than at national level.

Reed Elsevier/Harcourt could have raised similar problems. Reed Elsevier is an Anglo/Dutch business, Harcourt was American. The parties have a range of business activities. They overlapped in the provision of scientific, technical and medical (or STM) journals. The primary language of STM publications is English and the market is worldwide. The market is changing quite rapidly because of the growing importance of electronic publishing. Overall, on some definitions the parties appeared to have 40 per cent of the STM journals market (and there are respectable arguments for saying that the relevant markets for STM journals should be drawn more narrowly). The parties' market power might also have been even greater than this implies, given the quality and range of their publications and the relatively small size of competitors. Entry into the market is not easy – there are substantial reputational barriers – there is little buyer power (indeed some institutional subscribers are quasi-captive), and electronic marketing gives opportunities for bundling. Indeed, Reed Elsevier had developed a highly sophisticated system for the electronic delivery of material which, with the acquisition of Harcourt, raised questions about whether it might be able to entrench its position in the market. Notably, the market had also seen large increases in prices over an extended period, and there were widespread customer concerns about competition.

As ever, the primary question for us was whether there was a significant possibility, requiring further investigation, that the merger would substantially lessen competition in the relevant markets serving UK customers. We concluded that this merger did raise sufficient concerns to warrant a second-phase investigation. A divided Competition Commission concluded, by a majority of two to one, that the merger was unlikely to operate against the public interest, though it was (unanimously) sufficiently concerned about the rise in prices to invite the OFT to consider a wider review of the industry.

Again there is the hypothetical question: if the Competition Commission had concluded that the merger was likely to have adverse effects, how would they have been remedied? The competition authorities in the UK are able to consider only adverse effects in the UK, but the UK business of the companies is a relatively small part of their overall turnover. Would, therefore, prohibition or some other structural remedy have been proportionate or feasible for a national authority?

Lest you think that I want to export my in-tray to Brussels – I don't – I shall now mention two cases which I think were naturally scrutinized in the UK, although they were obviously international in a wider sense.

The first is Transocean/R&B Falcon. This case involved contract drilling in offshore oil and gas fields. The parties were incorporated in the Cayman Islands and Delaware, and at first sight one would expect this to be an international market, but things were a bit more complicated. We had first to consider whether the two main sorts of drilling rigs – 'jack-ups' and 'floaters' – were in the same market. As their names imply, jack-ups sit on extendible legs on the sea bottom, hence are only suitable for shallow waters, and floaters – naturally – float. Among floaters one can distinguish between semi-submersibles and drillships, but the key point is that only floaters can operate in deeper water. Jack-ups can operate in the southern North Sea, which is primarily producing gas. But only floaters can operate in the northern North Sea, which is primarily producing oil, which is much deeper and where conditions are much harsher. Of course the northern North Sea does not have a global monopoly of deep-water sites of interest to the oil industry. But the harshness of conditions there means that floaters built to operate in, say, the Gulf of Mexico would need substantial modification – as well as a long trip – to be substitutable. So while offshore drilling rigs may generally be an international market, arguably there was a smaller relevant geographic market – one limited to the UK and Norwegian sectors in the northern North Sea.

Moreover, if we (in relation to a remedy to avert a second-stage investigation) or the Competition Commission (following one) had sought remedies, there were 'local' ones potentially available – for example divestments of some North Sea floaters. However, it didn't come to that. We judged that there were enough competitive constraints on the merged entity for there to be no need for a second-stage investigation. So clearance was our answer. My claim is just that this broadly international merger raised some questions that it made perfect sense for the UK authorities to address.

Another recent case was Kodak/Bell & Howell (both US companies), where the business was the supply and servicing of micrographics equipment used for the capture, store and retrieval of information that has been substantially reduced in physical size. The market for such equipment was clearly international and we spent little time considering it. We also knew that some other authorities, including the US Department of Justice and the BKA, had cleared the deal.

Our focus was the market for servicing the equipment – particularly in relation to access to spare parts. This was an essentially national market. If it had been judged that, without remedies, the merger would have been detrimental to competition and the public interest, then remedies no more than national in scope would have been available. It made perfect sense for these national aspects of an international merger to be assessed by a national authority. Even if they had fallen to supranational consideration, the same questions should have been examined anyway.

On balance, we concluded that the merger was unlikely to be detrimental to competition provided competitors had continued access to spare parts, which in the circumstances (and in view of competition law generally) was reasonable to expect. So the merger was not referred to the Competition Commission.

These four recent 'international' cases all fell to national consideration. In two of the cases I think this was generally appropriate: the questions and (if it had been necessary) the answers were in some sense local. In two cases, however, supranational consideration might have made more sense. In such cases how could this be facilitated?

ECMR REFORM

The possible over-stringency of Article 9, and the fact that most Member States have never used it, and especially the deficiencies of Article 22 as a way of referring a case from Member States back to the Commission, lead to questions about ECMR reform. This could ease the movement of cases between the Commission and Member States so that the authority best placed to deal with a case does so. The freer movement of cases within the Community seems a fitting aim of competition policy for a single market.

The ECMR is in any case under review. One issue concerns the thresholds above which mergers go to Brussels rather than Member States for consideration. The last time thresholds were reviewed the Commission was strongly in favour of lowering them, and a number of Member States were quite strongly against. In the end a compromise was reached which led to the introduction of a new threshold for cases where the merger had substantial business in at least three Member States. Obviously, this new threshold was intended to draw more cross-border mergers within the ambit of the Commission. However, the new thresholds in Article 1.3 of the Regulation are pretty complicated to work out and these thresholds have so far drawn only a few cases into the Commission's ambit.

Although the Commission seems no longer to be seeking a general reduction in thresholds, it is worth noting that their level in real terms is anyway in long-term decline. Even low and stable inflation is still inflation, and over the 11-year life of the ECMR the European price level has risen about 30 per cent. So if the 5 billion euros threshold of 1990 had been price-index-linked, it would now be about 6.5 billion euros. A number of recent ECMR merger cases have been below 6.5 billion euros, so the point is not purely theoretical. Moreover, it would probably be more natural to benchmark the threshold against nominal GDP – the income and expenditure of the whole economy – than the price level. On this basis 5 billion euros in 1990 would now be more than 7.5 billion euros, an increase of over 50 per cent.

In noting this I am not pressing for upward revaluation or even index-linking of the thresholds. That said, I would suggest that the Commission should look carefully at the additional cases which it now garners because of the change in the real value of the thresholds, and should be prepared to revalue them if the additional cases that it is catching raise issues that are primarily national or subnational.

My main point, however, is that the focus now should not be the quantitative issue of threshold size but the qualitative issue of which types of merger are handled where.

Article 9, whereby cases can move from the Commission to Member States, is now working well but could work better still. At present there are disadvantages for the Member State – not only because of the problem of meeting a stringent test in three weeks but also in being bound subsequently by the Commission's timetable, which may not marry with that of the Member State. For instance, we find it virtually impossible to seek undertakings in lieu of a second-phase investigation unless these have largely been determined ahead of the making of an Article 9 request.

It is welcome that the Commission is already looking at Article 9. Especially now that the national authorities have built up capacity and expertise, the Commission's job is surely to concentrate its efforts on transnational issues, focusing on markets that are at least European-wide. It should be ready to pass back to Member States those cases that have a narrower geographic ambit. The Commission might usefully ease both the process of reference back and perhaps also the procedural constraints once that is done.

There is a case for a more far-reaching approach in respect of Article 22 – the unused route by which the Commission could be securing international mergers (such as Reed Elsevier/Harcourt and BASF/Takeda) that now escape its jurisdiction. Article 22 was originally designed to be used by individual Member States without their own merger control arrangements. This purpose is largely redundant now that all Member States except Luxembourg have adopted merger control arrangements. The Article was adapted in 1997 for cases of multiple notification. The adaptation was not entirely successful. As it stands there are oddities and uncertainties about who should and who could ask the Commission to act, how they should make the request, when they should make the request, and whether the Commission could then resolve all of the competition issues which arise.

These are genuinely difficult questions. But the prospective gains from a well-functioning Article 22 – in terms of both lower burden and greater effectiveness of merger control – seem sufficient to make this a priority for reform efforts.

Finally, in reviewing the Regulation I think it would be helpful to review the dominance test. Dominance is not an ideal test for considering the impact of a merger on competition. Narrowly interpreted, it would be far too permissive. The Commission has therefore been creative in applying the dominance test, particularly when looking at oligopolistic markets. But the concept of joint or collective dominance is not without difficulties.

When considering changes to UK merger legislation we were anxious to be *communautaire*, and would have adopted the dominance test had we thought it straightforwardly satisfactory. But in its merger reform proposals the UK has opted for the natural test readily available – substantial lessening of competition. I would welcome the Commission considering the same change. This would have advantages of straightforwardness and wider international harmonization. And the UK would end up being communautaire after all!

CONCLUSION

I conclude by summarizing some of the main themes of this discussion. The first is that international mergers – by which I mean mergers that potentially affect competition and consumers in multiple countries – are of different types. In particular, it is important to distinguish between those that raise competition issues in inherently international markets, and those that raise questions at national (or indeed subnational) level. Generally speaking, the former but not the latter may require international remedies. International mergers of both types may require information-gathering at national level in any event.

Second, while the burden of multiple notifications should of course be reduced where it is unnecessary, it is not the only – and perhaps not the most – persuasive argument for more internationalized merger control. The gains from burden reduction are significant but they are bounded. They are bounded by the need to gather sufficiently rich information to make good merger decisions – whoever takes them – and also by requirements of public account-ability in competition policy decision-making. Moreover, the public acceptability of international mergers as a whole in part depends on there being seen to be proper checks to ensure that they do not jeopardize the competitive process, and hence the interests of the general public as consumers.

Third, an important argument for more internationalized merger control is enhancing the effectiveness of remedies in those cases which, upon investiga-tion, call for international remedies, including prohibition.

Fourth, the question of which mergers posing competition problems call for international remedies is not a simple matter of deal size (and it can be hard to tell in advance which mergers fall into that category). It is welcome in Europe that more mergers that raise essentially national issues are now passing from supranational consideration in Brussels to national authorities. This is in keeping with the proposals for modernizing EC competition law enforcement, and the principle of 'best-placed acts', or rather 'best-placed investigates'. Conversely, it would be helpful if it were easier for national authorities in Europe, where appropriate, to remit certain international mergers for supranational consider-ation. Indeed, I would focus on this qualitative issue rather than the quantitative issue of ECMR thresholds, which have anyway steadily declined in real terms.

Finally, internationalization involves coordination, not just centralization, of policy decisions. Coordination – including the sharing of information and analysis where possible – has greatly increased, but there is a long way to go. One helpful, but perhaps not essential, step would be convergence on substan-tial lessening of competition as explicitly the key test for merger appraisal.

National competition authorities neither should nor will merge into a single international block. But the joint venture is making progress and it should make more – for the sake of competition and consumers worldwide.

NOTES

1. This chapter was given as a paper at the Fordham Conference in New York in October 2001, and it was first published in B. Hawk (ed.), *Annual Proceedings of the Fordham Corporate Law Institute*, Julis Publications, 2002.
2. I am very grateful to Andrew White, former Director of Mergers at the OFT, for all that he has contributed to this chapter.

APPENDIX: PUBLISHED OFT ADVICE ON CLEARANCES AND REFERRALS TO THE COMPETITION COMMISSION, SEPTEMBER 2000 – SEPTEMBER 2001 (IN DATE ORDER)

Completed acquisition by Eastman Kodak Company of the services and micro-graphics businesses of Bell & Howell Company

Proposed acquisition by Govia Limited of Connex South Central Limited

Proposed acquisition by Kodak Processing Companies Limited of certain assets of Colourcare Limited

Proposed acquisition by Tessenderlo Chemie SA of the Widnes Plant and business of Atofina UK Ltd

Proposed acquisition by HCA International Limited of certain assets of the London Heart Hospital

Proposed merger between Halifax Group Plc and Bank of Scotland

Completed acquisition by SMG plc of 29.5% shareholding of Scottish Radio Holdings plc

Proposed acquisition by Duralay International Holdings Ltd of Gates Consumer and Industrial

Proposed acquisition by RCG Holdings Ltd of Doncasters plc

Proposed acquisition by Blockbuster Entertainment Ltd of certain assets of Apollo Video Film Hire Ltd

Completed acquisition by Denplan Limited of BUPA Dental Cover Limited

Proposed acquisition by British Airways plc of British Regional Air Lines Group plc

Proposed acquisition by Mersey Docks and Harbour Company of Heysham Port Limited

Completed acquisition by Octagon Motorsports Limited of certain assets of British Racing Drivers Club Limited

Proposed acquisition by General Healthcare Group Limited of Community Hospitals Group Plc

Acquisition by Transocean Sedco Forex Inc. of R&B Falcon Corporation

Proposed acquisition by Reed Elsevier Inc. of Harcourt General Inc.

Proposed acquisition of Abbey National plc by Lloyds TSB Bank Plc

Proposed merger between Abbey National plc and Bank of Scotland

Proposed joint venture between the Northern Ireland liquid milk and cream businesses of Express Dairies Plc and Golden Vale Plc

Proposed joint venture between BBC Resources Ltd and Granada Media Group Ltd

Completed merger of the surface seismic data acquisition and data-processing interests of Schlumberger Limited and Baker Hughes Incorporated

Completed acquisition by Scr-Sibelco Sa of certain assets of Anglo Pacific Group Plc, namely, Fife Silica Sands Ltd and Fife Resources Ltd

Completed acquisition by Bourne Leisure Holdings Limited of the Rank Holiday Division

Proposed acquisition by City Technology Limited of the gas sensors business of Marconi Applied Technologies Limited

Proposed acquisition by BASF AG of certain assets of Takeda Chemical Industries Ltd

Proposed joint venture between the Mayflower Corporation plc and the Henlys Group plc

Completed acquisition by Caik Holding Af 13.06.2000 A/S (now Icopal Holding A/S) of Icopal A/S

Proposed acquisition by Daimlerchrysler Rail Systems (UK) Limited (Adtranz) of Railcare Limited

The completed acquisition by Microsoft Corporation of 23.6% interest in Telewest Communications Plc

Acquisition by GWR Group plc of the radio interests of the Daily Mail and General Trust plc

Proposed acquisition by Stanton Plc of Biwater Industries (Coney Green) Limited (Published at the request of the Secretary of State)

Proposed acquisition by Grundfos Holding AG of certain assets of Baxi Partnership Ltd, namely its pumps manufacturing business (Myson Pumps)

Acquisition by Interbrew SA of assets of Whitbread Plc, namely the Whitbread Beer Company

Acquisition by Interbrew SA of assets of Bass Plc, namely Bass Holdings Limited

Proposed acquisition by the Thomson Corporation of Primark Corporation

Published advice can be viewed on the OFT website at: http://www.oft.gov.uk/Business/ Mergers/Advice/index.htm

9.   Liberalizing postal services

John Dodgson

1.   INTRODUCTION: PRESSURES FOR LIBERALIZATION

My aim is to review the arguments about liberalization of the postal services, for and against, assess progress in the UK so far, and identify major issues and concerns for the future.

Postal markets have so far been protected from competition because of the arguments surrounding the Universal Service Obligation (USO), but pressures for liberalization have been increasing. In the UK they have come from two sources – the European Commission and the 2000 Postal Services Act through the new regulator, the Postal Services Commission (Postcomm).

First of all, in its European Postal Directive (97/67/EC) of 15 December 1997, the Commission (1997) defined minimum standards for universal service provision in postal markets in EU Member States, and set out a timetable for completion of the internal market in postal services. The European Parliament and the Council were to decide no later than 1 January 2000 on moves towards further gradual and controlled liberalization of the postal market, in particular with a view to the liberalization of cross-border and direct mail, as well as a further review of the price and weight limits with effect from 1 January 2003. These decisions were to be based on proposals from the Commission to be tabled before the end of 1998. Although progress has been slow, on 15 October 2001 EU Ministers agreed that the current limit of 350 g set out in the 1997 Directive on Member States' postal monopolies will be reduced to 100 g from 2003, and to 50 g from 2006. There will be a review before 2006, when the Commission proposes a final stage of liberalization consistent with maintenance of the universal service. In the meantime, the Commission has become very active in the area of competition policy investigations and rulings in the competed part of the postal business (Baker and Dodgson, 2001, contains a survey).

Second, the 2000 Postal Services Act defines the universal postal service as the provision (except under exceptional circumstances) of at least one postal delivery every working day to all homes and business premises in the UK, and the collection of mail at least once every working day from each access point.[1] Postal services for the collection, sorting, transport and delivery of relevant postal packets must be provided at affordable prices determined in accordance with a public tariff which is uniform throughout the UK. The primary aim of the regulator, Postcomm, is to exercise its functions in a manner which it considers is best calculated to ensure the provision of this universal postal service. In addition, subject to this primary objective, the Commission shall exercise its functions in the manner which it considers best calculated to further the interests of users of postal services, *wherever appropriate by promoting effective competition between postal operators* (my italics). There is therefore a presumption in favour of competition. The Postal Services Commission has the power to issue licences to postal operators (as well as to Consignia), and has already started to do so. Postcomm issued a Consultation Document on promoting effective competition in UK postal services in June 2001 (Postcomm, 2001a).

Government aims, and Postcomm's views, were reiterated in a published exchange of letters in October. From the DTI: 'It is my aim to secure an outcome within an acceptable legal framework that provides for a process of phased liberalisation consistent with maintaining the universal service at a uniform tariff and compatible with our domestic regime.' In reply the Chairman of Postcomm, Graham Corbett, noted that

> whilst Postcomm has not yet reached a final decision on the approach to competition we doubt that simply reducing the licensed area in the UK (through a reduction in the weight/price threshold) would be an attractive option for providing effective competition. Distribution of mail volumes and revenues tends to be concentrated towards the lower end of the weight and price range and on this basis a reduction to 100 grams would only result in a limited opening – 13% of the market by volume – which would make it hard for competitors to offer a service that would be of interest to mailers.

2.   BARRIERS TO LIBERALIZATION: THE UNIVERSAL SERVICE OBLIGATION

The USO is central to the argument about liberalization. Postal services in nearly all countries of the world are required to meet Universal Service Obligations. That is, they have to deliver to every address (or nearly every address) in the land, often once a day, and they have to collect mail in such a way that citizens can all access the postal network. In addition, and this is crucial to the economics of the matter, they usually have to do this at a *uniform tariff*.

A diagram that appeared in the European Commission's Green Paper on postal services illustrates the matter in broad terms,[2] and is reproduced here as Figure 9.1.

The figure shows that at a uniform tariff of P_1 there will be a part of the business which covers costs, and a part that does not. However, if cross-subsidy

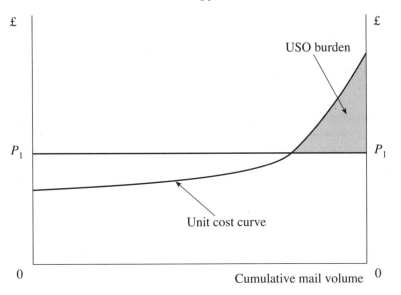

Figure 9.1   The burden of the USO

is permitted, the postal operator can meet the loss on the unprofitable business from the profits on the profitable business, and so break even (including earning a proper return on capital).[3]

The USO burden shown in Figure 9.1 can be estimated on a fully allocated cost (FAC) basis or on a net avoided cost (NAC) basis. If the unit costs shown in Figure 9.1 are estimated on an avoidable cost basis, then the area that shows the difference between revenue and avoidable costs in the left-hand part of the diagram must cover the loss on the unprofitable parts of the business plus fixed costs.

The traditional solution to the resulting cross-subsidization has been to protect the postal operator by defining a 'reserved area' where competition is not permitted. The justification has been as follows: the existence of some traffics whose revenue more than covers costs so as to cross-subsidize unprofitable traffics requires protection from competition in this low-cost sector. This is because an entrant could serve only a part of the market, and undercut the incumbent, provided that the entrant could achieve unit cost below the uniform price if the incumbent is not allowed to flex prices, but must continue to charge the uniform price for all business, or provided that the entrant could achieve a unit cost below the incumbent's unit cost in circumstances where the incumbent is not able to charge a price below its own unit cost.[4]

One relevant issue is the shape of the curve, since different shapes will determine the extent to which there would be opportunities for profitable entry.

NERA's estimates of USO burdens in our 1998 study for the European Commission (NERA, 1998) were based primarily on the way in which Royal Mail delivery costs (taken as 38.4 per cent of total letter mail costs in our study) varied across the network, on the basis of detailed data for a sample week on labour hours and items of letter mail delivered in the 1389 delivery offices in the UK. The resulting cost index of labour delivery costs per item delivered (with the lowest set at 1) is shown in Figure 9.2. This shows a relatively gently sloping curve, with a sharp 'tail' at the end, which represents what might be termed deep rural areas.

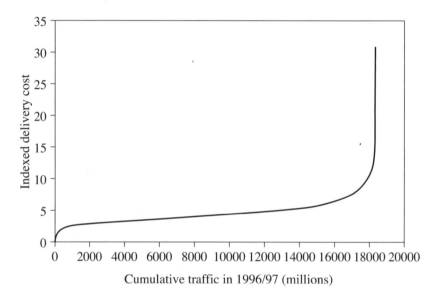

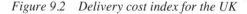

Figure 9.2   Delivery cost index for the UK

NERA's estimate of the burden of the USO in our 1998 study for the European Commission was £23 million at 1996/97 prices on a net avoided cost (NAC) basis, and £281 million on a fully allocated cost (FAC) basis (NERA, 1998, pp. 221–2). Using the same broad methodology, but more detailed data on Consignia's traffics, revenues and costs, Postcomm has estimated the burden of the USO on an NAC basis as around £80 million. Postcomm notes, however, that (i) this ignores benefits of the universal service, (ii) the estimates assume existing rather than optimal levels of efficiency, and (iii) distortions in the calculations might arise from levels of disaggregation across flows. Postcomm notes: 'It may be difficult at this stage to conclude that there is any net cost of the UPS or, if there is, that it is significant' (Postcomm, 2001b, pp. 32–3).

3. POSTAL SERVICE PROVISION IN THE UK

3.1 The Demand for Traditional Postal Services

It is useful to understand what has been happening in postal markets in the UK. Figure 9.3 shows Royal Mail volumes between 1991 and the present by two main types of mail: domestic first class and domestic second class. Figures have been adjusted to give a consistent series by allowing for a number of revisions to the published series which reduced recorded mail volumes.[5]

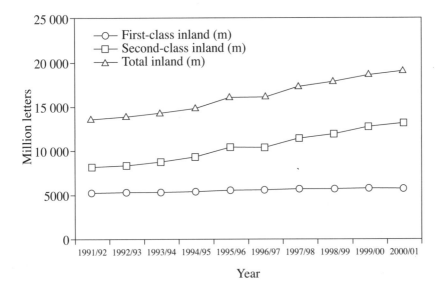

Figure 9.3   Inland mail volumes, 1991/92 to 2000/2001

The main feature of Figure 9.3 is how flat first-class mail volumes are. It is often said that electronic mail may see the demise of traditional postal services: certainly they may restrict hopes of growth. There is also little scope to increase mail volumes by pricing. Recent econometric estimates yield an overall price elasticity estimate for Royal Mail letter traffic of –0.2 if first- and second-class mail prices move in step, but an elasticity of –1 for first-class mail if second-class price is held constant, indicating (not surprisingly) substitutability between the mail types (Nankervis et al., 2001).

Contract letter service volumes where the sender receives a discount based on 'work-sharing' (and which are included in the first- and second-class mail volumes shown in Figure 9.3) have seen growth. There was a 10 per cent per annum growth rate in pre-sort traffic in the UK between 1981 and 1999

(Nankervis et al., 2001). According to Postcomm, by 1999/2000 contract letter services accounted for 57 per cent of total letter service revenue of £4614 million (Postcomm, 2001a, p. 107). About fifty customers account for 22 per cent of total mail volumes and the top 500 account for about 45 per cent (ibid., p. 75). This increase in work-sharing – that is, pre-sorting by senders – results from advances in computing which make it possible for senders to print out mail pieces in orders defined by Royal Mail's software and to add bar-codes that permit further mechanical sorting in Royal Mail's sorting centres. Indeed, under Walksort, a mailing can be sorted by the sender down to individual postmen's walks.

3.2   Costs and Productivity

Table 9.1 shows the split of Consignia's letter mail postal costs between activities. Delivery accounts for 43 per cent of directly attributable costs, sorting (both outwards and inwards) for 26 per cent, transport for 14 per cent, and collection for 5 per cent.

Table 9.1   Consignia letter mail postal costs by activity

	% of directly attributable costs
Collection	5
Outward sorting	12
Transportation	14
Inward sorting	14
Delivery	43
Support activities	12

Note: Directly attributable costs account for over 75% of total inland letter costs.

Source: Consignia, via Postcomm (2001a, p. 20).

There appear to be economies of scale and probably particularly of density in postal service operations. Consignia estimates that around 60 per cent of its total current costs can change over time with volume changes (Postcomm, 2001a, p. 34). Cost elasticities vary between activities: earlier Royal Mail estimates suggest cost elasticities[6] of 0.05 for collection, 0.84 for both inward and outward sorting, and 0.31 for transport (NERA, 1998, p. 48).

Consignia's regulatory accounts provide revenue, cost and hence profitability information for the three main categories of business (Consignia, 2001):

- the licensed USO business, that is, the part of Consignia's business covered by the 15-year licence granted by Postcomm on 23 March 2001, and covering the reserved area of items less than 350 gs and £1 (this part of the business accounted for 66 per cent of Consignia's postal revenue in 2000/2001);
- the unlicensed USO business, being the remainder of the business over which the USO applies (19 per cent of revenue in 2000/2001); and
- the non-USO business (the remaining 15 per cent of Consignia postal revenue in 2000/2001).

The regulatory accounts reveal a loss on ordinary activities before interest of £317 million on the licensed USO business, a profit of £518 million on the unlicensed USO business and a loss of £226 million on the non-licensed postal business (plus a loss on non-postal services of £94 million).

Mail services are still labour-intensive, especially in the reserved sector. Consignia's regulatory accounts for 2000/2001 indicate that 65 per cent of costs in the licensed USO part of the business are labour costs, compared with 40 per cent in the rest of the USO sector, and 45 per cent in the non-licensed, non-USO sector.

A simple form of labour productivity in terms of letters handled per staff operating hour is shown in Figure 9.4. Between 1991/92 and 2000/2001 letters handled per staff operating hour rose from 39.8 to 54.3, a rise of 36.4 per cent,

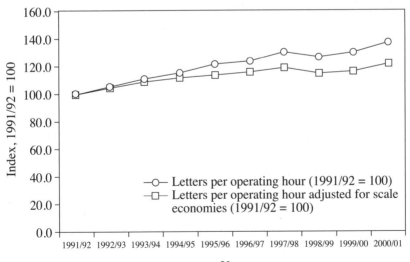

Figure 9.4   Labour productivity, 1991/92 to 2000/2001

an annual average growth rate of 3.5 per cent. However, adjusting for economies
of scale (since traffic in terms of letters posted rose by 38.6 per cent, and annual
operating hours did not change greatly) using the overall cost elasticity figure
of 0.6 means that underlying labour productivity growth over the period would
be reduced to 21.2 per cent, or an annual average of just over 2 per cent. In
addition, labour productivity should have been helped by (i) the fact that contract
mail volumes were growing faster than other mail, so the Post Office would
have been benefiting because of reduced labour needs due to work-sharing, and
(ii) the percentage of letters postcoded increased from 82.9 per cent in 1991/92
to 96.3 per cent in 2000/2001, which should have reduced sorting costs (these
two factors would have been related, since contract letters are postcoded letters).

4.   THE IMPACT OF LIBERALIZATION

4.1   How Can We Assess the Impact of Liberalization?

We have seen that provision of a universal postal service has required that
national postal operators be granted the protection of a reserved sector where
they are able to exercise monopoly powers. However, the protection that results
has led to deep concerns about postal operator efficiency and their willingness
to innovate, in a sector where demand has been growing slowly and where there
has been fierce competition for traditional postal services from alternative means
of communication, the telephone, the fax and now e-mail and the Internet. The
key issue is therefore to assess what will be the impact of liberalization on the
preservation of the universal service.

4.2   Alternative Forms of Liberalization: the EC Studies

There have been various proposals regarding the form that postal liberalization
might take, and in 1998 the results of the separate studies that the European
Commission had commissioned on the four main types of postal liberalization
were published. These were on:

- liberalizing direct mail (Arthur Andersen, 1998);
- reducing weight and price limits (CTcon, 1998a);
- upstream liberalization – liberalizing clearance, sorting and transport
  (CTcon, 1998b); and
- liberalizing incoming and outgoing intra-Community cross-border mail
  (PricewaterhouseCoopers, 1998).

These were complemented by a general modelling study of the impacts of
different liberalization scenarios (MMD Ltd, 1999). This study used data and

other information from the previous four studies, together with cost data from the NERA study, to model the impact of different scenarios on postal volumes, revenues and universal service providers' market shares. Results in the published version of the report are shown for the 15 Member States as a whole. The different scenarios were:

- scenario 1, a reference scenario in which there was no further liberalization, and underlying growth of 14 per cent in total mail volumes between 1997 and 2003;
- scenario 2, liberalization in 2003 of direct mail and weight bands greater than 50 g;
- scenario 3, liberalization in 2003 of direct mail, cross-border mail and weight bands greater than 50 g, that is, scenario 2 plus cross-border mail;
- scenario 4, full liberalization in 2003 of direct mail, cross-border mail and all weight bands; and
- scenario 5, two-stage liberalization, with direct mail, cross-border mail and weight bands over 50 g liberalized in 2003, followed by liberalization of all weight bands after 2005.

Results showed that under all scenarios the universal service provider was expected to retain more than 90 per cent of mail volume market shares in both 2003 and 2007, with one minor exception.[7] Given the assumed (fairly modest) underlying growth in mail volumes, it appears that universal service providers could be expected to be handling increased volumes of mail under the liberalization scenarios (though less than they would handle in the absence of liberalization). While these results all relate to the EU as a whole, it would be interesting to know what the model showed for the UK, and the detailed assumptions for the UK postal market on which these results were based.

4.3 Evidence from Other Countries

A number of countries have liberalized postal services, and a recent presentation by Ian Senior surveyed experience in four of them: Argentina, Finland, New Zealand and Sweden.

- In Argentina, the national postal operator Correo was privatized as a 30-year concession in 1997. It has just been placed in chapter 11 (a type of bankruptcy). It has lost business to private sector operators who do not have universal service obligations, and it claims that these operators do not respect social security and other regulations.
- In Finland the market was fully liberalized in 1994, but entrants would have to contribute to a universal service fund (USF). It appears that this

has acted as a deterrent to entry, though Postcomm claim that the threat of entry led to improvements in Finland Post's efficiency. (In our 1998 study we were critical of the use of USFs.)

- In New Zealand the market was fully liberalized in 1998, and New Zealand Post has 98 per cent of the market for letters. It retains a universal service obligation, for which it is not compensated. A competitor, National Mail, exited the market in December 2000.
- In Sweden the market was fully liberalized in 1993, and Sweden Post has 94 per cent of the market for letters. Prices rose, though, in part due to imposition of VAT, and profitability fell.

Evidence on experience from other countries is rather mixed, but it shows that incumbents are generally able to retain significant market share.

4.4   Modelling the Impact of Liberalization

A number of studies have been concerned with modelling the impact of entry into postal markets, the main one being the 'entry pricing approach' developed over a number of years by The Post Office (see, for example, Robinson and Rodriguez, 2000 and Rodriguez and Storer, 2000). The approach seeks to model the impact of entry into a postal market where the incumbent is required to provide a universal service at a uniform price. Entry will then occur in the low cost parts of the market. Entry will depend on two main factors:

- the assumed level of costs of the entrant; and
- the response of the incumbent.

If the incumbent is not permitted to respond (because a uniform price really does mean a uniform price – no discounts), then entry could occur even if the entrant cannot match the incumbent's costs. If the incumbent were X-efficient (in which case we might not worry about liberalization so much!) and there were economies of density, then the entrant might well not get costs down to those of the incumbent, but could still undercut the uniform tariff.[8]

If the incumbent can react and can charge any price above its own costs (to avoid accusations of predatory behaviour), it can undercut the entrant's costs unless the entrant can somehow build up sufficient volumes to match the incumbent's own costs.

If the incumbent is not X-efficient, then entry is easier (and more desirable), but the entrant still has to match unit costs and needs to beware of predatory behaviour. The EC ruling earlier this year on the case of Deutsche Post (Box 9.1) provides a precedent, though not one that should give complete comfort to entrants.

BOX 9.1   THE DEUTSCHE POST PREDATORY
PRICING RULING

In March 2001 the European Commission issued its first formal decision in the postal sector under Article 82, concluding that Deutsche Post AG (DPAG) had abused its dominant position by engaging in predatory pricing and granting fidelity rebates in the market for business parcels services. As a result DPAG had to create a separate legal entity for business parcels services, with a system of transparent and market-based pricing between DPAG and the new entity for services provided between them. (In addition DPAG was fined €24 million for the foreclosure resulting from its long-standing scheme of fidelity rebates which provided substantial discounts to large mail-order customers who sent all, or a sizeable proportion, of their mail-order parcels business via DPAG.) The decision follows from a complaint lodged in 1994 by UPS (Universal Postal Service) that Deutsche Post was using revenue from the profitable letter mail monopoly to finance below-cost selling in the competitive parcels business. The Commission's decision rules that any service by the beneficiary of a monopoly in open competition has to cover at least the additional or incremental cost incurred in branching out into the competitive sector. Any cost coverage below this level is predatory pricing and breaches Article 82. The investigation revealed that for five years DPAG had indeed not covered the incremental costs of its mail-order delivery service. However, the Commission ruled that DPAG did not have to make any contribution from its competitive business to cover any of the costs incurred in its provision of facilities needed to provide 'over-the-counter' universal service provision of parcels in Germany. 'DPAG is required only to cover the costs attributable to the provision of mail-order parcels services. This means that these operations are not burdened with the common fixed cost of providing network capacity that DPAG incurs as a result of its statutory universal service obligation.'[1] This might mean that a universal service provider is at an advantage compared with an entrant who has to incur overhead costs in setting up a network, since they could claim that the DPAG ruling means that they could cut prices to their own incremental costs in response to entry.

1. Commission Decision of 20 March 2001 relating to a proceeding under Article 82 of the EC Treaty (Case COMP/35.141 – Deutsche Post AG).

Despite the small size of existing USO burdens, Consignia argue that liberalization will open up the floodgates to competition and so Consignia will lose traffic and/or revenue. Consequently they will not be able to earn profits in order to cover their USOs. These conclusions are based on the entry price modelling approach, which requires a number of assumptions about:

- cost levels of entrants;
- the extent to which existing consumers will switch to entrants if entry occurs;
- the response that the incumbent will make to entry; and
- the extent to which lower prices in response to entry stimulate total demand for the services supplied.

A key driver in terms of the impact on incumbent profitability is the extent to which the model presumes that costs are fixed. If entrants do compete away a significant proportion of the excess of revenue over avoidable costs, and there is a substantial amount of fixed costs, then a postal incumbent that was breaking even without competition would find itself facing substantial losses. Consignia has argued to Postcomm that 40 per cent of its total costs would not change with volume and that these costs represent the 'unavoidable' costs of maintaining the potential for nationwide access and delivery, that is, the universal service provision (Postcomm, 2001a, p. 34). Postcomm's response was that Consignia should be prepared to re-optimize its business and develop more innovative cost structures in order to be flexible to competition (ibid., p. 35).

The entry pricing approach regards the cost of the USO as the difference between profits earned by an X-efficient postal operator under a liberalized regime without a USO, and profits earned by the same operator with the same liberalized regime but with a USO at a uniform price. One clear difficulty in operationalizing the concept is to determine the value of the first of these profit levels, since it represents the counterfactual case where liberalization occurs, the postal operator has become X-efficient (how do we know it is?), but it does not have USO/uniform price requirements. In light of this, another difficulty is that a postal operator with a USO and a uniform price requirement in a liberalized environment might claim that it is X-efficient and that all its losses are due to its USO/uniform price requirements.

But there are also problems with the method itself:

- Most of the modelling seems to assume that the entrant will have the same marginal costs as the incumbent, but this presumes they can take advantage of economies of density by building volumes. This will be difficult, and the entrants will have to judge before entry whether they will be able to do this. In making decisions about entry they will also want to be able to cover their own fixed costs, so they will need to assess whether they will be able to charge prices that enable them to do so.

- Consignia has benefits of ubiquity, it serves every address in the country, and interchanges mail with most (if not every) national postal administration in the world. It therefore offers customers, including major mailers, a 'one-stop shop'.
- Consignia has the advantage of its well-known brand names, especially that of Royal Mail.
- Customers have a reasonable expectation of what standard of service they will get from Consignia, since detailed quality-of-service statistics are published.[9]
- The entry pricing modelling generally assumes that the incumbent is X-efficient, but the major driver for liberalization is to improve efficiency in the operation of postal services. If actual or potential competition improves the incumbent's efficiency, this is a major benefit of liberalization.[10]

This all suggests that the risks of permitting serious competition may not be as great as the entry pricing approach suggests. But what is clearly important first is to establish the 'rules of the game' in regard to what competitive responses Consignia is permitted to make. Clearly predatory reactions are not permitted by competition law and precedents, but the question of other pricing responses needs to be answered. Postcomm have indicated:

> Consignia might reasonably be expected to have a degree of pricing flexibility in terms of its work share discounts and its ability under the Act to offer bulk discounts, subject to not being anti-competitive. (Postcomm, 2001a, p. 38)

This is already anticipated in the Postal Services Act, which notes that provision of a universal service does not prevent 'the conclusion with customers of individual agreements as to prices'. Condition 11 (on promotion of effective competition) in Consignia's licence states that the Licensee, in the terms on which it supplies or offers to supply postal services to customers,

- (i) shall not show undue preference to any person or class of persons, and
- (ii) shall not exercise any undue discrimination against or seek to impose any undue restriction on any person or class of persons, and
- (iii) shall not set terms or charges for the supply of postal services
  - (a) which are excessive, or
  - (b) which are predatory.

But the key issue is how far Consignia can react to specific entry, an area on which clear rules will need to be established.

5.   THE WAY AHEAD

The present legislation and the Regulator (and the general climate of opinion) appear to be pro-competitive. Consignia appears to be widely regarded as not being efficient. Nevertheless, there are concerns that liberalization might still jeopardize the provision of the universal service, and there is still rather limited evidence by which to judge the potential outcome of liberalization.

There is sufficient uncertainty to indicate that it would not be sensible to rely on competition alone. It is also difficult to believe that 'effective competition' means anything other than large-scale competition. In practice, actual competition might be patchy in its impact. Consignia might take action to protect its business from major customers, but may pay less attention to overall efficiency and to quality of service provided to private consumers of postal services.

There is also the danger that Consignia might use the entry pricing argument *ex post*. Postcomm liberalizes the market, entry and serious competition occur, Consignia's financial position gets worse, and, in effect, it tells the government:

> we told you so: we have lost profits as a result of liberalization because we were required to provide a universal service at a uniform price, and now we must be compensated because these losses are the direct result of liberalization: they are a direct measure of 'the cost of the universal service obligation'.

I believe there are two main implications of the arguments set out in this chapter.

First, Postcomm should encourage liberalization as much as possible, and should not be deflected from its objective of encouraging effective competition. Postcomm have already indicated that reducing price and weight limits is not enough, and tables in their consultation documents (reproduced here as Tables 9.2 and 9.3) indicate how Consignia's business might be affected by different relaxations.

Second, Postcomm should give greater weight to the potential for stronger regulatory intervention. The Postal Services Act gives the Postal Services Commission the duty to 'exercise its functions in the manner which it considers is best calculated to promote efficiency and economy on the part of postal operators'. So far Postcomm seems to have rather downplayed the role of regulation: 'Though regulation can help deliver consumer benefits, it may give less powerful incentives to operators than competitors to change behaviour and innovate' (Postcomm, 2001a, p. 2), and

> regulation without competition may not be well suited to identifying and achieving the quality of service and price package that different customers will desire. An important rationale, therefore, for choosing competition over regulation is to enable customers, rather than the regulator, to decide what is in their own best interests. Another reason for choosing competition over regulation is that effective competition is more likely to incentivise Consignia to focus on tackling competitors and

innovating in customers' best interest. Regulation, without competition, risks providing incentives to battle with the regulator, in Consignia's own interest, which may not necessarily be aligned with the best interests of customers. (Postcomm, 2001a, p. 15)

My argument is that both competition and regulation are needed. The danger is that even both together may not be enough. This is because Consignia may not react to the incentives in the appropriate way. It may blame universal service obligations for loss of profitability. It may not react appropriately to a price regime such as (RPI–X), an approach that has been designed for use on private sector firms.[11]

I believe that this will reopen the debate as to whether Consignia should remain in the public sector.

Table 9.2 Distribution of Consignia inland letter traffics by weight band, 1999–2000

Weight band (g)	Volumes (mn)	Cumulative % of total volumes	Cumulative % of total revenues
0–20	8 032	36.2	31.5
21–50	7 627	70.6	51.2
51–100	3 108	84.6	63.3
101–150	1 301	90.4	71.0
151–350	1 546	97.4	85.8
Over 350	576	100.0	100.0
Total	**22 190**		

Source: Consignia, via Postcomm (2001a, pp. 66–7).

Table 9.3 Distribution of Consignia inland letter traffics by price band, 1999–2000

Price band	Volumes (m)	Cumulative % of total volumes	Cumulative % of total revenues
20p or less	12 971	58.5	34.3
Over 20p to 27p	6 239	86.6	64.5
Over 27p to 50p	1 989	95.5	79.5
Over 50p to £1	701	98.7	89.5
Over £1 to £5	289	100.0	100.0
Over £5	0	100.0	100.0
Total	**22 190**		

Source: Consignia, via Postcomm (2001a, p. 68).

NOTES

1. The USO also requires provision of a service for registered mail.
2. Figure 3.1 in Postcomm's consultation document on promoting effective competition (Postcomm, 2001a, p. 31) is equivalent.
3. Without the uniform tariff the operator could simply charge more for higher-cost business, but this does not guarantee that cross-subsidy (though on a lesser scale) would not be needed because there might be some activities where economies of scale and low levels of demand might mean that no price will ensure cost recovery (that is, a downward-sloping average cost curve lies everywhere above the demand curve).
4. This raises the important question of the proper definition of predatory behaviour in postal markets, a matter on which the European Commission issued a formal decision in relation to Deutsche Post AG (DPAG) in March 2001.
5. Information on mail volumes is published in Consignia's annual accounts. The latest 2000/2001 accounts include a series of letter traffic from 1996/97 to 2000/2001, with traffic numbers restated to reflect a change from the previous year in the basis of calculation of inland letter volumes. There were previous changes in the basis of calculation in 1998/99 and 1992/93, and I have spliced the series together by assuming that growth rates between years are a fair reflection of changes in mail volumes. Consignia may still be having some problems measuring its letter volumes, since their regulatory accounts note: 'Consignia recognises that there are inadequacies in the current traffic measurement and statistical procedures and have ongoing initiatives to improve the processes.'
6. That is, elasticity of cost with respect to output: a value less than one indicates economies.
7. Universal service providers' combined market shares would fall to 89 per cent in 2007 under scenario 3.
8. Entrants might have difficulty reaching the traffic volumes necessary to take advantage of economies of density. See Postcomm (2001a, p. 25) on overseas experience.
9. Customers may, or may not, be satisfied with these standards of service, but it will be more difficult for consumers to establish in advance what quality of service they can expect from entrants.
10. The paper by De Donder et al. (2002) does consider what percentage improvements in incumbent efficiency would make entry desirable. One version of the entry pricing model does assume a 10 per cent improvement in Consignia efficiency, but this does not seem to be included as a benefit of liberalization.
11. In addition, it seems likely that any (RPI–X) regime would need to incorporate service quality factors.

REFERENCES

Arthur Andersen (1998), *Study on the Impact of Liberalisation in the Postal Sector: Direct Mail*, November.

Baker, S. and J. Dodgson (2001), 'Market definition in postal services', in D. Geradin (ed.), *The Liberalisation of Postal Services in the European Union*, The Hague: Kluwer Law International, pp. 121–37.

Consignia (2001), *Regulatory Financial Statements of the Post Office 2000–01*.

CTcon (1998a), *On the Liberalisation of Clearance, Sorting and Transport*, August.

CTcon (1998b), *Study on the Weight and Price Limits of the Reserved Area in the Postal Sector*, November.

De Donder, P., J. Cremer and F. Rodriguez (2002), 'Funding the universal service obligation under liberalisation: an analysis of the postal market', in M.A. Crew and

P.R. Kleindorfer (eds), *Postal and Delivery Services: Pricing, Productivity, Regulation and Strategy*, Boston, MA: Kluwer Academic Publishers.

European Commission (1997), *Directive 97/67/EC of the European Parliament and of the Council on Common Rules for the Development of the Internal Market of the Community Postal Services and the Improvement of the Quality of Services*, OJ 21.1.98.

MMD Ltd (1999), *Modelling and Quantifying Scenarios for Liberalisation*, February.

NERA (1998), *Costing and Financing of Universal Services in the Postal Sector in the European Union*, a report to DGXIII, NERA, London.

Nankervis, J., S. Richard, S. Soteri and F. Rodriguez (2001), 'Disaggregated letter traffic demand in the UK', in M.A. Crew and P.R. Kleindorfer (eds), *Postal and Delivery Services: Pricing, Productivity, Regulation and Strategy*, Boston, MA: Kluwer Academic Publishers.

Postcomm (2001a), *Promoting Effective Competition in UK Postal Services: a Consultation Document*, June.

Postcomm (2001b), *An Assessment of the Costs and Benefits of Consignia's Current Universal Service Provision: a Discussion Document*, June.

PricewaterhouseCoopers (1998), *Liberalisation of Incoming and Outgoing Intra-Community Cross-Border Mail*, December.

Robinson, Richard and Frank Rodriguez (2000), 'Liberalization of the postal market and the cost of the universal service obligation: some estimates for the UK', in M.A. Crew and P.R. Kleindorfer (eds), *Current Directions in Postal Reform*, Boston, MA: Kluwer Academic Publishers, pp. 107–32.

Rodriguez, F. and D. Storer (2000), 'Alternative approaches to estimating the cost of the USO in posts', *Information Economics*, **11**, 285–99.

CHAIRMAN'S COMMENTS

Graham Corbett

John Dodgson has presented an extremely thought-provoking assessment of the issues and challenges facing Postcomm in liberalizing the UK postal services market. He questions whether Postcomm is giving sufficient attention to regulation in contrast to competition. I would comment that we are certainly not ignoring it, but I hope we are being quite clear-eyed about how far economic regulation is likely to be effective against a wholly government-owned entity. Finally, he questions whether Consignia should remain in the public sector, but that is a matter for the politicians.

To stimulate the debate, I now offer three questions that concern us particularly.

UPS AND UNIVERSAL TARIFF

The first goes to the heart of the need for a regulatory regime at all. The Universal Postal Service concept is, rightly, hard-wired in to every developed postal system, and in many countries, the UK among them, it carries an attendant requirement for a uniform tariff. There is a widespread assumption that the UPS is an endangered species, calling for careful preservation and protection from marauding beasts. Indeed, so powerful has been the influence of this assumption that it has served to preserve the postal monopoly for over 350 years.

So on the basis that nothing deserves closer examination than a universally acknowledged truth, it's worth asking whether, if the UPS didn't exist, commercial pressures would be likely to bring it about *de facto*. To any operator covering 90+ per cent of the country, what are the benefits and the attendant costs entailed in being able to claim coverage of 95 per cent, or 99 per cent or 99.9 per cent?

The same goes for the application of a uniform tariff to the basic service. It's worth reminding ourselves that Rowland Hill was able to introduce the concept of a very simple pre-payment system in 1840 only because his exhaustive costing studies had shown him that the factor of distance played a far less important role than could be justified by the administrative costs and uncertainties entailed in a price-by-distance system. The result was a huge popular boost in the amount of mail being carried.

If we were to conclude that both the UPS and the uniform tariff might owe as much to commercial self-interest as to dictat, would it not be right for the regulator to test these findings by a progressive relaxation of the measures designed to protect the UPS and the uniform tariff from competitive erosion?

And if it were to become clear that the UPS and the uniform tariff were actually quite capable of sustaining themselves without intervention, Postcomm might find itself in the running for the Haskins Regulator of the Year award by having disappeared like the Snark even before the award could be bestowed – although it might well by then have been renamed as the Callum McCarthy award.

LEVEL PLAYING FIELD FOR NEW ENTRANTS

The second concern is whether Postcomm's focus does not therefore need to be at least as much about ensuring a level playing field for new entrants as about preserving the universal service capability of the incumbent.

Successful competition needs successful entrants. So introducing competition has to be about giving potential entrants to the market a proper chance to succeed and to pass the benefits on to postal users. One of the key lessons we have learnt from the experience of market opening in other countries is just how limited entry to the market tends to be, even where there is full liberalization.

Competition in postal markets has yet to produce one market that does not remain dominated – 90 per cent or more – by the national operator. Undoubtedly factors such as economies of scale and customer loyalty play a large role in this, but national operators have also strongly contested entry to the market by legal challenge, restricting access to the network, and aggressively responding on prices, often to the detriment of competition.

It seems to me that to counter this potential imbalance takes more than the regulator simply making some encouraging noises about opening the market. There must be real steps to ensure that the potential for competition leads to vigorous rivalry between operators that creates efficiency and value for money for postal users.

CULTURAL TRANSFORMATION

My last point is to recognize that introducing competition and supporting the universal service must be about more than systems and processes. It involves an important cultural transformation for the UK postal industry and its workforce – a change of mindset. The ways of yesterday with a comfortable monopoly cannot be the ways of the commercial marketplace. This may sound obvious, but it is in fact a tremendous challenge facing Consignia.

We often hear that competition is a threat to Consignia. Quite to the contrary. Competition itself is not the main threat. The real threat, as Dodgson has pointed out, comes from a reluctance to change and to provide better and more reliable postal services to customers. If they don't respond, customers will seek their own solutions. And that is likely to be damaging not just to Consignia, but to the whole postal service industry. So we in Postcomm are every bit as anxious to see Consignia responding successfully to this challenge as are Consignia themselves. Perhaps the question for us is then: what regulatory framework is best placed to encourage this change?

Index

2G licences 157
3G auctions 140, 157–8
Advisory Bodies – Consumer Panel 153
Advisory Committees on Telecoms 153
Affuso, L. 44
Africa 79
agricultural price supports 177
air quality 12–14
Airline Deregulation Act 166
airport landing rights 176
Algeria 107, 113, 116
AngloAmerican/Tarmac 207
Annual Report 153
Argentina 68
   Correo 227
asset ownership operations 191–3
asynchronous digital subscriber line 140,
   154–5, 156
AT & T 141, 180
Australia 61, 62, 68
   National Electricity Code
      Administrator 68
   National Electricity Market 83
   Victoria 72, 78
Austria 209

Baker, S. 219
BASF/Takeda 210, 211, 215
Baumol, W.J. 128–9
Becker, G. 165
Beeching rationalizations 24
Beesley, M. xxi, 67, 188–9
Belgium 127
Bell 172
   Canada 141
Better Regulation Task Force 186
Birmingham North Relief Road 29
Blinder, A.S. 128–9
Boeing–McDonnell/Douglas 179
Britain
   Central Electricity Generating Board
      67

competition policy 121, 124–5, 128,
   130–31, 134
economic regulation, demise of 162,
   186
electricity 62, 66, 68, 71, 74–5, 77–81,
   83, 88–9
and the European Commission 206–7
mergers 203, 204–6, 209, 210
mutualization and debt-only vehicles
   193, 194, 197
National Power 67
Nuclear Electric 67
postal services liberalization 223–6
PowerGen 67
telecommunications 140–41, 143–4,
   146–7, 154–6, 158, 160–61
   see also gas supply and demand;
      postal services liberalization
British Gas 115, 195
British Petroleum 100, 111
British Rail 59
British Roads Federation 40
British Telecom 140–1, 143–4, 147–8,
   155–7, 160–1
   see also Cellnet
broadband 140, 154–6
Brussels 160, 206, 209, 212, 213, 216
Burns, T. 193
buses 20–21
Byatt, I. 188, 200, 202
Byers, S. 158, 187, 188

C3D Rhone/GoAhead 206, 207
cable television monopoly 169–71
Cable and Wireless 148
California
   Assembly Bill IX 75
   Department of Water Resources 75,
      76
   economic regulation, demise of 173–4
   electricity 62, 67, 69, 71, 72, 73–7, 79

Poolco model 78
PUC 75, 76, 77
Canada 141, 146, 210
    Bell 141
    Radio, Television and Communica-
        tions Commission 147
Capex 192, 196
carbon dioxide emissions 11–12
cash-out prices, single/dual 82–4
Cayman Islands 212
Cellnet 140, 158, 160
Central Electricity Generating Board 80,
    89
centralized trading 80–82
Channel Tunnel 48
charging 29–30
Chataway, C. 187
Chicago School 123
China 211
Co-op movement 191
Coates, J. 10
COBA 39
Commission for Integrated Transport 10
commuter rail services 30–31, 32
competition 121–37
    Britain 121, 124–5, 128, 130–31, 134
    and economic regulation 179–82
    Europe 127, 128, 130–31
    France 130
    Office of Fair Trading 125, 126–7,
        130, 134
    United States 121, 123, 124–5, 127,
        128, 130–32, 134
    see also electricity
Competition Act 161
Competition Commission 57, 130,
    135–6, 147, 153, 157, 202
    mergers 204–5, 206, 211, 212, 213
Comprehensive Spending Review 37
Confederation of British Industry 126
congestion charging 29–30
    and hypothecation of revenues 2–3
Conservative government 7, 20, 25–7,
    29–30, 35–6, 38, 50–52
Consignia 220, 222, 224–5, 230–33,
    236–8
Consultation Document 1–4, 12, 17, 20,
    22, 27, 39, 220
Corbett, G. xxiv–xxv, 220, 236–8
corporate control 190–91

Crandall, R. xxiii, 162–83, 186
Cruikshank, D. 155
Currie, D. xxiii–xxiv, 80, 83, 187–98,
    199, 200, 201, 202

data local exchange competitors 155
debt-only vehicles *see* mutualization and
    debt-only vehicles
decentralized trading 80–82
demographic factors 5
Demsetz, H. 168, 173
Denmark 154
Department of the Environment,
    Transport and the Regions 2, 3, 17
Department of Trade and Industry 68–9,
    93, 103, 105, 220
deregulation, benefits of 166–7
deregulation, complete and conse-
    quences 167–74
    electricity 172–4
    telecommunications 171–2
    United States and cable television
        monopoly 169–71
*Developing an Integrated Transport
    Policy see* Consultation Document
digital subscriber lines 154
Docherty, I. 40
Dodgson, J. xxiv, 219–34, 236, 237

East Coast Main Line 23
Eastern Europe 79
economic rates of return 43–4
economic recessions 179
economic regulation 162–83, 186
    deregulation, benefits of 166–7
    deregulation, complete and conse-
        quences 167–74
    and economic recessions 179
    government controls, cost of 175–8
    modern theory 165–6
    in response to international disruptions
        178
    sectors, other 164
    to promote competition 179–82
    traditional regulation 163–4
Edmonds, D. xxiii, 160–61
electricity 61–90
    competition in generation: conduct
        and structure 68–71

competition in generation: initial
  restructuring 66–8
competition in retail supply 71–8
  costs and benefits 72–3
  direct access to wholesale spot price
    in California 73–5
  suspension in California 75–7
  transitional retail price cap 77–8
deregulation 172–4
Germany 63–4
New Zealand 64–6
overall trends 61–3
wholesale trading arrangements 78–84
  centralized verus decentralized
    trading 80–82
  New Electricity Trading
    Arrangements 79–80
  single/dual cash-out prices 82–4
electromagnetic spectrum 175–6
Ellig, J. 166, 167
Elliott, K.A. 177
Energy Contract Company 103, 106
Enron Corporation 162, 166
Enterprise Bill 60
environmental policy 11–12
Europe 79
  competition policy 127, 128, 130–31
  Eastern 79
  economic regulation, demise of 162,
    164
  electricity 68, 88
  gas 91, 106–7, 114, 115, 116
  mergers 204, 205
  telecommunications 140, 141, 158
  transport policy 7
  see also European
European Commission 62–3, 106–7,
    112, 114, 116, 131
  and Britain 206–7
  gas 91
  Green Paper on postal services 220
  mergers 213–15, 216
  postal services liberalization 219, 222,
    226–7, 228–9
  telecommunications 141, 144
European Community 62
  Merger Regulation 206–7, 208, 209,
    211, 213–15, 216
European Council 72, 219
European Parliament 155, 160, 219

European Postal Directive (97/67/EC)
    219
European Union
  economic regulation, demise of 179
  gas 113
  mutualization and debt-only vehicles
    188
  postal services liberalization 227
  telecommunications 155, 156, 160
Evans, A.E. 16

Federal Aviation Administration 176, 178
Federal Communications Commission
    146, 166, 169–70, 180, 181
finance/funding 47–50
Finland 227–8
  Post 228
Fletcher, P. xxiv, 194, 199–202
Foster, C.D. 3, 17
France 72, 73
  Electricité de France 68
  mergers 203, 210
  mutualization and debt-only vehicles
    192
  telecommunications 154, 155
franchise negotiations, delayed 22–3
freight 27–9
fuel
  costs 11
  road 10–11
  tax escalator 7–8
  tax protest 9–10
  taxation 7–8, 11–12, 13–14
fully allocated cost (FAC) 221, 222

gas supply and demand in Britain
    91–117, 119–20
  background 92
  balance of production and demand
    103–6
  contracts 113–16
  European gas import dependence
    106–7
  infrastructure provision 107–13
  potential production 92–9
    data and methodology 92–5
    results by field category 95–7
    results by producing area 97–9
  size and location of production and
    National Transmission System
    capacity 99–103

Gazprom 114, 115
General Electric 127, 131
General Electric–Honeywell 179, 210
Germany
    Bundeskartellant (BKA) 209
    Deutsche Post 228–9
    Deutsche Telekom AG (DTAG)
        155–6
    electricity 63–4, 68
    Federal Cartel Office (BKA) 64, 213
    mergers 203, 209
    RegTP 156
    telecommunications 154, 155–6
GFU 113–14
Glaeser, E.L. 177
Glaister, S. xxi, 1–54, 56, 59, 60
Glas Cymru 188, 189, 190, 194, 199,
    200, 202
government controls, cost of 175–8
government intervention 27
Govia/Connex 207
Graham, D. 5–6, 14
Great Depression 179
Great North Eastern Railway 23
Greater London
    Assembly 2, 30, 31, 32, 48, 53
    Assembly Act (1999) 30
    Authority 34
    Authority Act (1999) 2
    Council 33
Greece 209

Hanson/Pioneer 207
Harvey, S. 69
Haskins Task Force on Better Regulation
    157, 160
Hatfield accident 16, 25, 26, 45, 52, 56,
    57, 58
Hathaway, P. 8
Hausman, J. 172
Hay, D.A. 128, 135
Health and Safety Executive 188
Hicks, J.R. 122
Hill, R. 236
Hogan, B. 80, 82
Hogan, W. 69
Honeywell 127, 131
    see also General Electric–Honeywell
Hufbauer, G. C. 177

Independent System Operator 79

India 62, 79
infrastructure
    gas 107–13
    investment in 37–40
Institution of Civil Engineers 42
integrated services digital network 154,
    155–6
integration 17
Interbrew/Bass 207
international disruptions 178
International Energy Agency 91, 107
international mergers 203–18
    Britain 204
    Britain and European Commission
        206–7
    European Community Merger
        Regulation 213–15
    practical examples 208–13
    procedures in Britain 205–6
    reform in Britain 204–5
Internet Service Provider 155
Iran 116
Ireland 209
Italy 68, 154, 155, 203, 209

Japan 180, 203
Jenny, F. xxi
Joskow, P.L. 69, 78–9
Jubilee Line Extension 35, 48

Kahn, E. 69
Kelda proposition 189, 199–200, 202
Kemp, A. xxii, 91–117
Kingston 148
Kodak/Bell & Howell 213
Kolasky, W. 131
Korea 154

Labour government
    mutualization and debt-only vehicles
        187, 191
    and traffic 8–9
    transport policy 1, 50, 54
        air quality 13
        buses 20
        fuel taxation and environmental
            policy 11
        infrastructure investment 38, 39
        integration 17
        local transport 40
        London 30, 32, 33, 35, 36

railways 23, 24, 25, 26
road traffic 10
safety 15, 16
social inclusion 18
transport policy charging 29
Lafarge/Redland 210
Laffont, J.-J. 141–2
liberalization *see* postal services
liberalization
Littlechild, S. xxi–xxii, 61–87, 88, 89, 141
Livingston, K. 29
local transport 40–42, 43
London 12, 16, 30–37
Authority for London 2
commuter rail services 30–31, 32
rail franchises, renegotiation of 31–2
Railtrack 36–7
Regional Transport 17, 30, 51
Underground 17, 22–3, 30, 32–8, 47,
50–51, 53, 56, 60
see also Greater London
Long Run Incremental Cost 148, 155
Luttmer, E.F.P. 177

MacAvoy, P.W. 167
McCarthy, C. xxii, 119–20
MacKerron, G. 73
Mandelson, P. 158
Market Abuse Licence Condition 68–9
Marshall, A. 121–2
Marshall, E. xxii, 88–90
Masson, J. 44
MCI Executive 146
Mercury 147
mergers *see* international mergers
Mergers Panel 206
Mergers Task Force 207, 209
Mexico 62
Microsoft 179
mobiles 140, 157
mobility, benefits of 5–6
Modigliani–Miller theorem 189
Monopolies and Mergers Commission 153
Monte Carlo technique 93, 94, 95
Monti, Mr. 131
Morris, D. xxiii, 128, 134–7
Morrison, S.A. 166, 176
mutualization and debt-only vehicles:
RPI-X regulation 187–202
asset ownership and operations,
separation of 191–3

corporate control and mutuals 190–91
debt-only vehicles 189–90
regulatory context 193–4
regulatory system, future of 195–7
mutuals 190–91

Nankervis, J. 223–4
National
Air Traffic Control Services 22
Audit Office 72, 73
Balancing Point 110
Economic Research Associates 73,
157, 222, 227
Gas Corporation 189
Grid Company 82–3, 84
Transmission System 99–103, 107–10,
112
net avoided cost 221, 222
Netherlands 61, 72, 211
Gasunie 112, 115
*New Deal for Transport: Better for
Everyone see* Transport White
Paper
New Deal for Trunk Roads in England, A
39
New Electricity Trading Arrangements
79–80, 81–2, 89, 188
New Zealand 62, 64–6
Commerce Act 65
Commerce Commission 64
Contact Energy 67
electricity 61, 72, 88–9
Electricity Corporation 67
Electricity Governance Board 65
Energy Market 83
Guiding Principles 65
Minister for Energy 65
National Mail 228
Post 228
postal services liberalization 227–8
Transpower 65, 67
Newbery, D.M. 173
Newbury, D. 44
Nigeria 116
Norsk Hydro 113–14
North America 141
see also Canada; United States
North Sea 92, 94–5, 97–9
Northern Line 35

Norway 61, 72, 75, 83
  gas 92, 100, 107, 113, 114, 115, 116,
    117
  mergers 209, 212
  telecommunications 154

Ofcom 139–40, 146, 153–8, 195
  3G auctions 157–8
  broadband 154–6
  mobile 157
Office of Fair Trading
  competition policy 125, 126–7, 130, 134
  mergers 203, 204, 205, 206, 209, 211,
    212, 217–18
  telecommunications 147, 161
Office of Passenger Rail Franchising 3,
    22, 31, 51, 57
Office of the Rail Regulator 57
Office of the Regulator General 78
Ofgas 195
Ofgem 77–8, 80, 82, 108–11, 196, 201
Oftel 78, 143–6, 147–53, 154, 155, 157,
    158, 160, 161
Ofwat 190, 195, 200, 201, 202
One2One 157
Opex 192, 193–4
Orange 157, 160
Organisation for Economic Cooperation
    and Development 91, 107, 178, 179,
    180
Organisation of Petroleum Exporting
    Countries 178, 179

Paddington accident 56
Panel of Economic and Financial Experts
    153
Panels of Users 153
partnership 35
Peltzman, S. 165
Petoro 114
Philippines 62
PJM 83
Pools 78, 79, 80, 81–2, 83, 89, 90
Portugal 209
Posner, R. 165
Post Office 226, 228
Postal Service Commission (Postcomm)
    219–20, 222, 225, 228, 230–32,
    236–8
Postal Services Act (2000) 219, 231, 232

postal services liberalization 219–34,
    236–8
  barriers: Universal Service Obligation
    220–22
  cultural transformation 237–8
  future prospects 232–3
  impact 226–31
    alternative forms of: European
      Commission studies 226–7
    assessment 226
    modelling 228–31
    other countries, evidence from 227–8
  new entrants 237
  pressures for 219–20
  provision in Britain 223–6
  Universal Postal Service and universal
    tariff 236–7
Power Exchange (PX) 79
Prescott, J. 10
Private Finance Initiative 33, 35, 47, 48,
    53
privatization 24–5
Proctor and Gamble/Clairol 209
Public Accounts Committee 153
public transport fares 30
public–private partnership 2, 49, 52

Qatar 116

rail franchises, renegotiation of 31–2
Railtrack 16, 22–3, 26–7, 51–2, 56–60
  and London Underground 36–7
  mutualization and debt-only vehicles
    187, 188, 189, 199
  Network Management Statements
    (1999 and 2000) 44
  Periodic Review 26, 44, 45, 46
  Regulatory Asset Base 45
railways 22–7
  catastrophic decline 25
  commuter 30–31
  failures 25–7
  franchise negotiations, delayed 22–3
  government intervention 27
  growth under privatization and under
    Ten Year Plan 24–5
  Strategic Rail Authority, delayed 22
  Strategic Rail Authority, lack of 23–4
  see also Ten Year Plan and the railways
Railways Act (1993) 3
rate-of-return 141, 142

Reed Elsevier/Harcourt 210, 211, 215
Regional Development Agencies 32
regulation 191–3, 195–7
Regulatory Office 88
regulatory regime 34–5
rent control 176–7
retail price cap, transitional 77–8
retail supply *see* electricity
road fuel prices, political economy of
    10–11
road taxes 29
road tolls 29
road traffic 4–10
    fuel tax protest 9–10
    growth of traffic 4–8
    Labour government, effect on 8–9
    reduction of traffic 4
roads, benefits of 39–40
Robinson, C. xxi–xxv
Robinson, G. 47
Robinson, R. 228
Rodriguez, F. 228
Rowlatt, P. xxiii, 186
Royal Mail 222, 223–4, 231
RPI-12 per cent 157
RPI-X 146, 233
    see also mutualization and debt-only
        vehicles: RPI-X regulation
Ruff, L. 80, 81–2
Rural Bus Grant 20
Russia 92, 107, 113, 114, 115, 116, 117

safety 14–17
Sansom, T. 12
Schroder, Salomon, Smith, Barney 114
Schumpeter, J. 71
Scottish Power 200
Select Committee 153
Senior, I. 227
Shaw, J. 40
Sherman Act (1890) 121
Shin, R.T. 168
Shuttleworth, G. 73
Singapore 154
Smith, A. 131
social inclusion 18–19
Spain 68, 155, 209
State of the Nation 42
Statoil 113–14
Stelzer, I. xxii–xxiii, 121–33, 134, 135,
    136, 137

Stephen, L. xxii, 91–117
Stigler, G.J. 165
Storer, D. 228
Strategic Agenda 23
Strategic Rail Authority 3, 17, 22–4, 26,
    30–32, 45–6, 51, 53, 57–8
    Planning Criteria 43
    Strategic Agenda 44
subsurface lines 36–7
Swalec 194
Sweden 154, 227–8
    Post 228
System Buy Price 82
system marginal price 80, 144
System Operator 82
System Sell Price 82

taxes, road 29
Technical Expert Advisers' Panel 153
Telecom Act (1984) 146
telecommunications: regulatory
        incentives and deregulation 138–61,
        171–2
    background 140–41
    Ofcom and policy appeals 153–8
    Oftel 147–53
    regulation and incentives 141–7
        incentives for the regulator 145–7
        regulatory creep 144–5
        regulatory game 143–4
Telecommunications Act (1996) 153,
    170, 180
Ten Year Plan 3, 52–3, 56
    charging 29
    finance and funding 47–50
    local transport 41
    railways 23
    road fuel prices 11
    safety 14
    social inclusion 18
    transport infrastructure 37, 40
Ten Year Plan and the railways 24–5, 42–7
    balance between modes and economic
        rates of return 43–4
    freight, prospects for 45–6
    future funding, security of 46
    growth, unrealistic ambitions for 44–5
    physical problems 45
    risk assumptions 42–3
    Treasury, burden on 46–7
    without inflation 42

Terra 155
Thailand 62
Thameslink 2000 44
Tirole, J. 141–2
Total Element Long Run Incremental
    Cost 180
Towers Perrin 161
Trade Act (1974) 177
trade protection 177
traffic growth 38–40
Transco 100, 101, 103, 105, 106, 107–12
    mutualization and debt-only vehicles
        189, 196
Transocean/R&B Falcon 212
Transport 2010 see Ten Year Plan
Transport Act (2000) 3, 20
Transport Bill 22
Transport for London 17, 30, 31, 32, 48,
    51
    Board 2
transport policy in Britain 1–54, 56–60
    air quality 12–14
    buses 20–21
    charging 29–30
    freight 27–9
    fuel taxation and environmental policy
        11–12
    infrastructure, investment in 37–40
    integration 17
    local transport 40–42
    London 30–37
    policy development 1–3
    railways 22–7
    road fuel prices, political economy of
        10–11
    road traffic 4–10
    safety 14–17
    social inclusion 18–19
    Ten Year Plan: finance and funding
        47–50
    Ten Year Plan and the railways 42–7
Transport White Paper 3, 11–12, 14, 17,
    20, 22, 24, 27, 47, 53–4
Trunk Roads Programme 40
Turkmenistan 116

Uff-Cullen recommendations 46
UK Continental Shelf 92, 93, 94, 95, 97,
    109
United Financial Group 114

United States
    and cable television monopoly 169–71
    Chicago University 165
    competition policy 121, 123, 124–5,
        127, 128, 130–32, 134
    Delaware 212
    Department of Justice 179, 210, 213
    economic regulation, demise of 162,
        172
    electricity 61, 68, 78, 81–2, 88
    Massachusetts 72
    mergers 203, 210
    mutualization and debt-only vehicles
        199
    San Diego 74, 75
    Supreme Court 180
    telecommunications 146, 154, 155
    Texas 72
    see also California
Universal Postal Service 229, 236–7
universal service fund 227, 228
Universal Service Obligation 219,
    220–22, 225, 230
universal tariff 236–7
Utilities Act (2000) 187

Vickers, J. xxi, xxiv, 122, 203–18
Virgilio 155
Virgin 23, 59, 60
Vodafone 140, 157, 158, 160

Walton, W. 40
Wanadoo 155
water 176
Waverman, L. xxiii, 138–59, 160
Welsh Water 199
West Coast Main Line 27, 45, 58
White Paper
    A Mayor and Assembly for London 2
    New Deal for Tansport, A 3
    see also Transport White Paper
wholesale spot price 73–5
wholesale trading arrangements *see*
    electricity
Winsor, T. xxi, 56–60
Winston, C. 165, 166, 167, 176
Wood MacKenzie 113

X-efficiency 228, 230, 231

Ying, J.S. 168